Who Killed Christopher Robin?

Who Killed Christopher Robin?

The Truth Behind The Murder Of Brian Jones

Terry Rawlings

BⒺXTREE

First published in 1994 by
Boxtree Ltd
21 Broadwall
London SE1 9PL

10 9 8 7 6 5 4 3 2 1

Typeset by SX Composing Ltd, Rayleigh, Essex
Printed and bound in the UK by The Bath Press, Bath

ISBN 0 7522 0989 2

A catalogue record for this book is available from the British Library

Contents

1   A Normal Day For Brian   1
2   From The Cotswolds To Queensway   2
3   The Blues Came From SW10   23
4   Down The Road Apiece   44
5   Sweet Li'l Innocent Brian   65
6   The Road To Morocco   85
7   Gimme Shelter   103
8   Through Cotchford's Past Darkly   129
9   Death At Pooh Corner   142
10 Who Killed Christopher Robin? – Parts 1 & 2   157
11 Jig-saw Puzzle   184

APPENDIX   195

   Tom Keylock affidavit   197
   Brian Jones' Certificate of Death   198
   Brian Jones' Certificate of Birth   199
   Forensic Pathology report dated 17th March 1994   200
   Pathology reports from July 1969   201
   Inquest verdict   211
   Witness statements   214
      Frank Thorogood
      Tom Keylock
      Albert Evans
      Janet Lawson
      Anna Wohlin
      Lewis Blount Jones

Thanks and acknowledgements go to the following who have made this book possible – it wasn't easy.

LESLEY BENSON: For living with me and Brian Jones for the duration of this writing.

JANE PASCOE: For her tireless word processing and endless supply of note-pads.

PAOLO HEWITT: For making sense of the whole thing.

ELAINE BUSTIN: For her marathon processing session.

PAT ANDREWS: For tireless enthusiasm.

NICKY ROBERTS: For common sense.

ART WOOD: For phone call.

JERRY STONE: For answering it!

PAUL WELLER: For opening doors.

REG GANZ: For his uncanny ability to decipher my writing.

NIGEL FOSTER: For his many theories.

TOM KEYLOCK, FRANK THOROGOOD.

GERED MANKOWITZ: For being an all round good guy.

CHRISTOPHER GIBBS, KEITH ALTHAM, KENNY JONES, TREVOR KEMPSON, PAUL JONES, NOEL REDDING, MICK AVORY, TERRY DORRAN, DICK TAYLOR, HELEN COLBY, DICK HATTRELL, SUE WHITE, PETER JONES, DONOVAN, LINDA LAWRENCE.

MARY, LES AND PAULINE HALLETT.

JANET DUCKETT, MICHAEL HALL, JOHNNY PERKINS.

STATESIDE: SUE ANDERSON, ROSEANNE FONTANA, ROBERT WEINGARTNER.

PAUL HALLUM, GEORGE DOSWELL.

A SPECIAL MENTION TO: STEVE MARRIOTT, STEVE HOWARD, KIPPER, TOM DUFFY.

PHIL GOSNEL, and ANDREW NEIL: For initial inspiration and interest.

DENNIS BURKE, KEITH BOOKER, MR & MRS JOHNS AT COTCHFORD FARM, RUSSELL TWYMAN, JAMIE BAILEY, CHRIS CHARLESWORTH.

THE MERLIN GROUP: RAY SANTILLI, SANDRA BOYER, HARRY MAGUIRE, VICKY MURPHY.

1

A Normal Day For Brian

In Billy Wilder's classic 50's Hollywood movie, Sunset Boulevard, the director opens his masterwork with William Holden lying dead in a swimming pool, shot in the back by a crazed Gloria Swanson. It is from the silence of his watery grave that Holden relates the story leading up to his untimely death.

If Brian Jones could be afforded such artistic licence, then surely his untimely and tragic death by drowning on the 2nd of July, 1969, would not be shrouded in mystery or tainted with rumour and counter rumour.

In Hollywood's hands, the beautiful and talented boy who started the most successful rock 'n' roll band in the history of music would have exorcised his personal demons, overcome his massive reliance on drink and drugs and emerged, like his friend Keith Richards, to live a folk hero.

But life is not a film and Brian Jones' death left behind many unanswered questions and conflicting reports. It is the contention of this book that the official version of Brian's death was wrong. The sinister truth is that he was murdered.

2

From The Cotswolds To Queensway

When Prime Minister John Major stated in a recent speech that in 50 years time, Britain will still be the country of warm beer, cricket matches and old ladies cycling to church in the Sunday morning mist, he may well have been thinking of Brian Jones' home town.

Cheltenham, Gloucestershire, is a grand, spacious, beautiful English town that sits snugly at the foot of the Cotswolds, about 100 miles west of London. Throughout its history, the town has always been portrayed as the essence of genteel English life, an unassailable bastion of middle class mores and values.

Cheltenham first gained importance after the English Civil War, when the surrounding area was turned into a flourishing tobacco plantation. Unfortunately, the town's prosperity was short-lived. The Government of the day, fearful that the home produced crop would harm the economic development of their new colonies in America, especially Virginia, passed a law prohibiting the growing of tobacco in England. The law still stands today.

Cheltenham turned to its market trade to survive until 1716, when a Quaker farmer, William Mason, discovered a natural source of spring water and secured Cheltenham's future prosperity. He set up a bottling firm and sold the water to all the surrounding areas, including London.

In 1736 the Cheltenham Spa was opened, instantly attracting dignitaries and royalty alike to the baths. With them came the money to start the construction of an elegant Regency styled town. Buildings were laid out on a grand, almost regal scale whilst tree-lined promenades and luxurious flower gardens were utilised to separate and border the street, thus giving rise to Cheltenham's reputation as the flower garden of England.

Cheltenham is not only proud of its place in the horse racing calendar but also of its heroes. Dr. Edward Wilson, who accompanied but died with Captain Scott on his ill-fated Antarctic expedition, is commemorated by a statue in the new town centre. In Trafalgar Street there is a plaque where Nelson's famous companion Captain Hardy once lived, and even the house where Jane Austen spent a few weeks bears a public acknowledgement.

No wonder then that the Government should choose this town to build their top secret G.C.H.Q. (Government Communications Headquarters) building.

In 1853, the famous Cheltenham Ladies College was opened, an educational institution that is still renowned for its ability to impart a thoroughly traditional education to its high fee paying pupils. About a mile to the east of the college is Hatherley Road, the street where Brian Jones grew up.

He was born Brian Lewis Hopkin Jones on the 28th of February, 1942, to Lewis Blont and Louise Beatrice Jones. Brian was the couple's first child. The second Paulene, tragically died of leukaemia at the age of two. Their third child, Barbara, was born four years after Brian.

Brian's father, Lewis, worked as an aeronautical engineer and Louise taught the piano. Like all aspiring Cheltenham families, their values were upper middle class and Brian soon learned that the best way to win the love of his parents was to conform to these ideals.

Yet a creative and rebellious streak, which soon surfaced, made such an accommodation highly fraught and triggered a behavioural pattern, that of acceptance and rejection, which would remain with him until his death.

Brian was a strange and sometimes sickly child. At the age of four he contracted a case of croup which left him with severe asthma. At five, his mother recalled Brian painting the family cat with blue food colouring, a feat he would repeat on a goat some years later.

When he wasn't altering the natural colour of the family pets, Brian delighted in lining up his collection of toy soldiers on tin trays and melting them down with lighter fuel. He also developed an early and lasting fascination for buses.

His father actually made him a large double-decker bus out of wood and Brian would spend hours ringing its bell and flashing its lights. He kept this bus well into adulthood.

When Brian was 6, his mother started teaching him the piano. The lessons lasted until he was 14 although, by his mother's own admission, he was never fully engaged by the instrument, much preferring the clarinet, despite his bouts of asthma.

When he was 11, having been tested with an IQ of 135, he won a place at Cheltenham Grammar School. It was here that Brian learned to read music. He also studied music theory and gained a place in the choir as first clarinetist. It was clear by now that music was Brian's only interest, the one subject of any importance to him both in and out of school.

Other subjects, discipline and attendance, became obstacles to be gleefully manoeuvred around. Subsequently, he was twice suspended from school, once for using his mortar board as a boomerang and a second time for organising a rebellion against the prefects he despised so much.

He spent most of his suspension time at the Cheltenham Lido, developing his swimming skills before returning to school as something of a notorious hero to his school mates. His father tried to talk to Brian about his disruptive behaviour and the seemingly endless stream of letters from complaining and exasperated teachers, but it was all to no avail.

Brian had firmly cast himself in the early James Dean/Marlon Brando rebel stance and it suited him well.

"Look Dad," he would point out in the midst of another blazing row, "they're only teachers. They have never done anything. You want me to do the things that you did but I can't be like you. I have to live my own life."

Yet, despite his unyielding independent stand, Brian was sensitive enough to take note of his parents' anguish. At the age of 16, with his all-important 'O' levels looming on the horizon, he surprised everyone by applying himself to his studies. He duly passed his exams with flying colours.

A year before sitting his examinations, Brian had joined his first group, a classroom skiffle ensemble. In 1957, a skiffle craze, spearheaded by acts such as Lonnie Donnegan, had gripped Britain's youth. The music was easy to play and the required instruments were cheap and affordable. Most 60's British musicians had first cut their teeth playing skiffle and Brian was no exception.

In his first group, he played the washboard but the group soon petered out. By dint of passing his exams, Brian was allowed into the sixth form to study for two 'A' levels. Whilst there, he received an education of another kind.

With the death of skiffle, jazz had taken over as the popular music amongst his school friends. Brian was soon borrowing records and taking them home to play repeatedly. Artists he admired included Coleman Hawkins and Charlie "Bird" Parker.

Such was his enthusiasm, that he finally persuaded his parents to buy him a saxophone and taught himself to play by blowing along to these records.

It was the stimulation he needed to form his own group. Jones put together a jazz outfit that rehearsed after school and played a couple of local gigs before calling it a day.

As Brian's love for music intensified so his cursory interest in school declined even further, his neglect for studies and discipline reaching an all time low. His father was not impressed.

"I saw music as a positive evil in his life, undermining his school work," he said. "I saw it as evil because he became so obsessed."

But music wasn't the only thing on Brian's mind. On his 17th birthday, his parents gave him a cheap Spanish guitar that cost three pounds. He returned the favour by using the happy occasion to inform them that his current 14-year-old girlfriend was pregnant by him.

Brian had actually tried to keep the affair quiet whilst simultaneously attempting to persuade the girl to have an abortion. She refused but was brave enough to acknowledge Brian's obvious lack of fatherly commitment. She turned to her family for support. They, in turn, contacted Brian's parents.

A meeting between the families was quickly arranged. Both parties understood that a scandal had to be avoided at all costs. The result was that Brian's relationship with the girl was immediately terminated and she was sent away for the duration of her pregnancy to France. Neighbours and friends were told that she was studying there.

Once she had given birth, she could only return home under the strict proviso that the baby be adopted.

Brian's sentence was a fortnight in Germany whilst his parents anguished over his future. Brian accepted his punishment with mixed emotions. He certainly felt a sense of banishment and shame from his own family but he couldn't deny a huge sense of relief that the mess was to be cleared up in his absence.

Meanwhile, a paid trip to Germany was not exactly a hardship and he could always look forward to his rogue status at school being greatly enhanced upon his return.

The girl eventually returned to Cheltenham and stuck by the arrangement of having nothing else to do with Brian. She later said of their relationship, "I was Brian's girlfriend for about three months before I got pregnant. I had our baby adopted and realised the love Brian claimed to have for me didn't exist. I am not really sure if mine did either. It was all a foolish mistake."

Brian also returned home. He had rightly anticipated a frosty welcome from his parents but he certainly hadn't anticipated the same reaction from his schoolmates. In the minds of his middle class friends he had gone too far, and far from bestowing even further notoriety upon him, they rewarded him with the cold shoulder.

A school friend of his at the time commented, "The kids that had once been sort of impressed by Brian now thought of him as a bad influence and just ignored him and left him out in the cold."

Brian spent his few remaining months at school as a loner and, consequently, he turned to spending his time with the much older crowd that frequented Cheltenham's coffee bars, such as El Flamingo, The Waikiki, The Aztec and the town's jazz clubs cum drinking dens such as The Barbecue, The Studio, The Patio and probably the most famous Cheltenham hang-out, No 38 Priory Street.

It was here that the young, disaffected middle class children, attracted by the bar's jukeboxes, regularly assembled. From eight in the evening until the early hours, Brian would hang out with a collection of beatniks, jazz enthusiasts, CND supporters and avid readers of Jack Kerouac's books.

Given his alienation at school coupled with an almost pathological loathing of conformity, it was no surprise when, as soon as he had completed his 'A' levels, which he passed, Brian quit formal education for good. He made the decision final by turning down the chance of attending university. The thought of three more study-filled years horrified him.

After a period of gainful unemployment, John Appleby, one of Brian's new found coffee bar friends, told him of a vacant position as a conductor on the buses. Brian needed some prompting to apply for an interview but his love of buses won him over. John saw Brian the next day and he excitedly told him that he had been taken on. John wrote of Brian's early days with a wonderful insight in his short "Sortofautobiography" *38 Priory Street and All That Jazz*, "He was a star to be and already taken with the pleasures that life offered in and around Cheltenham. He had girlfriends that he would bring around to my house in London Road for coffee. His enthusiasm was quite contagious and extended across a range of subjects he enjoyed, like serious music and jazz. It was the call of music that seriously concerned his parents who wanted a career for him in commerce and it was his parents that called on me to encourage him to apply for the bus conductor's job, for Brian was quite prepared to do little or nothing except hang around." He lasted three weeks in the job.

Part of Brian's decision to quit had been induced by a series of highly embarrassing meetings on the bus with the parents of his ex-girlfriend. They clearly hadn't forgiven him for his past indiscretions and the prospect of bumping into them on a haphazard basis proved too much.

In order to escape his past, Brian fled to Scandinavia. On his own. It was a trip which allowed him to fully indulge in his two main passions: music and sex. Busking by day, at night, Brian found his fantasies about nubile Swedish girls not only based in reality but enthusiastically fulfilled.

He eventually returned to Cheltenham broke and exhausted and was forced once more to undertake a series of dead end jobs that included messenger boy, shop assistant and errand boy. Typically, each job lasted a matter of weeks, if that. A spell at the local music shop seemed to be the perfect answer to his problems but even that failed.

Another coffee bar acquaintance, Dick Hattrell, says, "Brian desperately wanted to earn a living with his music, maybe to prove to his father that what had started out as an interest could finally become a career. But anything remotely artistic musically was considered too Bohemian and was frowned upon in Cheltenham. The place was so painfully uptight. To give you a prime example, my father was a retired brigadier army officer who became a lawyer in Bedford Row, Tewkesbury. He took over a small practice there. I would often take Brian to a meeting at his office and over to our house for dinner. It was always very proper and civil but Brian could hold his own and talk about Shakespeare and poetry with my father which pleased him greatly. Brian could turn on these impeccable manners. My father, like Brian's father, hated our interest in music – well, our brand of music, Jazz and blues. I think chamber music would have been acceptable.

"I remember that very first TV appearance that Brian did on *Thank Your Lucky Stars*. I rushed home to see it and called my father into the sitting room to watch Brian and I don't think he knew what to expect. He was so used to this polite, perfectly-mannered young man visiting. He sat very quietly right in front of the TV and when it was over, he went into this complete rage. He was incensed. He stormed out of the room and came back with his old service revolver and shot the TV into a thousand pieces and scowled at me, 'Never, never let that moron near my house again!'"

As a regular amongst Cheltenham's late-night coffee bar habitués, it wasn't long before he was accepting various offers to sit in with many of the town's informal trad jazz groups. He may have hated the music but the chance to perform in public was not to be sniffed at, especially when engagements, such as a date at The Wooden Bridge Hotel in Guildford brought with it the chance of a quick liaison with a married woman of 23. This act of infidelity on the woman's behalf resulted in the birth of Brian's second illegitimate child.

Within the various group line-ups, Brian would play either saxophone or guitar and by all accounts acquitted himself with a certain aplomb. His unorthodox appearance also guaranteed that the younger members of the audience took special note of Brian.

"You couldn't help notice him," Pat Andrews, a local 15-year-old brunette recalled, "because all the guys he played with were these old jazz guys much older than him or us, thirty plus, and there was Brian standing out like a sore thumb."

Pat belonged to a section of Cheltenham's youth that Brian had no contact with. He rarely attended after-gig parties, preferring instead to go home and practise. He was dedicated to music first, pleasure second. Later on in life he would combine the two to such an extent that the lines became quickly blurred. At this stage, however, his fierce allegiance to music meant that if he fraternised with anyone it would be the older musicians, the ones who could teach him something.

The teenagers at The Aztec coffee bar, intrigued by Brian, decided to bring him into their circle. They chose Pat Andrews to put their plan into action. One night, Brian had just finished playing a local barbecue when a note was pressed into his hand.

It was a message asking him to go to The Aztec the following evening and meet Pat, a female admirer who worked there. The note certainly intrigued and excited Brian. His standing with the local girls had considerably worsened of late thanks to his reputation and the inevitable gossip that circulates in tight knit communities. A blind date at The Aztec was too good a chance to miss.

The next night found a nervous Brian sitting in one of the bar's darkened alcoves, sipping coffee whilst Pat saw out her shift behind the counter, serving hot dogs and drinks.

"I used to sometimes help out the man who owned The Aztec," she explained, "mainly when he wanted to nip across the road to the pub. One of the gang had fixed up a date with Brian and as I had just packed up with my boyfriend, who had gone to Germany, I thought why not? I nearly died when I saw him. He looked like old man. He had short hair and was wearing a brown herringbone suit and a tie, just like a bank manager. I thought, no way. He looked just like someone's dad."

Pat managed to suppress her initial horror and the two chatted happily away for the rest of the evening. They arranged to meet the following night, a Sunday, at the town's cinema. The local custom for first time dates was to meet inside the cinema. That way the potentially embarrassing and public spectacle of who was going to pay for who was neatly avoided.

Brian and Pat sat through Kirk Douglas in *A Town Without Pity* and then returned to The Aztec to arrange a further date. Brian Jones, despite his fearsome reputation as a cold-blooded Casanova, now had a steady girlfriend.

It was at this point that Lewis Jones felt he could no longer stand by and watch his son's aimless progress in life as he trudged from one low-paying job to another. He arranged an interview in London with an ophthalmic firm and accompanied his son up to town. The firm had a shop in nearby Newport but Brian would only consider London.

At the interview, Brian turned on an impeccable display of behaviour which convinced his father that the firm would soon offer his son worthwhile employment. On the way back to the station, Brian asked if he could hang around London for a bit so that he could visit a few jazz clubs. He promised to return home to Cheltenham at a reasonable hour.

Lewis, feeling that one good show of faith deserved another, reluctantly agreed. Brian came home at six the following morning, igniting his father's suspicions that any hopes he had for his son to pursue a respectable career were wildly misplaced.

It was also obvious, after spending time with him in the capital, that Brian had acquired an insatiable taste for life in London.

Brian now started making regular trips to the capital where the variety of music on offer, the buzz of club life and the sheer excitement of big city life was enough to dazzle any teenager's eyes. For any independent and determined person, unlucky to be born outside of the capital and into the restrictions of small town life, London has always symbolised escape and the golden chance to make something of yourself. Brian was no exception and it was on one of these trips that he met a like-minded individual. His name was Paul Jones and he would later hit the big time as the singer with Manfred Mann.

"I first met Brian on one of his trips to London," he recalled. "I would travel down from Oxford and Brian would travel from Cheltenham, so it became easier to meet halfway and travel down together. He would stay over at my flat, mainly when there were parties. We would get-together a band and play at these parties. We called ourselves Thunder Odin and the Big Secret."

Jones also recalled that from the outset, Brian always made it clear that these impromptu get-togethers were for fun only. Despite Paul's repeated invitations to turn the group into a serious proposition, Brian always turned him down.

"Brian would always say to me, I don't join other people's bands, I only help them out or form my own. He always had this air about him that he was above you musically and he probably was. He would say that his only reason for going to London was to recruit musicians for a band he was planning. He was always on at me to join him, to be in his band. He hated the idea of not being the leader."

It was through this collaboration that Brian made his first

recordings. With some of Paul's Oxford musician friends in town the group recorded a few songs featuring Brian on guitar, George Khan on saxophone, Roger Jones on bass, Chris Elkington on drums and Ben Palmer on piano.

"We played the tape back," Jones said, "and we all thought it sounded great so Brian wrote a little note and gave it to me saying, 'Send the tape to clubs in London and see if we can get some gigs.' I don't think we even had a name for ourselves then, we were so naive. We assumed this band was so good that we would call it something after we were besieged with offers of work."

Naturally, the boys were to be disappointed with their perceived shortcut to fame. But, more importantly, directly through his London trips, Brian had slowly been exposed and then turned on to the blues, signalling a major musical shift away from jazz. He began frequenting clubs such as The London Blues and Barrelhouse or Studio 51 and especially admired the sounds of such musical giants such as Howling Wolf or Muddy Waters.

Back in Cheltenham, Brian and Pat continued seeing each other, meeting regularly either at The Aztec or the cinema. "We would watch any bloody thing at the pictures every week, it didn't matter if it was James Bond in *Dr. No* or Doris Day," Pat recalled.

"There really weren't any places to go in Cheltenham other than the coffee bars and you didn't always fancy a cup of coffee. I was too young to drink so we had to be quite inventive on our dates. Brian had a friend who worked in a signal box, a really old guy of about fifty. He would work nights because he hated his wife. So we would go and visit him and he would let Brian pull the handles and switch the switches. He was like the biggest kid in the world. He loved trains."

By now, Brian was sure that he had been unsuccessful in landing a job with the ophthalmic firm in London. Instead, he took a job at a local factory. Every morning, he would be picked up by the factory van and driven to work. One morning, the van crashed and Brian sustained bad injuries to his legs. He also lost a front tooth.

After being patched up at the hospital, he hobbled into the local branch of Boots, the chemist where Pat was now working. With his hand covering his mouth, he told her that he had been involved in an accident and would be unable to see her that night. Pat became immediately suspicous.

11

"You could never tell with Brian," she explained, "because he was a notorious liar. So I said I would go to his house that night instead of going out."

As she made the journey to Brian's house in Hatherley Road on a freezing November night, she was sure that Brian's parents would not know of either her or her impending visit. Arriving at the house, she was greeted by Brian who ushered her into the dining room, explaining that his mum had made them some tea.

"I couldn't believe it," Pat recalled. "She had made tiny cucumber sandwiches and cake. Very nice but he had just had his front tooth knocked out and she was giving him cake and sandwiches, and cucumber ones at that, in the middle of winter."

With tea finished, Brian then brought Pat into the living room to meet his parents. The first thing that Brian's mother asked was, "What she do for a living?"

"After I told her that I worked in Boots the chemist, that was that. A shop girl. It was so obvious I was considered not good enough. As for my father, he worked for the same firm as Brian's dad, Dowty Rotel, the aeroplane firm, but on the shop floor. Brian's dad was management. That just about finished it off. I don't think they said another word to me. Brian's father didn't even offer to drive me home."

After such a frosty reception, Pat steered clear of Brian's home, the couple preferring to spend time at Cheltenham coach station where the back seats of the unlocked coaches provided a warm and private space for the lovers' nightly rendezvous.

This arrangement worked fine until Brian lost his job at the factory and, without telling his parents, promptly took a job as a coal man. It was a calculated move designed in the long run to upset his long-suffering mother and father. He knew full well that such lowly employment would stretch the limit of his parents' patience and irrevocably upset their parochial values. At first, Brian managed to keep up the pretence of factory life by visiting the local baths to wash and change before returning home.

However, when the baths closed down for Christmas, Brian's secret job was revealed. Naturally, Lewis and his wife were outraged. They told Brian in no uncertain terms that they had not raised a son to become a coal man and refused to speak to him. In turn, Brian became all the more determined to stick it out on the coal wagon. The crisis reached its zenith on 22nd of December,

1960, the date of Pat's 16th birthday. To mark the occasion, the couple had planned a romantic night out. Meeting each other after work, Brian surprised Pat with a beautiful green pearl necklace. They then decided to make a brief stop at Brian's home so that he could change before heading out.

When they reached his home, they were amazed to find the house in darkness and locked up as tight as a drum. Searching for a way in, the perplexed couple came across a suitcase hidden behind a hedge in the driveway. Attached to the case was a note from Brian's parents explaining to their wide-eyed son that they had gone to Wales for Christmas. Brian had no key and the electricity had been disconnected.

Pat was speechless. Brian broke in through a window at the back of the house and after changing his clothes, the pair continued their now sombre date. After seeing Pat home, Brian returned to his house, reconnected the electricity and went to bed. Minutes later a loud knock at the door signalled the arrival of the police. They had been alerted by the neighbours who had been told by Brian's parents that the house would be empty for Christmas.

Brian finally managed to convince the law of his identity and they left. Later on that week he went to Pat's sister Betty and her husband Bernie to spend Christmas. He stayed on as a lodger. Pat Andrews is convinced that it was this incident which prompted Brian to subconsciously sever all remaining ties with his parents.

On Boxing Day, the couple met up and celebrated Christmas by spending their first night together. Brian had a friend who owned a pub, The Norwood Arms, on the outskirts of Cheltenham. Somehow, Brian had managed to, in Pat's words, "wangle the keys".

Through his relationship with Pat, Brian had now started mixing with the crowd who had secretly brought them together in the first place. Many of them were art students attending the Pitfield Pumproom College. Nine months after moving in with Bettie and Bernie, Brian, reasoning that a place at the college would give him the time to pursue his musical interests without the distraction of work, applied for a position. He was rejected. Unknown to him, there was a hidden reason behind the college's decision.

Bernie, his landlord, had become so fed up with his wayward lodger that he had actually contacted the college and filled them in with the salacious details of Brian's past, pointing out, in high moral tones, that the father of two illegitimate children was hardly the student type they should be seeking. The college agreed.

As it was patently clear that Brian was no longer welcome at his digs, he started looking around for a new home. A couple of the students he now mixed with offered him a room on the first floor of a flat they shared at 73 Prestbury Road close to the college. Brian gratefully accepted their offer and moved in, taking Dick Hattrell along with him as rent assurance.

As his coal man job no longer had the desired effect of upsetting his parents, Brian quit and began a short-lived career as a trainee architect with the local county council.

The job's lengthy hours left Brian little time for playing music but, even so, Brian knuckled down to his work. He was now making reasonable money and even paying the rent on time. It was the first sign that Pat had ever seen in her boyfriend of a mature acceptance of responsibility.

Encouraged by this unexpected change, Pat thought that the time had finally come to tell Brian the news she had been deliberately keeping back from him for weeks. She was pregnant.

Brian greeted the news with his usual warm understanding. He told Pat she should have an abortion. He knew a woman at the local hospital and he was sure she could help them. Pat refused.

"Although I knew I was pregnant," she said, "I kept trying to convince myself that I wasn't. I used to look at my older sister and her family and think, it only happens to these people, proper families with proper husbands, not me and Brian."

After stating her firm intention to give birth to their child, Brian changed tack and began to warm to the idea. The couple agreed to keep the news to themselves whilst they began the search for suitable living quarters.

"I remember feeling really grown up, almost important," Pat recalled. "I felt I loved Brian and having the baby would sort everything out. I thought everything was going to be wonderful."

Over the next few weeks the couple planned for the forthcoming birth, although Brian was also keen to restart his musical ambitions. When Pat was seven months pregnant, he rang Paul Jones in Oxford and asked him if he had received any reply from the tapes he had sent out in London.

"Of course we hadn't," Jones said. "I had sent a copy to Alexis Korner who ran a club called The London Blues and Barrelhouse. But he hadn't replied or even sent it back. Considering how much Alexis encouraged young R & B bands and musicians in those days, to not even send it back must speak volumes as to how bad it must have been. In fact, Ian Stewart, who was a friend of mine in those early days, told me some years later he had actually heard the tape. He said it was pretty grim."

After telling Brian this news, Paul then suggested the band get together the following weekend and perform at a party some friends were throwing in Oxford. They would also record the set. Brian's reaction was one of sheer enthusiasm. He arrived in Oxford, excited at the prospect of making another tape. Disappointment soon set in amongst the band members when it became apparent that the party was so manic that taping became a virtual impossibility.

Brian, however, was determined to play regardless of the situation. He began blowing relentlessly on his saxophone. Suddenly his pallor turned a deathly white and he collapsed. Paul was the first to reach him.

"He could hardly speak. I had to put my ear to his mouth and managed to make out the words, asthma attack. He was telling me he couldn't breathe and that he had left his pump at my flat. I stole a bicycle and rushed home to get it. I'll never forget it. It wasn't like the little asthma pumps you get nowadays. This was like a fucking great wooden box with a tube at one end with a ball you squeezed. It looked old-fashioned then. God knows what it would look like now. I remember thinking, good God this bloke's really ill. I've never seen anyone with asthma like Brian had it."

Brian recovered and sat out the rest of the party before returning home the next morning to Pat and Cheltenham. Neither one of the couple had yet told their respective parents of Pat's condition and she had miraculously managed to evade detection. But the pretence was proving impossible to maintain.

Pat told Brian that she was going to tell her parents that she was pregnant. She also suggested that Brian try and heal the rift with his folks and lay the way to telling them. Brian, who was by now well schooled in the art of informing his mother and father of their impending status as grandparents, knew that the matter would not be resolved so easily. Even so, he agreed that they could delay the news no longer.

On the night they had planned to attend the neighbouring village of Bishops Cleeve's annual dance, they decided to stop off at Brian's house and talk with his parents. There was no-one home when they arrived but the door was on a latch, so they let themselves in. As they waited, Brian asked Pat to iron a shirt for him. Just as she was putting the finishing touches to his top, Brian's mother walked in.

Brian knew that his mother would not take the news well but even he, a veteran of such moments, was visibly shocked by her wild reaction when he told her the news.

"She became hysterical," Pat recalled, "picking things up and throwing them at Brian and screaming at the top of her voice, telling him what a bastard he was. Then she ran into Brian's old bedroom, grabbed his guitar and started smashing it. It was a terrible scene."

It was at this point, with Mrs. Jones seemingly out of control, that her husband Lewis walked in. His appearance sparked off even wilder behaviour on her behalf.

"She was still screaming," Pat recalled, "and calling me all the names under the sun. Then she told him that Brian had come in and started hitting her, which was a complete lie. I just grabbed my coat and Brian's arm and told them that they would never see the baby so long as I was its mother and as far as I was concerned they weren't fit to be parents, let alone grandparents."

As the fleeing couple raced up Hatherley Road, they could still hear Brian's parents screaming. Glancing back at the house, and noticing the neighbours twitching their net curtains in a kind of crazy morse code, Pat swore to herself she would never go back on her vow.

Despite the upsetting scenes they had just witnessed, the couple decided to go on to the dance in Bishops Cleeve. By the time they reached the venue, the dance was in full swing. At one end of the old barn, propped up on a makeshift stage of bailed hay, there was a jazz band playing its heart out. The group were from London. The vocalist was black and he had the audience eating out of the palm of his hand.

"As silly as it may seem now," Pat recalls, "the only bands, especially jazz or trad bands, you got to see outside London in those days were all white. Everyone associated jazz with the likes of Kenny Ball or Acker Bilk. So this black guy was blowing their minds."

After the gig, Brian's troubles seemed a million miles away as he chatted to the band and enthusiastically insisted that they move on to his flat for an impromptu party. Pat was amazed.

"Brian was so excited by that band it was as if nothing had happened earlier. He just had to get more of it. About thirty or forty kids went back with Brian and squeezed into the tiny flat he was sharing. About an hour later the band turned up with all their equipment. You couldn't move in there as it was. Brian was over the moon."

Brian soon had the band unpacking their gear and with his battered guitar slung over his shoulder, he started playing. So eager was he to impress his new musician friends that when Pat looked closely at Brian's hands she noticed they were covered in blood from the ferocity of his playing. After they had finished playing, the band's lead singer then offered Brian a small polythene bag of powder. Brian asked him what it was. "Cocaine," came the reply, "it's the only way to keep going, man."

The band also had in their possession a whole array of mind bending substances including uppers, downers, cocaine and grass. It was Brian's first real encounter with drugs and he made the most of it. That night, he sampled them all. He took a dab of this and a snort of that. He took a black pill. He took a purple pill.

For Brian, it didn't matter. He was like a greedy child locked in a sweet shop and his reverie was only interrupted when one of the revellers suggested the whole crowd should go skinny dipping across the road at the lido.

"It was like a scene from *Hair*," Pat recalled. "All these beatniks and students leaping about naked in the pool. I was too fat by now and anyway I had told my parents I was staying at a friend's house for the night. It wouldn't have done to go home pregnant *and* with pneumonia, so I curled up on the sofa." It was about seven o'clock when the last of the guests left. Brian woke the exhausted Pat and took her to his room. It was there he asked her to marry him. Pat happily agreed to his proposition. Fortified by Brian's declaration of never ending love, she finally broke the news of her imminent motherhood to her amazed and shocked parents. "My dad went completely mad and forbade me to ever see Brian again, but there was no way I was having that. After he calmed down he was alright about the baby but he said I was still banned from seeing Brian."

A month passed and Pat, with the help of her parents, prepared for the baby's arrival. One Sunday morning Pat crept out of the house and sneaked over to Brian's flat. His friend Richard Hattrell answered the door and told her Brian was asleep. Pat said that was fine and that she would wake him but Hattrell was insistent, waving his arms around and saying, no, no. Pat knew instinctively what was wrong and raced to the kitchen. "I knew he had a girl in there. I grabbed the biggest knife I could find." She pushed past the worried looking Richard and burst in on the sleeping Jones. Brian was laying on top of the bed naked, his arm draped over a girl no older than fourteen. Pat went into a blind fury.

"I was going to kill him," she later stated. Richard and a flatmate forced the seething Pat into the kitchen and tried to calm her down, telling her to think of the baby and not Brian. He was to blame. By the time a timid Brian emerged from his room, three hours later, a sobbing Pat had been taken home. "I heard a tapping noise at my window later that day. I looked out and it was pouring with rain. There was Brian sopping wet throwing pebbles at my window. He wanted to say sorry and make it up." Pat refused to speak to him and pulled her curtains tight. Over the next few weeks she avoided him as best she could, hoping to discourage his pathetic attempts at winning her back by ignoring his phone calls and tearing up his notes, which involved considerable risk in delivering as Brian had already been hit over the head with a umbrella by Pat's mum on one such mission.

Pat was rushed to the Victoria Nursing Home in Cheltenham, at midnight on the 22nd of October, 1961. Some four or five hours later, Brian's third child was born, a boy. "I had given up on seeing Brian when this huge bunch of flowers appeared at the end of the ward, all you could see were these little legs sticking out from underneath. I couldn't see who was holding them until he put them down." Brian had sold his only possession other than his guitar, his record collection, to pay for the flowers. Under the watchful, unimpressed glare of Pat's mother and father, the two were reunited. They decided to name the baby Mark Julian Jones, Julian after Brian's favourite jazz musician Julian Cannonball Adderley, and Mark from Pat's baby name book. "Brian sulked because he wanted Julian first but it seemed too grown up for such a tiny baby, he just didn't look like a Julian. My dad took me to register Mark but once we got there he wouldn't let me register him in Brian's name. I couldn't even enter his name as the father." Pat, with the baby, continued to live with her parents while Brian stayed on at the student flat, the plans for their wedding temporarily on hold.

One morning, the local paper carried an advert that caught Pat's eye. The Chris Barber Jazz Band were playing Cheltenham Town Hall. She knew Brian had seen them play once before and thought this time they could go together. Barber was a thirty year old trombone player who had formed his own band since splitting from the equally popular Ken Colyer Band. Although essentially a jazz band, Barber's group were one of the earliest bands to promote R & B in Britain, only they called it Country Blues. Barber had a musical policy of having an interval slot which showcased the talents of up and coming soloists. He had already helped the career of banjo player Lonnie Donnegan and brought to England's attention a harmonica player from Chicago called Sonny Boy Williamson. This time around it was the turn of a guitar player called Alexis Korner. Korner had already earned a name for himself having originally played with Ken Colyer and for running the London club, The Blues and Barrelhouse.

Alexis Korner was born in Paris on 19th April, 1928. His mother was Austrian and his father Greek. The family moved to England after the war and settled in the Hammersmith area of London where Alexis attended St Paul's Catholic School. He began his musical career at the comparatively late age of 25, playing blues guitar on the London pub circuit, before getting his first break by joining the established Ken Colyer Jazz Band. It was while playing with Colyer that he met another young musician, a harmonica player called Cyril Davis whose interest in playing the blues matched Korner's own.

Korner left Colyer and, teaming up with Davis, they played their first gig in 1957 at the London Blues and Barrelhouse Club, which was situated in the upstairs room of a pub called the Round House, on a corner of Wardour Street. They played to an audience of three people, one of whom was the pub owner. Despite the poor attendance, he was impressed enough to offer Alexis and Cyril the chance to run the club! This they did successfully for the next three years, until being fired for the heinous act of introducing amplification into their set.

Following their dismissal from The Barrel House in 1960 they joined the Chris Barber Band, who was still enjoying a high profile on the strength of an unexpected top ten US hit entitled *Petite Fleur* a year before.

It was soon obvious to Barber that his two new recruits were on an entirely different wavelength to himself. Musically, they were poles apart. Yet Barber didn't let their differences cause a problem. Rather, instead of letting two excellent musicians leave, the adventurous leader created a special thirty minute slot for Davis and Korner at the end of each gig. It was an inspired decision which allowed Davis and Korner to show off their skills although in reality it was the latter name that benefitted the most. As the only electric guitarist in England much of the 30 minutes was naturally given over to Korner.

By accepting and promoting this style of music, Chris Barber deserves an awful amount of respect for being the probable founder of what was to become the British rock scene.

As a surprise for Brian, Pat bought two tickets for Barber's Cheltenham concert. After nagging her mother into babysitting, the pair set off for the Town Hall.

Barber's band played to a capacity crowd and won over the usually hard to impress audience. At the end of their set, Barber introduced some members of his band who were "now going to perform a short blues set." He then introduced Mr Alexis Korner. "Well," Pat recalls, "Brian went mad clapping and whistling and stamping his feet, I looked round and everyone was looking at us like we were lunatics."

Korner's short set totally altered Brian's musical state of mind. Every major musician has one or two memorable musical experiences which determine their outlook forever. This was Brian's. It was as if a vision that only he could see had appeared in the packed Town Hall and he sat there in a total state of transfixation. Naturally, after the closing notes had died away, Brian had to meet Korner. He rushed to the stage door but without the neccessary passes to get past the security. Fortunately, his face was well enough known on the Cheltenham music scene to have little trouble getting backstage. His main mission was to find out if the tape that Paul had sent off had reached Korner.

Hanging around the dressing room, a backstage worker who knew Brian told him that he'd heard the band were going across the road to the Patio Wine Bar and he should go across there if he wanted to meet Korner.

Pat saw little point in protesting the fact that both she and Brian should return home to see Mark. She was reluctantly and hurriedly walked home. Brian gave Pat a peck on the cheek and raced off to the wine bar. There he introduced himself to Korner, who regrettably informed him he couldn't remember receiving a tape but was none the less chuffed that someone from as far out as Cheltenham had heard of him. The two musicians sat comfortably talking for hours about the blues and Brian's plans to form a band. Brian was adamant that Korner should hear him play and badgered the guitarist mercilessly until he finally agreed. Brian raced home to the flat and grabbed his guitar, returning to the wine bar completely breathless. Despite this puffing and panting, Brian's playing was faultless and a sufficiently impressed Korner gave Brian his phone number and address in London. He told the elated Brian to give him a ring next time he was in town, adding he would show him around and maybe meet some people.

Brian didn't need any more encouragement. The very next weekend Brian was sitting on a train bound for Paddington, Alexis' phone number etched into his memory. The surprised but happy Korner was as good as his word and showed Brian around the clubs introducing him to his family and friends, some of whom included musicians Alexis had brought together to form a band he himself was planning, called Blues Incorporated.

Alexis and his wife Bobbie put Brian up at their flat in Moscow Road and the rest of the weekend was spent sitting around and talking and playing through Korner's impressive record collection. Alexis played Brian *The Sky Is Crying*, a record by Elmore James, and the effect was so dramatic that it stopped Brian dead in his tracks.

"Elmore James is the most important discovery I've ever made in my life," he told the slightly undervalued Pat, as he proudly showed baby Mark the new electric Hofner Committee guitar he had bought on his return to Cheltenham. "It was like the world shuddered on its axis when I heard him." James was Brian's new hero, his latest obsession. When he wasn't talking about him, he was listening to him or playing slide guitar for hours on end, to the accompaniment of one of Elmore's albums, only stopping when he was satisfied he had mastered one particular phrase or chord change. Pat was used to Brian's obsessive nature but even she gave him a worried stare when he began signing his name Elmore Jones.

Brian began visiting the Korners in London practically every weekend, enjoying feeling an accepted part of a family again. He was hinting more and more that he wanted to move down to the city permanently, always emphasizing how he now hated Cheltenham completely. The people there, Brian felt, cramped him and he was sick and tired of the restrictions his parents had tried to impose on him. He wanted to get as far away from them as possible.

Each time Brian brought the subject up, Alexis tried to discourage him from making such a move, telling him he didn't think Brian was ready to deal with life in London. He might as well have held a red flag to a bull. Pat recalls, "Brian was spending so much time up in London it was inevitable that he would end up staying. Then one day he turned round to me and said he had quit his job and Alexis had found him a flat in London and he was moving." Brian told Pat as soon as he got himself a job he would send for her.

Brian announced his departure from Cheltenham by throwing a party. It began shortly before midnight, a moderately noisy but uncrowded event that by one o'clock had become a seething, packed-to-capacity high-decibal riot. It was, not surprisingly, broken up by the police after they received numerous complaints from the neighbours. Brian slipped away unnoticed, leaving his flatmates to clear up the mess.

3

The Blues Came Up From SW10

Brian moved into a two room flat in Bath Road, close to where the Korners lived. Once again he shared with a student. It was here that he celebrated his 20th birthday on 28 February, 1962.

By now, Korner had left Chris Barber's band and was looking to branch out musically with his own group. He had never been wholly comfortable playing the jazz part of Barber's set so the split had been inevitable. But it was to have unforseen economic consequences for the guitarist. He quickly found out that there was a serious lack of clubs and venues willing to book anything other than jazz or trad jazz bands.

The live music circuit, especially in London, was divided up pretty evenly between the Aker Bilk and Terry Lighfoot style jazzers and the "poppy" end of the rock and roll scene, which was sewn up by the likes of Cliff Richard, Marty Wilde or Tommy Steele. Even the lightweight Jim Dale could be relied on to pull in the punters. In the eyes and experience of the club owners and booking agents only the smallest minority would be interested in watching anything else. Fads like rhythm and blues were not to be given any consideration. Minority taste meant small crowds and small crowds meant small money. This frustrated Korner, who knew there was a huge untapped audience of Rhythm and Blues and blues fans that were not being catered for, not only in London but throughout the country.

In order to get his message across, and with a wife and new daughter to support, Korner was forced to become a bit of an entrepreneur. He began staging one night a week blues clubs where he could hire out a back room of a pub or club and charge an admission fee. He always made sure he promoted the club under a name other than the name of the venue that housed it, thereby ensuring it retained its own individual identity, much the same as he had done at the Barrelhouse.

He started out using the back room of the A.B.C Bakery in Ealing Broadway, calling it the Ealing Club. He placed two adverts, one in the *New Musical Express* and the other in *Jazz News* which read:
Alexis Korner Blues Incorporated
The most exiting event of the year
Ealing Broadway Station
turn left, cross the zebra and go down the steps
between the ABC Teashop and the jewellers
Saturday at 7.30pm

Brian had returned to Cheltenham a couple of times since moving to London in order to visit Pat and Mark. He stayed at his old flat near the college. On one particular visit, Brian made the acquaintance of another fourteen-year-old school girl. The two were often seen walking arm in arm around the town. Despite the danger, Brian lapped up the attention her school uniform attracted from passers-by.

Naturally, these sightings were soon flashed to Pat. She went to the flat to confront Brian. Without batting an eyelid, Brian denied any knowledge of such a girl's existence and swore nothing was going on. Pat wanted to believe him but knew better. She returned to the flat early the next morning and inspected Brian's room. She found a girl's ring by his bed and once again confronted him. With his customary charm and smoothness, he told her he had picked it up while cleaning the flat, and that it actually belonged to his flatmate's girlfriend.

It was a nice try but he knew Pat hadn't bought a word of it. He finally admitted there was a girl but, he added, it was purely a platonic relationship. He went on to explain that the girl lived with her mother in Cheltenham. The mother was very well off and she was giving Brian money to meet her daughter from school and take her out.

Brian laughably pointed out to Pat that the girl was under age and the mother trusted him. Apparently, she believed Brian was a nice boy and all she wanted was her daughter out of her hair for a few hours. In return, the mother, who also had a flat in London, would stop off at Brian's and cook for him whenever she was in town on business. As Brian hadn't the faintest idea of how to cook, he thought it an excellent arrangement.

"I knew it was complete rubbish but I wanted to believe it," Pat recalled. "I desperately wanted to be able to trust him when he was away, so I tried to put it out of my mind." Brian went back to London and found work as an electrical appliance salesman at Whiteleys Department Store in Queensway. He wrote to Pat and told her the news but gave no indication of when she would see him next. "It was about a week before Easter and one of Brian's friends invited me to a barbecue," Pat said. "He asked me if I had heard from Brian and I said I had received a letter some days ago and nothing since. Then he told me he had seen that school girl Brian had been taking out when he was last in Cheltenham and she had told him she was going to London to spend the weekend with Brian."

Pat bought a single coach ticket to London on the Easter Saturday. She waited for her mother to go out before packing up as much of Mark's belongings as she could. Leaving a note on the table, and with only a handful of change in her pocket, she set off for the coach station.

The coach didn't leave until three the next morning so Pat and the baby hid out at a friend's house, knowing her mother would be frantically searching Cheltenham. As the coach pulled out Pat crouched low in her seat and watched in horror as her mother, escorted by several policemen, entered the station only seconds too late to stop her.

At 8.00am on Easter Sunday, an exhaustated Pat arrived in London. She then had to catch another bus in order to reach Brian's flat. Unfortunately, she got off at the wrong stop. "I stopped some guy and asked him where I was and told him where I wanted to get to. I must have looked such a pathetic girl. He gave me a lift right to Brian's door."

Brian opened the door as cool as ice. He had no need to be worried. He was alone at the flat. "I felt such a fool but it didn't matter, I was happy to be back with Brian. I found out later that the girl's mother in Cheltenham had been tipped off as to what was happening when my mother was going around the town frantically looking for me. She had rung Brian and he had sent the girl packing before I arrived."

Alexis Korner's Blues Incorporated had played their first gig at the Ealing Club to a crowd of over a hundred but within a month their audience had more than doubled and matched the club capacity of 200 people. Rhythm and Blues and blues fans were travelling the length of the country to hear Korner's band. The leader was soon promoting the club as the only Rhythm and Blues club in Europe. Brian was now more determined than ever to get his band together.

Although Brian had acquainted himself with a surprisingly wide circle of friends and musicians in the comparatively short time he'd lived in London, he really only had one friend he could call on whom he felt could join his band.

It was Paul Jones (who was now calling himself Paul Bond – "We got fed up of explaining we were not brothers") that Brian called and suggested he join up with him. "I went round to see him. He was calling himself Elmo Lewis now. We made another tape and called it Elmo and Paul." Brian took the tape to Korner and pleaded to be given a chance to play the interval spot for Blues Incorporated.

Alexis couldn't deny Brian a break, so, on March 1962, Brian sat in with Korner's band for the first time.

By chance, Korner had also invited another young musician down to the Ealing Club. His name was Mick Jagger. Jagger had sent Korner a tape and made the same request to fill the interval slot after reading about the Ealing Club in March's edition of *Jazz News*.

In the same issue there was a reply to the editor of the letters column from Brian concerning a previous debate on Rhythm and Blues. Jack Good, a popular TV and radio presenter, whose appraisal of the subject had obviously clashed with Brian's own, was suitably dismissed by the budding Blues guitarist, who ended his reply by saying, "please play this man a Muddy Waters record so he can see what Rhythm and Blues really is."

Jagger's tape entitled "Little Boy Blue and the Blue Boys," had been successful in grabbing Alexis's attention and he had agreed to giving the singer a spot after hearing him sing. The tape recording also carried the earliest efforts of another guitar hopeful named Keith Richards.

Michael Philip Jagger was born on 26 July 1943 in Dartford, Kent. His father, Basil Joe Jagger, came from the north of England, Lancashire, and his mother, Eva Mary, was born in Australia. He had one brother, Christopher, who was born on 7 December 1940.

Mick went to Wentworth Junior Country Primary School, where he made an early friendship with another Dartford lad named Keith Richards.

Keith Richards had been born on 18 December, 1943. His father, Herbert William Richards, and his mum, Doris, were a staunch working class couple from Walthamstow in the north-east end of London.

After completing school, Mick had won a scholarship to the London School of Economics to study law while Keith took a place at the Sidcup Art College.

Since entering higher education, the two lads had lost touch with each other until a chance meeting at Dartford Train Station reunited the old friends. Mick invited Keith to his house and the two friends discovered their mutual love of music, playing Mick's Chuck Berry records late into the night. It was the first of their many get-togethers that was to result in the band "Little Boy and the Blue Boys".

The pair had formed the band along with school friends Dick Taylor, Bob Beckwith and Allan Etherington. They concentrated on imitating early Jimmy Reed and Chuck Berry records.

By all accounts the tape was every bit as dreadful as Brian and Paul's but something in Jagger's voice had persuaded Korner to invite him along. In the meantime, Brian had agreed to Pat and the baby staying with him at the flat in Bath Road. It was a bit of a squeeze but they were sure they could manage. All was fine until his landlord pointed out that according to the rules of Brian's tenancy, babies weren't allowed in the building and he told them they had to leave.

Faced with the prospect of returning to Cheltenham, Brian and Pat felt they had no choice but to put Mark up for fostering.

After agonizing over a decision, a home was found for Mark in nearby Mill Hill. Brian set about looking for larger accommodation while Pat looked for a job.

She found work in a laundry in Notting Hill Gate and, together with Brian's wages from Whiteleys, the couple were able to rent a flat in Powis Square. It was no larger than their previous one but it allowed children to live on the premises. Mark was brought back from Mill Hill and the family was united once again.

With his domestic commitment back under control, Brian was able to concentrate on his musical plans. One of these involved grabbing a second spot guesting with Blues Incorporated. It was on 7 April 1962 that Alexis Korner announced to a packed and hushed crowd at the Ealing Club: "Ladies and Gentlemen, we've got a special guest to play some guitar tonight. He's come all the way from Cheltenham just to play for you. Would you please welcome, Elmo Lewis."

At that precise moment, Mick Jagger, Keith Richards, Dick Taylor and Allan Etherington walked through the door.

It was as if someone had hit the foursome right between the eyes. Brian's guitar playing froze them to the spot. They were literally awestruck. Brian finished his short set and, after bowing to the sound of riotous applause, walked triumphantly to the bar to join Paul Jones. Keith, Mick and the others waited for Brian to cool down before nervously venturing over.

After introducing themselves, the foursome started plying Brian with half pints of bitter. Then the little crowd retired to an alcove at the rear of the club. In Mick, Keith and Dick's eyes, Brian was a professional. He was only a year older than themselves in age but he was clearly years ahead of them musically. Even Dick Taylor, who earned a reasonable reputation as a guitarist in and around Dartford, had to begrudgingly concede to Brian's obvious talents, albeit with a mixture of admiration and jealousy.

The group sat talking in the alcove of the Ealing Club for a couple of hours, good naturedly arguing about the varying quality of their blues and rock influences. By all accounts, Brian greatly impressed the trio with his superior knowledge of blues artists such as Jimmy Reed, Muddy Waters and, of course, Elmore James.

Keith, a devout Chuck Berry fan, couldn't help showing his amazement, and a little smugness, when he discovered Brian knew little to nothing of his St Louis duck-walking hero. Brian's slight slip was more than made up for, however, when it was revealed he'd fathered three illegitimate children, all before the age of 20. In Keith Richards' estimation that excused Brian's ignorance of Berry.

This first historic meeting allowed the men who would eventually form the world's greatest rock 'n' roll band time to acquaint themselves with each other. But it also left the three Dartford lads feeling a little undermined. Brian, during the course of the evening, had mentioned several times that he was booking a rehearsal in order to start a band of his own. Not once did he suggest that his new friends should drop by. He was already making it clear that he thought his aspirations were far and above that of Jagger and company.

In the May '62 edition of *Jazz News*, Brian placed an advert asking that musicians interested in forming a R&B group should attend rehearsals at the back room of the White Bear public house just off Leicester Square.

Jazz News was Soho's 'What's On Where' trade paper and the day the ad appeared, Brian proudly took a copy to show Pat at her laundry. On his arrival he discovered, much to his disgust, that she worked with a handful of young men. In a fit of jealous temper he demanded that Pat leave her job.

"His jealousy was ridiculous," she recalled. "He couldn't stand anyone showing me any attention yet he loved getting it himself, he even went into my purse and tore up all the photos I had of my previous boyfriend."

Pat gave up her job in the laundry and took another at a company called Leo Computours, a subsidiary of Joe Lyons' Corner House, while Brian added yet another column to his CV by going to work at the Civil Stores record department in the Strand.

Brian Knight, a singer/harmonica player whom Brian knew from drinking in the Ealing Club was one of the first to see him after reading his ad.

"I had originally been asked to join Blues Incorporated by my mate Cyril Davis whom I worked with as a panel beater. Blues Incorporated were like the biggest deal then but I misunderstood what they wanted from me. I thought they wanted me to come up with a whole set of songs so every time I would see one of them, I would make up some excuse and put them off because I didn't have any. So in the end, they stopped asking me and got Art Wood."

Brian had heard that Alexis had been keen for Knight to join his band and assumed the singer had turned them down. He asked Knight if he would be interested in trying out a rehearsal the following Monday.

"It was the first time I had spoken to Brian but I had seen him around quite a bit and I was feeling really pissed off at blowing my chance with Blues Incorporated especially as the line up at that point was so good," Knight recalls. "They had Charlie Watts on drums, Graham Bond playing horns and Long John Baldry. They were really something and there I was kicking my heels. So when Brian asked me – I was more than happy to oblige."

Knight went along to the White Bear pub accompanied by his mate, a guitar player named Geoff Bradford who was playing the occasional gig with Alexis but was on the look out for permanent work.

"Geoff was a really serious blues guitarist," said Brian Knight. "He was very into the idea of getting a pure blues outfit together. He had seen Brian play and thought this would be it."

The two arrived at the pub and were met by the strange spectacle of a thick set, square jawed man wearing a pair of shorts, seated at an old battered pub piano. His name was Ian (Stu) Stewart, a piano player from Cheam in Surrey.

"I found out later they were cycling shorts," said Brian Knight. "Ian went everywhere on his push-bike. He worked for ICI as a clerk and he used it to duck out of work and get to rehearsals."

Ian had a lighthearted and easy-going nature that at first seemed at odds with the obsessive and petulant Brian. But if Brian had been harbouring any reservations as to Ian's ability as a musician they were soon forgotten as Stu thundered away brilliantly at the piano.

Stuart became the band's first serious fixture and, after as little as two rehearsals, Brian was referring to the burly piano player as both his band's anchorman and his friend. Throughout May of that year, Brian, Geoff, Stu and Knight started rehearsing two or three times a week. They had moved their centre of operations to another pub – The Bricklayers Arms – off Wardour Street, owing to Brian being caught red-handed behind the bar at the White Bear loaded down with cigarettes and bottles of beer.

At the end of the month, the teen magazine *Disc* ran a short news item that read: "A nineteen-year-old Dartford rhythm and blues singer named Mick Jagger has joined the Alexis Korner group "Blues Incorporated" and will sing with them regularly on their Saturday dates at Ealing plus their Thursday session at the Marquee."

Over the following weeks, Brian and Stu scrutinized over a dozen players other than Bradford and Knight. This proved too much for the patience of Knight who had laboured through every rehearsal before finally quitting in exasperation.

"Brian was very particular about whom he played with," Brian Knight recalled. "They had to rate very highly. We auditioned for about eight weeks. I didn't think he was ever going to get it together."

Knight decided to form his own band, 'Brian Knight's Blues by Six'. After poaching Alexis' drummer, Charlie Watts, he put his band to work playing the Marquee's Monday night residency. Brian's particular brand of perfection was having its drawbacks. Even Paul (Pond) Jones had given up waiting for Brian to get his show on the road and had gone back to live in Oxford where he found work doing a regular vocal spot at a local dance hall.

"This guy who owned the hall," Jones says, "was always telling me with every breath, how convinced he was that I was going to be a star and that he knew exactly how I should go about it. So I thought – well, he knows what he's talking about, I'll stick with him. I couldn't see how in his wildest dreams Brian was going to make a living out of R&B. It seemed I was wasting my time with a no hope dreamer, so I told him in no uncertain terms – I'm off."

Brian and Stu's rehearsals were now well known among Soho's music crowd. It was inevitable, therefore, that Mick Jagger, who was now singing three nights a week with Blues Incorporated, would ask either one of them how they were going. Ian grabbed his chance and suggested Jagger came along and see for himself. Stuart also mentioned during his talk that Korner never paid his musicians very much and that Brian's outfit could also accommodate Mick's firm ally Keith.

Stu knew Mick and Keith were virtually inseparable as friends and that Mick's singing with Blues Incorporated had separated the two. He figured the offer of both joining Brian's band would be a big enough carrot to dangle in order to get both down to rehearsals. He was right.

Along with Dick Taylor, who went with them, they successfully auditioned for Brian, much to the dismay of the long-suffering Geoff Bradford. Bradford's level of perfectionism easily matched Brian's and he clearly considered all three to be mere amateurs.

To make matters worse, Keith made no secret of the fact that he considered Geoff's idealism as particularly childish. He deliberately went out of his way to disagree with everything the guitarist said or suggested, always safe in the knowledge that his two friends would always back him up.

Geoff hated rock 'n' roll as much as he hated Keith. Keith's persistent Chuck Berry riffs were the final straw in sending the disenchanted blues man packing. Keith reasoned to the others that, "two guitarists in this band were quite enough anyway. Thank you". The next time Brian saw Bradford, he was happily playing in Brian Knight's "Blues by Six".

With his band complete, Brian turned his attention to the more difficult task of persuading a drummer to throw in his lot with him. Brian had found that there had been no shortage of willing front men and guitarists eager to join him in a share of the spotlight. But a drummer who owned a kit and more importantly, transport for it, was an altogether different matter.

Another ad was placed, this time in the *Melody Maker*. It attracted a reasonable response, but most fell prey to Brian's professional inspection. They would timidly tap along self-consciously before hurriedly leaving the session. Brian eventually settled on and recruited a drummer named Mick Avory. At last, Brian had a full band. Now all they needed was a name.

By mid-1962, Alexis Korner's Blues Incorporated were a big enough live name to attract the attention of the BBC who were putting out a weekly radio show called *The Jazz Club*. The producers of *The Jazz Club* approached Korner and asked him to do the show. It was their biggest break to date and Korner leapt at the offer. There was one problem. The broadcast clashed with the group's Thursday night residency at the Marquee.

Korner explained his dilemma to the Marquee's owner, Harold Pendleton, who unobligingly refused to give them the night off. He told Korner in no uncertain terms, "no gig no residency." The quick thinking Korner came up with a compromise.

News that Mick Jagger had left Blues Incorporated wasn't yet widespread, certainly not to the BBC. Korner told Pendleton that if Mick turned up as usual but with a new band it wouldn't cause too much of a disappointment. He modestly added that with Thursday's familiar front man still in attendance, no-one would be that bothered if the backing band's line up had inexplicably changed.

Pendleton, somewhat sceptically, agreed to the proposition. Korner rang Brian and explained the position. Brian wasn't at all happy with the fact that it was Jagger's status that had swung the gig for them but he accepted the booking. To make sure his authority wasn't being overlooked as leader, Brian was adamant he should choose the name of the group.

He chose The Rolling Stones after a favourite Muddy Waters song, *Rollin' Stone Blues*. All the band hated it, especially Stu who cringed when he heard it, but they accepted it because it was, after all, Brian who had formed the group. On the 11th of July 1962, *Jazz News* printed in its gig info column, that "Mick Jagger, R&B vocalist is taking a rhythm and blues group called The Rolling Stones into the Marquee tomorrow night (Thursday), while Blues Incorporated is doing *The Jazz Club* radio Show. 'I hope they don't think we're a rock and roll outfit,' says Mick. The line up is, Mick Jagger (vocals), Keith Richards and Elmo Lewis (guitars), Dick Taylor (bass), Ian (Stu) Stewart (piano) and Mick Avory (drums). A second group under Long John Baldry will also be playing."

With his diary boasting The Stones' first and only finalized booking, Brian felt accomplished enough to pay a lightning and unexpected visit to Cheltenham in order to see his parents. Pat was still too annoyed to see him. In the case of his parents, the months of silence had gone some way to healing the rift between them. Indeed, Brian's father couldn't help feeling a little bit proud of the fact that his son's determination to play jazz was paying off, even if he was a touch misguided as to just what sort of musicians these freshly named Rolling Stones were.

Brian knew the band's live debut at the Marquee was going to be tough going from the minute they walked out on to the dimly lit stage. The atmosphere was decidedly uneasy. The club's die hard jazz and blues clientele had been respectful of Alexis Korner's brand of professionalism but were making it clear they weren't about to be taken in by this unknown band of scruffy R&B fadsters.

The resentment of the club's predominantly jazz oriented crowd was wholly reinforced when, mid way through The Stones set, a large group of curious Mods entered the club. The immaculately attired scooter riders contemptuously eyed the goatee bearded jazzers up and down. Then they barged their way to the front of the stage where, after admiring Brian and Keith's Muddy Waters and Chuck Berry guitar riffs, they gleefully attacked the audience. Violent chaos ensued.

Harold Pendleton was seething. Pendleton was a leading member of the country's national jazz league to which the club belonged and he made it clear he was holding The Stones personally responsible for such an outrage. Pendleton had made the mistake of booking The Stones without seeing or hearing them play a single note. Now that he had experienced a Stones concert he was irrevocably against the group. Accordingly, Brian doubted the chances of ever being asked back but nonetheless regarded the gig a personal success.

A few nights later back at the Ealing Club, with Brian once again propping up the bar, he was offered another spot there, but this time with his own band. This was The Rolling Stones' second official outing and an important breakthrough for the group. The engagement led to a succession of five more gigs in as many weeks. These gigs built up The Stones' reputation and following to a such a size that the group's obvious popularity was enough to sufficiently interest Harold Pendleton to risk putting the band on a second time at the Oxford Street Club. Pendleton's change of heart didn't stretch any further than the Marquee's box office. He still hated The Stones and made it obvious by the choice of dates he booked for the band. He organised several fifteen minute interval slots covering far more established artists. When he didn't cancel them at the last minute, which he did more often than not, the ploy enabled him to capitalise on the already sizeable number of Stones fans without having to pay the band a headlining fee.

If Pendleton loathed and despised The Stones then there was no great love lost so far as the band were concerned. However, being desperate and downright grateful to take on any work offered them meant swallowing any amount of the venue boss's treatment and chiding, except for Brian who felt it his duty, as the group's leader and spokesman, to make his and their feelings known. He wrote another letter to *Jazz News* in the hope of exposing some of the juvenile and snobby prejudice that bands like The Stones and Blues by Six were suffering at the hands of people like Pendleton and his precious Jazz crowd at clubs like the Marquee. He finished his crusading speech on behalf of R&B by stating – "Rock is a direct corruption of Rhythm and Blues where-as Jazz is negro music on a different plane, intellectually higher but emotionally less intense . . . Elmo Lewis."

By now, Brian was working all week with extra gigs and re-hearsals taking up at least four nights a week of Brian's time. Left at home at Powis Square, Pat was feeling lonely and isolated. "The friction between me and Brian started to get really bad. He was leaving me on my own with the baby and no TV or radio at this tiny flat in Notting Hill night after night, I was going potty. We were too young to cope with that sort of situation. Then he lost his job again." The overspill of regular late nights meant Brian's habitual bad time keeping had resulted in a constant dock-ing of his wages which he compensated for by making up the difference out of the record department's till. This illegal arrange-ment survived until the day he was caught and dispensed with on the spot. Not that Brian was unduly worried about losing his job at the Civil Service Store. The band was gigging frequently now and Pat's wages were regular. What was more important to him was finding another drummer. Mick Avory, whom Brian had re-cruited just in time for the first gig at the Marquee, had since left, surfacing some months later playing with the two brothers from Muswell Hill in a heavily Stones influenced R&B band called The Ravens, who later changed their name to The Kinks.

His place on The Stones vacant drum stool had been filled by Tony Chapman, who had turned up at rehearsals after Brian had placed another ad in the Melody Maker. Chapman wasn't a great drummer but his influences were the same as the rest of The Stones, so his pedigree was good enough for everyone else except Brian who had someone else in mind.

The Store manager at the Civil Service Stores had not prose-cuted Brian and the errant Stone soon found himself another counter job fairly easily. He went to work a couple of hundred yards up the road in a branch of WH Smiths Newsagents in Kingsway, Holborn, still within handy walking distance of their rehearsal room at the Bricklayers Arms.

It was after one late night rehearsal that Brian decided he couldn't face the long trek back to his nappy sodden flat across town. He and Stu opted for a night out on the town and planned to go straight to work after. When he did return the following evening the place was empty. Pat and Mark were gone. There was a hastily scribbled note on the table.

"I had eventually had enough," Pat recalls. "I left him and went to stay with some girlfriends I had met at work in a flat in Maida Vale. The last straw was when Brian didn't come home and at about four o'clock in the morning Mick turned up at the door looking for Brian, knowing full well he wasn't there, and tried to get into bed with me. It was pathetic, he was all spotty and really drunk, I just laughed at him."

With Pat and the baby gone, the landlord, who had never liked the look of Brian anyway, gave him a day's notice to get out. Brian found himself homeless once again until Mick came to his rescue and found Brian a basement bedsitter flat with a kitchen in Brackley Road, Beckenham, a short distance from drummer Tony Chapman.

Pat hadn't mentioned anything in her note to Brian about Mick's early morning visit although Mick was unsure as to what Brian knew about his drunken pass at Pat. Frightened of reprisals, Jagger was bending over backwards to help Brian out. The accomodation arrangements that Jagger had sorted out were to be short lived, however, as Brian hated living so far out of the city. Having to catch the last train back to Beckenham every night was sorely cramping Jones's newly acquired bachelor status. Also, having to travel back and forth to rehearsals with Tony, whom Brian felt sure knew of his plans to replace him, made the boring journey even worse.

It was Brian's non-existent domestic aptitude that was to solve his commuting problem. One night he managed to convince a girl he'd just met to stay with him for the weekend in order to cook and clean. All his life, Brian chauvinistically assumed all women to be born naturals in the kitchen. On this occasion he was wrong. He returned home one night to find out that she had burnt half the flat down.

Brian continued to live in the flat's burnt out shell by successfully avoiding the owner for the next few days until Mick came to his rescue once again. This time he found them both a flat back in London, number 102 Edith Grove. This flat consisted of two spacious rooms on the middle floor of a large white-fronted terraced house in the fashionable Chelsea, SW10 area. In August, 1962, Mick and Brian moved in.

The rent was sixteen pounds a week. Although the area may have been fashionable, unfortunately the same could not be said for the actual flat. It was completely run down, damp and cold. Bare light bulbs hung down from the yellow, decaying ceilings and the wallpaper peeled off the walls in sheets. The rancid communal toilet was situated between the second and third floors and was accessible only by candle light. The most frequent visitors were rats. They would scatter along the skirting boards whenever anyone entered.

Despite the rundown condition of the house the rent was still exorbitant. Even with Mick's grant from the L.S.E and Brian's wages from Smiths, it was still a struggle to meet the weekly demand. The two Stones decided to move in a third party. The obvious choice was Keith who, having just finished his last term at Sidcup Art College, was anxious to leave home.

He had got used to spending time crashing out at Brian's flat in Beckenham and the thought of returning to live with his parents didn't appeal to him at all. Richards moved in.

Unfortunately for Brian and Mick, Richards didn't relish the prospect of finding a job so, with the rent still a problem, it meant taking on yet another flatmate. He came in the shape of a mysterious red headed printer who answered to the name of Phelge as neither Brian, Mick or Keith could ever remember his name. Brian later lengthened his moniker to Nanker Phelge which became an early pseudonym for group compositions, a nanker being a hideously funny face invented by Brian which involved sticking fingers up his nose.

Keith, out of work and completely broke, would spend his days alone at the flat practising his guitar for as long as the electric meter allowed, often ending the day sitting in the dark waiting for one of the others to return in order to feed it. Happily he wasn't to want for company for long. Brian, true to form, had been caught with his hands in the till again. He was fired. Now, with both Brian and Keith not working, the perpetually hard-up living conditions at the already disgusting flat deteriorated further and at an alarming rate. Food became an incidental luxury, mainly supplied in the form of parcels sent up to Keith by his mum, Doris, while heating and lighting were restricted to near non-existent lengths of time.

That year, 1962, brought with it an exceptionally harsh winter. The boys spent hours huddled together under blankets on a large mattress in the middle of the floor to keep them warm. To entertain themselves, they would play imaginary games like tearing up sheets and making sandwiches out of them. The freezing conditions made bathing and washing a nightmarish chore to the point of its exclusion altogether, except for Brian's incessant hair washing. Rehearsing was also virtually impossible due to their finger tips instantly turning blue and then bleeding on the strings.

Things didn't look like they were going to get any better as Brian's diary for October had only two forthcoming gigs pencilled in, both at the Ealing Club. The weeks slowly and painfully crawled by as the three sat around wrapped in blankets watching their cold breath rise towards the cracked ceiling, the true horror of their desperate situation finally dawning on them. Even Keith considered finding a job, resigned to the fact that they were never going to make a living playing Rhythm and Blues. He collected his portfolio of artwork from Sidcup in readiness to look for work. As leader, Brian needed to do a bit of morale boosting.

After lengthy discussions, it was decided to give the band one year in which to make it, Brian reasoning that if they didn't crack it by then, "well at least they would have tried." Keith breathed a sigh of relief and threw his large black folder back into a corner.

There was only one way to avoid freezing to death and that meant getting out of the filthy Edith Grove ice box and into somewhere warmer on a daily basis. To that end, Brian had taken to spending much of his time at the home of Cyril Davis, where he was learning and quickly mastering playing the mouth organ. This was Brian's first real step towards becoming the multi-instrumentalist the world would later know.

Mick was spending his days at college studying for his forthcoming exams, leaving Keith more often than not shivering alone in the empty flat, pacing up and down while vowing to buy a revolver in order to shoot his companions, the rats.

Faced with near starvation and failure, Brian set about harassing clubs for gigs for the band. With renewed vigour he battled tirelessly against the club scene's continued resistance against booking anything other than jazz. Even though the jazz era was obviously over and finished, the venue owners were clinging on to its memory like a departed loved one and paraded the same tired old acts night after night.

Despite this widespread defiance, Brian miraculously started to pull in the work anywhere and everywhere. Church halls, suburban sports club dances and back room pub gigs. They all mounted up to a small but regular income which Brian, as self-appointed treasurer, would share out among the band after skimming an additional payment off the top for himself for services rendered as leader, agent and manager.

One of these gigs was at an old wooden barn of a dance hall on Eel Pie Island in the middle of the Thames at Twickenham. The island was only accessible by crossing a rickety footbridge or by boarding an equally rickety ferry which cost sixpence. The band would travel to gigs in Stu's ancient pre-war Rover that was big enough to carry the band plus the drums and amps so long as they stacked it right. They would arrive outside clubs looking like a hill-billy family on the move.

One of their constant worries at this stage was their equipment. The majority of it was on hire purchase and the repayments had mounted up quickly. The band had developed a routine of putting a percentage of their meagre gig money in an old tea caddy back at the flat, but this was never enough to cover the gear repayments. Unfortunately, Brian's pilfering habits by now knew neither boundaries nor loyalties.

At the end of September 1962, Mick recieved his exam results. He had passed well. This set the singer thinking hard about his future. He was about to start a second term at the L.S.E., so study was important. Looking around the squalid Edith Grove flat, Mick weighed up the prospect of conventional employment as opposed to wasting away physically and mentally in the pursuit of musical fulfilment.

He knew that he was not about to quit the group as his involvement in it did not yet jeopardise his future. As a compromise, he decided to take a more relaxed backseat role and leave the motivation to Brian and Keith, whom, he figured, had nothing else to do anyway.

Keith's more pronounced up-front role with the band got off to a good start when, following their next appearance at the Marquee, Harold Pendleton's sarcasm finally got the better of him. Richards walked over to the sniggering club owner and promptly smashed him over the head with his guitar.

This was the end of any Marquee dates for The Rolling Stones for the foreseeable future.

Repercussions from Keith's action were quick in coming and they manifested themselves from the most unlikely quarters.

Cyril Davis, who had befriended the band from the very beginning, instantly dropped them from a promised support slot on
any of his forthcoming gigs. So did Ken Coyler who had lined
them up for a show at his club, Studio 51.

The loss of people like Davis and Coyler from the Stones'
corner, coupled with their ban at the Marquee was enough to persuade Dick Taylor to chuck it all in. He told Brian he wanted to
concentrate on his college work. "I was completely neglecting my
work at the Royal College of Art where I was a student, I simply
had to make a choice," he recalls.

Without a bass player, Brian needed to do some quick thinking
in case Dick's departure started a trend amongst the others. He
raided the last of the tea caddy's resources and booked an hour's
studio time for the band at Curly Clayton Studios near the
Arsenal football ground in Highbury in an ambitious attempt to
make a demo.

In the meantime, Pat had moved with Mark to a flat of their
own in Ladbroke Grove. She had no idea where Brian was and
had made no effort to find out. She continued to work for Leo
Computers until one day she was taken ill. She collapsed suffering with a case of Peritonitis. "I was rushed into hospital where
they contacted my parents who came straight up to London to
collect Mark and took him back to Cheltenham so I could recover."

The band, without Taylor, entered the studio on October 27th
and put down three tracks, Bo Diddley's *You Can't Judge A Book By
The Cover*, Muddy Waters' *Soon Forgotten* and Jimmy Reed's *Close
Together*.

Brian's next step was to take a leaf out of the enterprising Alexis
Korner's book and to start a club on their own. Starting off with a
Saturday night and Sunday afternoon gig at the Red Lion pub in
Sutton, Surrey, they followed up with a string of appearances in
the area. They plastered the place with bold home-made posters
that announced "Rhythm and Blues with The Rolling Stones."

For these dates Brian managed to convince Dick Taylor to stand
in long enough for him to audition a new bass player.

It was Tony Chapman who said he knew of a bass player who
had played in his previous band, The Cliftons, and who might
possibly be interested in an audition. Brian told him to get him
down to the next rehearsal. The band had now moved their rehearsal room closer to their home base at Edith Grove. Money

had been scarce and making the ten minute trip to the Bricklayers Arms public house at Worlds End, Chelsea, cost nothing.

It was here on the 7th December, 1962. that Tony introduced Brian, Mick, Keith and Stu to Bill Perks, a bass player from Lewisham.

William George Perks was born on the 24th of October, 1936 to William Senior and Kathleen Perks, a working class couple from south-east London. William junior was the first of five children. He had two brothers, Brian, (who the family called John) and Paul, along with two sisters, Anne and Judith. At eighteen he was called up for National Service and entered the RAF, leaving two years later with a change of name to Bill Wyman, inspired by an RAF pal. He also had a wife, a girl called Diana whom he moved in with at a flat above a petrol station in Penge.

By 1962 he was playing bass semi-professionally in a band called The Cliftons, who backed the then impressively billed "England's answer to Little Richard", a lacklustre signer who went under the unfortunate name of Dickie Pride.

Bill was older than the other Stones, married and the proud father of a baby son, Stephen. It was an achievement that caused Brian to raise an eyebrow, but no more.

Brian auditioned Bill twice before asking him if he wanted to join the band, more impressed with the bass player's equipment than by his actual playing ability. Bill had a huge VOX 850 bass cabinet that was large enough to accommodate a guitar as well as his show-stealing VOX Phantom bass. All of the equipment was his own.

Bill thought Brian's offer over while munching a bag of chips which he shared with the other four back at the Edith Grove slum before eventually agreeing. "Good," said Brian, "your first gig is next Saturday. Call round for us here at six."

Dick Hattrell, Brian's old room-mate and friend from Cheltenham, had recently moved up to London where he had signed up with a branch of the Territorial Army. He began staying on and off with the lads at Edith Grove, chipping in money towards food rations. Royal feasts of pork pies and potatoes would often be thrown, normally after Dick had donated all his wages. He also fed the starved electricity meter that seemed to swallow coins like a one-armed bandit in Las Vegas.

Brian treated Dick Hattrell like a complete lackey. He came

from a very well-to-do background, even by Cheltenham standards, but this didn't bother Brian who, in an unusual show of compassion, befriended him and took him under his wing. Brian's friendship with Dick hadn't been a problem for him during his carefree wandering days in Cheltenham. But now, in London, surrounded by his poor but eminently cool musician cronies, Brian viewed the association with acute embarrassment. He became intent on exploiting his trusting pal to the full.

He started by commandeering his army pay and relieving him of his regulation army great coat which he then gave to Keith. The winter of '62 was now being extolled as the worst Britain had faced in a hundred years, not that Brian, Keith and Mick needed newspapers to tell them.

They were still huddled together in Edith Grove where the plumbing had frozen solid, the lavatory wouldn't flush and icicles were hanging down like beaded curtains in every window and doorway. The ever-inventive Brian had got hold of an electric fan heater which he would train on the water pipe long enough to thaw it out in order to wash his hair daily and then, standing in front of it, dry it.

Dick would suffer numerous indignities at the hands of Brian for only as long as his wages permitted. As soon as Brian had spent the last penny of Dick's money, Dick would be dismissed. One night Brian pulled two completely harmless wires from the back of a speaker and crept over to where Dick was asleep. He woke him with a shake and standing above Hattrell brandished the two bare wires ends at him, threatening to electrocute him. Fearing for his life, Hattrell was sent running naked to the door and out into the snow. Dick remembers those days with a perhaps strange, on reflection, affection.

"Brian had this very cruel side to his nature," says Hattrell, "but I regarded him as a very true friend, although he could go to complete extremes. At times he would wait for me to come back to the flat and take my wage packet and make me walk behind him in the street."

It was into this madness that Bill Wyman returned on the 15th of December in order to play his first gig as a Rolling Stone at a youth club in Putney.

After the show, Brian informed him that his wages were to be donated to the Edith Grove ration fund. Tony Chapman, the drummer, enjoyed the next few gigs, happy to be reunited with his old Clifton's band member once again.

Wyman and Chapman started travelling to gigs together. One gig was at the Ricky Tic club in Windsor. After the show Brian casually informed Tony he was fired. The reason for Chapman's dismissal centered around Brian's efforts to get Brian Knight's drummer, Charlie Watts, to join the band. But his overtures had proved unsuccessful. However, Brian's constant badgering was slowly paying off. His latest ploy was to let Watts know that The Stones were now drummerless and, within the pipeline, they really were in a fix.

Charles Robert Watts was born on 2nd June of June 1941, the son of a lorry driver, Charles Richard Watts and his wife, Lillian. He was brought up in London's King's Cross area, until moving to Wembley in 1952 and starting at the Tylers Croft Secondary School. Leaving school in 1957 with one 'O' level in art, he gained a place at the Harrow School of Art and eventually a job with the advertising agency Hobson and Grey. By 1960 Watts, a sharp-suited Mod with an extraordinary knowledge of jazz and art, had immersed himself in London's coffee bar and jazz club scene. He joined Alexis Korner's Blues Incorporated in 1962, before moving on to Brian Knight's Blues By Six and then The Stones.

Brian Knight's memory of Charlie was that, "Charlie was always troubled by making a 100 per cent decision involving his music or art. He loved his job as a graphic designer and didn't want to give it up, and vice versa. He left Blues Incorporated and joined up with me when Alexis got really popular and Charlie found he was playing most nights of the week. His work began to suffer and we were playing more than the Stones and Blues Incorporated put together. He decided to join The Stones because they only played around twice a week."

Whatever the true reason behind Charlie's joining The Stones, join he did. "I just got a call from him one afternoon," said Brian Knight. "He was at work and he said, 'I've joined The Stones.' I thought, good luck to you."

Charlie set up his first kit with The Stones for his gig on the 14th of January 1963 at The Flamingo Club in Soho, thus completing a line up that would remain intact until 1969.

4

Down The Road Apiece

Before Tony Chapman was so callously abandoned by Brian in January 1963, he had sent the band's 3-track demo to England's major established record companies, EMI and Decca. They were turned down flat by both companies. Decca responded with the curt reply, "great band but you'll never get anywhere with your singer", while EMI simply and politely returned the acetate accompanied by a "form" letter of the, "it's very nice, needs more work," variety.

EMI's A&R department had already gone out on a limb with a new signing from Liverpool, who they at first thought were German, called The Beatles. Their first single *Love Me Do* was hardly setting the charts alight, limiting the chances of EMI signing some more long-haired hopefuls from slim to none.

It was the beginning of a new year, 1963, and the band had a full twelve months to run before their agreed time limit was up. Despite their disappointment over the lack of record company interest, January and February were looking like turning out to be good months for the band, gig wise. Brian's diary was showing a healthy list of dates coming up including a double return to the Marquee, which Brian had underlined triumphantly.

Brian had also become friendly with a London club promoter called Giorgio Gomelski whom he had first met when The Stones played at his venue, the Piccadilly Jazz Club, the previous year. The Club had since folded and Giorgio was now running another club in the back room of the Station Hotel in Richmond called The

Crawdaddy Club. Brian set about persuading Gomelski to book The Stones.

Giorgio Gomelski was a large, bearded, 29-year-old man of Franco-Russian descent. His involvement with music began during the 1950's after landing a job working for Chris Barber. From here he moved on to experimenting with a crude early form of promotion video before turning finally to club management and ownership. He had liked Brian immensely from their first meeting, but unfortunately, in Giorgio's opinion, that couldn't be said for the rest of The Stones. He thought they were terrible.

At every meeting, Brian persisted in trying to persuade Giorgio to re-book the band. He finally convinced him to at least watch them one more time, but not at his own club. Instead Gomelski travelled down to The Red Lion Pub in Surrey. Giorgio was amazed at the progress The Stones had made since he had seen them last, but still offered them nothing. Instead, he had something more important in mind: management.

Meanwhile, Brian, not one to pine for female company since the departure of Pat, had started dating a young 15-year-old schoolgirl called Linda Lawrence, whom he had met after playing at the Ricky Tic in Windsor.

"I was into jazz," Linda recalled. "I hated pop, Cliff Richard and all that, so we used to go to this tiny jazz club called The Ricky Tic, a little informal room above a pub in Windsor that served as a club. One night the usual jazz group cancelled and it was said that a rhythm and blues group would take their place. I never knew what R&B meant but I was curious enough to find out so I went along and it was The Stones. I hadn't ever heard of The Rolling Stones and certainly never understood what rhythm and blues meant but it was terribly exciting. I danced all night long and had a great time. Afterwards Brian asked me if I would like a drink at the bar. I was amazed at the way he played harmonica so I told him his music was fantastic and how much I'd enjoyed it."

Brian told Linda that the band had a gig the very next night in London.

"Brian asked me to come down and he would get me in, so I did".

Linda's family originally hailed from Reading in Berkshire before they moved to Windsor where Linda attended school. Following that first weekend encounter she began accompanying

Brian to most Stones's gigs, but only if they didn't fall on school nights.

A few weeks later, Brian had to do a double-take as he walked on stage with The Stones at the Ealing Club. As he peered out into the darkness of the club there in the front row was Pat Andrews cradling his baby son.

"I had gone back to Cheltenham after getting out of hospital to pick up Mark and returned to London in March," she recalls. "On the Saturday, Easter Saturday, I was shocked to suddenly realise it had been a year to the day since I first made the move to London to be with Brian, so I went to the Ealing Club after reading that The Stones were playing there. It was as if we had never been apart."

It was a shock for Brian, too. He had gone to the Ealing Club with his new girlfriend, Linda. But after seeing Pat and his son, it was enough for him to send Linda home with a muttered promise to explain everything later. Pat then moved back in with Brian at the Edith Grove flat, naturally taking one of the two rooms for themselves and Mark, cramping Mick, Keith and Phelge into the other in the process. Pat still had her job and the extra regular money she brought home, plus her cooking and cleaning, which she really had no choice but to do – "Not one of them could cook a thing" – enabled life at number 102 to take on a form of normality that hadn't been seen since Brian's arrival.

In the meantime, Giorgio had assumed an informal management role with the band. He began booking dates for the band that finally included a Sunday night spot at his own Crawdaddy Club. This relieved the pressure from Brian, who was, so far as anyone could see, enjoying living with his reunited family once again. Brian knew that with the respectability of Giorgio at the band's helm, clubs would be keener to book the group. Jones's assessment was correct. Within a month, Giorgio had taken The Stones from playing as a two-nights-a-week curiosity to a regular five-night-a-week circuit attraction.

With Giorgio behind them, Stones' gigs started to sell out. Hordes of scooter-riding Mods were beginning to converge on any venue that hired the band. They would arrive at gigs in a mass of blinding headlights, chrome and mirrors.

The Stones were offered a Sunday night residence at the Crawdaddy for a guaranteed one pound per gig following their first showing there in March when they sold out the place, pushing over the club's capacity of 300. Things had never looked so good.

The following week Giorgio took out a self penned ad in *The Melody Maker* announcing to the world the arrival of the craziest new sound around, the Rhythm and Blues of the unparalleled Rolling Stones. The response to the ad the following week was outstanding. The Club was literally besieged.

As the band arrived in Stu's old Rover, they were amazed at the lines of fans that spilled out along the passageway and on to the Thames sidestreet. Teenage clans of all types and descriptions, from Mods and Rockers to Beatniks and Teddy Boys, were mingling together in an excited and friendly huddle as they shuffled closer to the club's door where Giorgio stood at the entrance, dressed in his finest nightclub owner's garb, collecting ticket stubs and money.

With his beaming face and a grin a mile wide, he looked to all the world like a respectable cousin of Popeye's Bluto. Giorgio was now in the full managerial swing of things, booking gigs and placing ads in the music papers with gay abandon, each one more outrageous that the last, culminating with his over-the-top proclamation advertising "THE THRILLING EXHILARATING GALVANIC INTOXICATING INCOMPARABLE ROLLING STONES".

Giorgio's logical next step was to capture the sound of The Stones on a demo in the studio. He booked them into his friend George Clewson's studio in Portland Place with a young engineer named Glyn John where they recorded five tracks in under three hours.

The five songs recorded were Bo Diddley's *Road Runner* and *Diddley Daddy*, Jimmy Reed's *Honey What's Wrong?* and *Bright Lights, Big City* and Muddy Waters', *I Want To Be Loved*. Brian was completely bowled over by the recorded results, taking them home and repeatedly playing them to Pat and Mark for hours on end until, as Pat succinctly puts it, "Thankfully someone destroyed the record player mysteriously."

On April 13th the band got its very first piece of independent press in Richmond's local paper, *The Richmond and Twickenham Times*. The paper's Barry May wrote:

"A musical magnet is drawing the jazz beatniks to Richmond. The attraction is The Crawdaddy Club at the Station Hotel, the first kind in an area of flourishing modern and traditional jazz haunts. R&B is replacing Traddy-Pop. The deep, earthy sound is typical of the best R&B, and gives all who hear it an irresistible urge to stand up and move. The four or five nights of jazz every week at Eel Pie Island have dwindled to only two at the weekend. Save from the swaying forms of the group on the spotlit stage, the room is in darkness. A patch of light from the entrance doors catches the sweating dancers and those who are slumped on the floor, the long hair, suede jackets, gaucho trousers and Chelsea boots. How sad and unfortunate that The Station Hotel is to be demolished. The Stones will go on rolling."

Brian carried the folded cutting around with him until it literally faded away.

Giorgio and Clewson, armed with a bundle of acetates and copies of the newspaper began tirelessly touting the demos around London's record companies, but all to no avail.

If, professionally, life was still a struggle at least Brian's domestic arrangements were working out fine. Pat and Brian were, it seemed, inseparable and, despite their dilapidated surroundings, Pat had performed a minor miracle in turning the Edith Grove hovel into something that resembled a home.

Keith, at this point, had started dating a young Indian girl named Aleema Mohammand whom he had met at one of their gigs and declared he was very fond of. Both she and Keith would often double date with Brian and Pat. "We were all so really close then," Pat fondly recalls. "It was always the four of us just going for a walk or to The Wimpy Bar. Keith used to have this thing about climbing up lampposts along the Embankment, while Brian, ever the proud father, pushed baby Mark along in his pram. Keith would get right to the top and look out over the sea, well the Thames, acting like a pirate shouting, 'Aaaaghh Jim Lad – up the crow's nest!' We all used to fall about laughing. We called ourselves the four musketeers."

Through Giorgio's past involvement with film, he had made a number of associates in the TV world. It was not surprising, therefore, when he told the lads that he had been invited to the ABC TV Studios in nearby Twickenham to watch the taping of a new pop music show called *Thank Your Lucky Stars*. What did impress the band, however, was the fact that the show was going out live and was to feature The Beatles.

The Beatles had surpassed their somewhat unremarkable debut single when they released their infinitely superior follow-up entitled, *Please Please Me*. This record had shot straight to the number one spot signalling the start of Beatlemania. Thousands of youngsters began wearing collarless jackets, adopting Liverpudlian accents and calling everything they liked 'fab'. The swinging sixties were well on their way.

The band hadn't given Giorgio's swanning off to the TV station a second thought. They were well used to his mentioning this producer or that director when talking of his contacts in the world of media and his great plans for the future of the band. But what really made them sit up and take notice was that when Giorgio returned he walked back into the club mid-way through The Stones set, beaming his famous grin and escorted by all four Beatles. They were shown to Gomelski's exclusively reserved table by the side of the stage.

The Stones had barely finished their very nervous and rushed set and thanked the seething and sweating crowd, before Giorgio frantically beckoned them over.

Giorgio stood with his arms around the shoulders of Brian and Mick like a proud father and introduced The Beatles one at a time to each of The Stones. The Beatles were only two singles and an album into their recording career but this was enough for Brian, who, although he never let on, considered them to be glamorous stars. He actually asked John Lennon for a signed photograph, but not for himself, you understand.

Both bands amicably chatted for several hours. In keeping with their characters, Brian and John traded musical compliments, while Paul fascinated Mick with the revelation that 90% of The Beatles repertoire was now original compositions, published by their own publishing house.

The Beatles were mid-way through a second tour of Great Britain and four days away from playing their first visit to the Albert Hall, where a change of chart position and billing had put them as the headlining act, topping the bill over American artists Chris Montez and Tommy Rowe. The Beatles invited all six Stones along.

It was typical that only Brian, Keith, Mick and Giorgio went along. Bill and Charlie stayed home with their respective partners, Diane and Shirley, while Stu was, as was fast becoming a habit with Brian, characteristically left out.

Entering the Albert Hall via the stage door, a huge scream rang out as the three Stones, at a distance, were mistaken for The Beatles. A large crowd of hysterical girls thundered towards them, clawing and grabbing at their hair and clothes.

Once in the safety of the auditorium, the three decidedly shaky Stones stared at each other in astonishment. Only Brian broke the silence. "That's what I want," he announced. "That's what I want."

Giorgio had witnessed the whole thing and his managerial determination was given a recharge of energy. Vowing that "if the record companies aren't interested, we'll make them interested," his next idea was to shoot a short 20 minute promotion film of the band performing their next gig back at the Crawdaddy. In preparation for the filming, he booked the band into proper rehearsal facilities at a studio in Morden.

The big gig filming extravaganza was set for Sunday 21st April and to give it an air of professional authority Gomelski contacted Peter Jones, a well known music columnist and writer for the pop paper *Record Mirror*. He went along to the club.

"I went down and met Brian, who was without doubt the leader," Jones recalls. "He came out and offered to take me round to the front of the club to the pub part and buy me a drink and have a chat. We got to the pub but Brian didn't have a penny on him, only a folded piece of newspaper which was like a review-come-article about the band. After I got the drinks I talked to Brian who was really fed up with the record companies taking no interest in his band. He talked about Muddy Waters, Jimmy Reed and all his influences. I could see he was really determined and he greatly impressed me. I told him I'd see if I could get some interest for him.

I knew a couple of guys I thought would possibly be into The Stones," Jones continues, "one of which was a guy called Andrew Oldham, who was quick on the mark where a good thing was concerned, had a great knowledge of music and an eye for trends. He had weasled his way to working as a bit of a publicist for The Beatles after bumping into Brian Epstein at a TV studio and literally talked himself into the job. He seemed interested but I never gave it too much thought. But I did convince a fellow columnist on the *Mirror* called Norman Joplin to go along the following week and do a piece on them for the paper."

Joplin wrote a fascinating, foresighted article which stated, "You may never have heard of The Rolling Stones but by gad you will. They are probably destined to be the biggest R&B band on the scene." Yet even this high praise and expectation wasn't enough to open the door to that elusive record company deal.

Giorgio's combined demo and promo film had failed again to inspire record company interest, including the old favourites, Decca, although one piece of good news arrived unexpectedly when Brian received a letter from the BBC.

Back in January he had sent a hand-written biography of The Stones explaining the band's make-up and influences, and a full listing of venues they had played, in the hope of getting an audition for the radio show, *The Jazz Club*. But so much time had since elapsed that Brian had all but forgotten it. The letter informed Brian they had been successful and to report to the BBC on the 23rd of April.

Panic set in on the day of the audition when, hours before the gig, Bill and Charlie told Brian they could have no more time off from their regular jobs. Since leaving the band to play as a four piece would have meant cancelling the gig, Brian, at the last minute, dragged along the Rhythm Section from Cyril Davis's band The All Stars. The audition was successful and they were booked for a later date.

One week after the BBC's A&R man, Norman Joplin, had gone to see The Stones, Peter Jones' friend, Andrew Oldham, arrived at the Crawdaddy. With him was one Eric Easton, former cinema organist and booking agent for Bert Weedon and the piano playing grandmother, Mrs Mills. Andrew was 19 and Easton 35.

This unlikely couple shared an office at Randor House, Regent Street, with the express intention of forming their own management company. Easton, though his management of Weedon and Mills was already firmly established, wanted to move in on younger acts. Andrew Oldham, with his youthful arrogance, represented the way in.

Both men stood at the back of the club and watched The Stones plough through an electrifying, high-energy, charged set of R&B standards, giving the songs their very own distinct treatment and drive. One half of the set was all Oldham needed to see. He was completely bowled over with the band. And he had already recognised something in them that hadn't even registered with themselves, that is their sheer animal magnetism mixed with a magical combination of natural sex appeal and musical arrogance.

In the interval, pushing through the crowd, Andrew managed to collar Mick Jagger and, after introducing himself and Easton, asked if the band had a leader or manager, anyone he could talk to concerning business matters.

Brian instantly sprang into view eyeing the pair up suspiciously but outwardly friendly enough to talk with Oldham and Easton for a few minutes before the band had to take the stage once again in order to resume their set.

During Andrew's probing questioning, Brian had made it abundantly clear that although Giorgio certainly looked out for the band, he far from considered him a manager. In fact, if anything, Brian's off-hand manner seemed to suggest the group had no confidence in him whatsoever. This might have had something to do with the fact that Giorgio was away in Switzerland attending the funeral of his father at the time. That suited Oldham fine.

After exchanging phone numbers, they parted. The next day, Oldham and Easton discussed the possibility of a joint management project concerning The Stones. They both agreed to give the plan a try. Oldham rang Brian at the Edith Grove flat and asked him to come up to their office in Regent Street in order to discuss some business and, possibly, management matters.

Brian jumped at the chance but, eager to play it cool, made the meeting hours late, going on to make a further four trips, conning lunch every time before admitting his interest.

Brian liked Andrew immensely. He was roughly the same age, quick and enthusiastic, and, to top it all, he had even worked for The Beatles.

On his fifth visit to Oldham and Easton on the 1st of May 1963, Brian signed a three year management contract on behalf of all six Stones. In addition to this, Brian struck a further private deal of his own. He secured with Oldham a separate contract that in effect entitled him to an extra £5 a week over and above anything the rest of The Stones would in future receive, whether it be salary or otherwise.

Brian broke the news to Pat and the whole band at the flat where Stu, for one, expressed serious reservations. Not surprisingly, he was more than slightly peeved at being signed away in such a nonchalant fashion without so much as being consulted. Despite this small oversight on Brian's part it was generally accepted by all that Brian held superior knowledge in such situations and he had done so much good for the band already that the deal was given the go-ahead.

Stu's reluctant acceptance of his new management team had only just sunk in when he was delivered another, more savage, blow. Oldham's superior wisdom had decreed he would have to go altogether. In his mind, he didn't look quite right. Stu's appearance, he told Brian, was all wrong for the band.

Unfortunately, following an operation for vitamin deficiency when he was a small boy, Stu had been left with a very prominent and jutting jawline. It was something of which he was painfully aware and shy about, and to have it numbered among the reasons for why he no longer fitted in with the group image was a painful and spiteful experience.

Things were helped very little when Brian, seeing how upset Stu was, offered his old mate a small gesture of compensation and thanks. He took him aside to happily inform him he could have the job of road manager and driver for the band. From now on, it would be his job to transport the group and their equipment to all forthcoming gigs. As this was something that Stu had been doing since their very first outing, being the only band member who owned any transport, he wasn't particularly over the moon with the offer. By all accounts, he only narrowly avoided hitting Brian.

Andrew, quick to spot any potential threat to his newly acquired protegees, stepped in with Henry Kissinger-like tact and decorum and told Stu that he would still be used on all future recordings as well as receiving a full 6th share in profits. This he begrudgingly accepted after assurances from Brian, who used all the sincerity he could muster to win Stu over. This could not, however, disguise the serious blow that had been dealt to Stu and Brian's friendship.

Stu then looked on open-mouthed as Oldham's next item on the agenda was the insistence that Keith dropped the "s" from his surname in order to give a punchier sounding ring to his name. More of a Cliff Richard overtone was needed, Oldham had decided.

This episode left things clear for the next inevitable problem which was the return of Giorgio Gomelski. For this eventuality the entire band had arranged to visit their 'manager' together in order to let their leader and spokesman, Brian, explain away all the recent developments.

Mick, Keith, Bill and Charlie arrived together and sat uncomfortably in Giorgio's living room, watching re-run after re-run of a newly edited version of the filmed Richmond gig, patiently waiting for Brian to show up.

Brian eventually arrived and, to their amazement, he was with Andrew. Giorgio, by now very suspicious of such an unexpected gathering, tactfully asked Brian to introduce his friend. The rest of The Stones held their breath and with all their eyes fixed on Brian, listened in amazement as he said, "Giorgio, I want you to meet an old school friend of mine, who has come up to visit me from Cheltenham. His name is Loog, Andrew Loog Oldham."

Giorgio had never once in the past tried to get the band to sign a contract with him. His advice, on the contrary, had always been the opposite, never let anyone get control over you, sign nothing, do it yourselves. Don't run the risk of someone taking you over.

Although Brian had lied about Andrew, the astute Russian knew him well enough to realise what had happened behind his back. He knew his well-meaning advice had gone only so far to drop himself out of The Stones parcel. But Stu and Giorgio weren't the only ones disgusted at Brian and Andrew's roughshod handling and insensitivity.

Pat was furious when Brian told her what had happened with both their tried and trusted friends. "I couldn't believe what Brian had done to Stu, let alone Giorgio," she recalls. "He and his wife, Edith, had been like a mother and father to Brian, Mark and me, and all the lads. That's what made it all worse. They were like advisors always taking such good care of them. They would always be eternally grateful to them and never forget the kindness, but Brian didn't seem to care." He had a goal and no-one was going to stand in the way of that.

For the band, it began to feel in those first few days of Oldham's management that no sooner had the dust settled on one decision that caused a major altercation, than another would raise its head. On the 4th of May, Andrew took the band down to the Battersea Park fun fair for their first professional photo session and gig under his care.

For the occasion Andrew had taken the entire band on a shopping spree down Carnaby Street and kitted the group out in identical mod stage outfits. Brian arrived together with Pat and Mark, a fact that greatly annoyed Oldham. "Brian was carrying Mark like he always did when he was being oh-so-proud, and Andrew went mad," Pat recalls.

"He took Brian aside and literally screamed at him, and told him he must never be seen in public with a girlfriend, let alone with a baby. It would ruin his image. What image? This was before they even had a record out. I thought it was ridiculous but I was really mad. Furious, Andrew was saying that Brian must always appear available, even if he wasn't. Brian did have some pictures taken with Mark just to get up his nose. I used to carry them in my handbag until it was stolen." Andrew would soon find out that Brian would always do the opposite anyone told him.

Andrew was moving in on The Stones very quickly. After Brian told him that the band had already demoed some material months before at the studios at Portland Place, both he and Easton went straight round and brought back the master, laying out £106 in cash on the spot. Then, after checking with Brian that there were no more skeletons in their collective cupboards, he produced a further contract, this time covering three years of exclusive recording with the company "Impact Sound". The deal gave the band a 6 per cent royalty clause which was to be divided evenly five ways. Brian and Andrew's sincere promise to Stu was already well forgotten.

Oldham's next step was a brilliantly manoeuvred record deal with Decca, the company that had already passed on the band twice. Dick Rowe, head of the A&R department, was instantly famous as the man who turned down The Beatles. He had recently been a panellist alongside George Harrison at a music talent contest in Liverpool where he had been told by George that he should check out a London band called The Rolling Stones. Not daring to make the same mistake twice, especially after being told by a Beatle, he did just that.

Andrew exploited the embarrassed company man mercilessly. Oldham had done his research and would only agree to a leasing deal with Decca whereby he and Easton retained ownership of all recorded material by the band, a deal that not even The Beatles had.

With the deal in the bag the next step was to get the band back in the studio. The band entered the huge Olympic Studios by the Thames in Barnes for the first time on the 10th of May. After compiling a list of their favourite songs picked from their respective record collections, they whittled it down to one, a Chuck Berry number entitled *Come On* backed with Muddy Waters *I Want To Be Loved*.

Andrew confidentially informed The Stones that he was going to produce the record and took up position in the control booth. After a couple of takes, Andrew's naivety was obvious to all. It took engineer Roger Savage to make it official. He informed Oldham that the band were running out of time and hadn't yet got a finished take. Andrew calmly replied, "Oh, just use the last one." "So what about the mix?" Savage innocently asked. Clearly bemused by the term, Andrew replied, "Yeah, do whatever it is and I'll pick it up in the morning."

If Andrew and Eric's arrival on the scene had signalled to Pat the start of Brian selfishly toying around with well established relationships, the next episode simply left past discrepancies well in the shade. Keith's girlfriend Aleema had taken to staying over at Edith Grove on the odd night. Keith had come down with a bad case of flu and returned home to his parents for a few days whilst Pat was at work and Mark with a minder.

"Aleema had been sleeping with Keith on and off for a few months," Pat recalls. "God knows how she kept it from her parents because they were Indian and very religious. She had told Keith she wanted to remain a virgin and to his credit he had accepted it. He was really shy with girls then, very awkward. Anyway, Brian comes home and gives her all the old chat and that was that. I came home and Aleema was in tears saying how sorry she was for sleeping with Brian. I packed up for good after that. I don't know if she ever told Keith. I didn't want to find out. I didn't even care. I just had to go. I couldn't believe how far he would go."

Pat's leaving affected Brian very badly. Their time together at Edith Grove had afforded him the time to forge a close and loving bond with his son, a tie, Pat claims, he found irreplaceable. "I heard some time later that he missed Mark so terribly that he started walking the streets all around Chelsea, stopping couples who had little blond kids, hoping it would be Mark, running up to them thinking it was us. But even if I'd known, I don't think I could have gone back." Pat finally returned to Cheltenham.

In the midst of this separation, on the 13th of May, Brian received a rejection letter from the BBC concerning The Stones' earlier audition for BBC Radio's *The Jazz Club*. The letter finished with "We regret that the performance wasn't suitable for our purposes." Brian pinned the notice on the wall next to his signed picture of The Beatles and laughed. Since that audition The Stones had signed a major record deal with Decca and gained a new team of managers. *The Jazz Club* now, in the wake of losing Pat and Mark, seemed hardly important.

The Rolling Stones's debut single, *Come On*, was released on June the 7th 1963. To coincide with its release, Oldham lined up interviews with just about every teenage pop magazine on the news stands. The journalists on *Rave*, *Fabulous*, *Beat* and *Sixteen's* waxed lyrical and wildly about the five long haired wild men who were set to become the new leaders of the nation's teenage sub-culture.

But while the teen mags took The Stones instantly to their hearts, the serious and more critical music papers were a lot more reserved. They reviewed the single with less than enthusiastic results, ranging from *Melody Maker's* "very ordinary" to *Pop Weekly's* "This one's a miss!" A miss it was, rising slowly and painfully up the charts to flounder at the number 26 mark.

None of The Stones were particularly surprised at its poor chart placing. Since its recording the band's reaction to the finished product had been unenthusiastic, to the point of them jointly refusing to ever play it live.

But there was one bright note amongst this combined negativity. One article in *Disc* magazine was a review which read "The Beatles, who recommended The Stones to Decca, may well live to rue the day. This group could be challenging them for top places in the immediate future. The sturdy beat will drive you mad this summer."

Brian, resigned to the fact that Pat had left for good, looked once again to Linda Lawrence for female companionship. She had since left school and had begun attending hairdressing college in Piccadilly while seriously considering a career in modelling. Brian at once tried to convince Linda to move to Edith Grove as an obvious replacement for Pat's sadly missed womanly touch around the place, but she wisely remained at her parents' home in Windsor.

Eric Easton knew the one sure thing to ensure a high chart placing for The Stones' lacklustre debut single was television. As luck would have it one of Easton's management clients was the radio compère, Brian Matthews, who had recently landed the link-man job on the Birmingham based T.V show *Thank Your Lucky Stars*. Easton approached Matthews and The Stones were booked to appear miming *Come On* on June the 16th.

As The Stones left the studios after the show, they were unaware of the massive reaction their ninety second appearance had caused. Seconds after appearing on screen, the ABC TV's studios switchboard had lit up like a Christmas tree, with callers across the nation protesting at their being subjected to such an unsightly and scruffy bunch of louts on their TV's, especially on a prime 'tea-time' show.

The band were also unaware, as they motored south down the M1 to London, that Giorgio Gomelski had some bad news in store for them. There were to be no more gigs at the Richmond Crawdaddy Club. Ind Coope, the brewers, had been tipped off that the club was breaking fire regulations by overfilling the venue with numbers regularly exceeding the 500 mark. They instantly had ordered its immediate closure.

When the band heard the news, Brian considered that to be that. There was no way Giorgio would do the band any more favours after being treated so badly by them. But he was wrong. Giorgio was made of sterner stuff. He loved the band and loved what they had done for him and his club. He was going to relocate the Crawdaddy to the nearby Richmond Athletic Ground.

The new Crawdaddy reconvened on the 30th of June, with an open air gig that had The Stones topping the bill over Cyril Davis, Long John Baldry and a new group that were being looked after in the typical fatherly fashion by Giorgio, called The Yardbirds. They featured a curious Brian Jones lookalike singer called Keith Relf, as well as a young guitar hero named Eric Clapton.

Eric Easton was now in full stride, labouring away at the Regent Street office, pulling in favour after favour for his protegées, including one from an old associate, music promoter/manager/impresario, Don Arden.

Arden had lined up a nationwide pop package tour featuring American acts Bo Diddley and The Everly Brothers. Easton got The Stones on to the tour, sharing third billing with singer Julie

Grant, above the Flinstones and Micky Most. It was a tremendous coup to appear on the same bill as acts of such stature, especially their own hero, Bo Diddley, and it was enough for Charlie, Bill and Mick to accept The Stones as their one and only form of work. (All three had hung on to their regular paying jobs with Mick still at college even after their signing with Decca).

Mick had an extra reason to hand in his resignation to The London School of Economics and reaffirm his commitment to The Stones. A rumour had started that Brian had on more than one occasion suggested replacing him, once in favour of his old friend Paul Jones, now lead singer for the Mann Hugg Blues Brothers, who later became the enormously successful Manfred Mann. Paul Jones remembered that, "Brian had organised a little rehearsal, a jam if you like, when Mick wasn't around. Brian said Mick had terrible laryngitis. I had deputed for Mick once before at Richmond anyway so it wasn't that unusual, so we played together for a few hours. Just jamming along and Brian was saying, 'Great, this is what we should be doing more often. Free flowing blues, R&B unrehearsed material.' It was the basic Stones line-up with a couple of others. I can't remember who it was, but it was all very good fun. Brian said, 'We must do more of this unstructured type of thing.' He was into this idea of having a variety of deputy singers, but of course The Stones were never going to agree to this so that was basically the end of it. Whether he was judging us on our musical talents or whether he reasoned Mick was a less easy person to have in one's band, I don't know. But it was very much Brian's band and if that's what was on his mind he was probably right."

Mick knew all about Brian's ruthlessness and was sure that, given the chance, Brian would replace him at the drop of a hat. He had already suggested as much following an unusually below par performance by Mick at an earlier Marquee gig where Ian Stewart overheard Brian saying to Eric Easton that Jagger's voice was too weak to sing night after night, so they would probably get rid of him now rather than later. This was the start of an internal conflict within the band that would dog Brian throughout his career as a Rolling Stone.

Throughout all of Brian's criticisms and underhanded manoeuvring, Jagger remained inexplicably loyal to him, still recognising Brian as the leader of the band, and even a little in awe of him. But an unavoidable shift was happening amongst the front line of The Stones, as it does with most groups fronted by a lead singer. It is inevitable that the spotlight will fall on the singer of the band every time and will do so with very few exceptions. The singer cannot help but commandeer the main focal point and therefore be regarded as the leader. Brian knew this and resented it. He began to feel threatened by Mick's antics on stage and would go out of his way to undermine Jagger's performance, trying to attract the attention of the adoring audience, every time at Mick's expense. Brian was under the firm opinion that respect should only be paid to those within the band who played an instrument, reasoning that everyone can sing and it required very little talent. All of this resulted in an incredible on-stage fight between Brian and Mick for the limelight, each desperately trying to upstage the other. This made life very difficult on the long drives up and down the motorways in Stu's new Volkswagen Traveller (his new tool for his trade), but it certainly didn't effect the band's performance. In fact, they benefited from the pair's prima donna behaviour.

A couple of days before the tour, Brian made another return visit to Cheltenham, this time to introduce Linda to his parents. He considered her the right sort of girl to gain their approval. She was a quiet, well-mannered and frightfully middle class county girl. "The visit was a disaster," Linda recalled. "Brian's parents made it clear that there was still little he could do in their opinion to amend their sheer disappointment in him. Hardly a word was spoken. Even when Brian suggested the group go out to a pub in order to liven up proceedings, the atmosphere didn't change."

It was as if Brian didn't exist. It hurt Brian terribly because he so wanted to reach them, he tried to get them to listen to his music but that didn't help. Even his sister it seems was discouraged from taking an interest.

Arden's tour snaked its way round the country, beginning on 29th September at the New Victoria Cinema in London and taking in the northern hospitality of Birmingham, Wolverhampton, Liverpool, Sheffield and Manchester. Then they ventured beyond to Scotland and two shows at the Odeon Theatre in Glasgow, a first visit outside of England for Keith who before the tour hadn't even been outside of London.

Brian got things off to an antagonising start by insisting Linda

Lawrence accompanied them on tour. "Brian wanted me to go along with him. I didn't realise it was going to cause an atmosphere but the others were really uptight and straight away their girls were quizzing them all, 'How come we can't go?' It started a lot of arguments and bad feelings."

The undoubted highlight of The Stones' careers so far was their playing on the same stage as their hero Bo Diddley, whose material made up a large proportion of The Stones' own repertoire. To qualify things at the outset, Brian announced to the press that on tour, "It won't be a case of the pupils competing with the master, we'll be dropping all the Bo Diddley numbers from our set. He's one of our biggest influences." Diddley was renowned for perfecting the chunky, pounding, driving rhythms that bear his name (Oh Bo Diddley) and was the main structure and heart of countless songs already plagiarised by dozens of English R&B groups, including The Stones, up and down the country. He was a pioneer of using controlled distortion, played at a furious speed on any of his own elaborately shaped custom-built guitars, and influenced Brian's acquisition of a pair of equally individual 'Vox pearl drop' guitars.

Brian's guitar playing so impressed the Chicago R&B giant that he instructed his manager to ask him, Charlie and Bill if they would back him in favour of his own band on a forthcoming radio broadcast for the BBC's *Saturday Club*. It was at this session that Brian first spoke to Diddley. Brian was in his element talking to the complimentary Diddley and gave him a pair of gold cufflinks, which he in turn had been given, only as a borrowed prop, at an Oldham organised photo session with photographer Dezo Hoffman before the tour.

On the 8th of September, the tour inevitably reached Cheltenham where they played two shows at the Odeon Theatre. Brian nervously scoured the audience for some sign of Pat, only to be told afterwards by some of his old town friends that she had been at the gig but left before the end in order to avoid a meeting. Brian was hurt and upset but managed to conceal his feelings from Linda.

Dick Hattrell, once again resident in Cheltenham after ill-health and appendicitis had forced him to move back home, had been at the show and had tried to get backstage to greet his old friend. "I wasn't allowed to get near the dressing rooms, so I left quite upset that I hadn't had a chance to see Brian. I knew that he wouldn't be able to resist going to one of his old hang-outs in the town, either The Aztec or The Waikiki. I went to the Waikiki first and there, sure enough, was Brian.

"I'll never forget how shocked I was when I saw him. He had this big fur coat on and was huddled in this dark corner clutching a drink, totally alone, just staring out of the blackness. He looked very haunted already. I went over to him and said, 'Hi, mate.' He perked up and said it was, 'lovely to see an old friend. Come on, let me buy you a drink.' Well, Brian got so drunk that night – totally smashed – because he always did this stupid thing of mixing his drinks. He always did it. In the same glass he would mix whisky with wine or beer with brandy, but this night it was whisky with champagne."

Midway through the tour The Stones' first united band versus management rebellion erupted when they refused to wear the wardrobe that Andrew Oldham had chosen for them. Their stage uniforms consisted of cuban heeled boots, black trousers and blue leather waistcoats, topped with the garish black and white dog-tooth check jackets. Oldham, for all his pioneering foresight, at this point subscribed wholly to Brian Epstein's school of thought regarding "band presentation". He attempted, quite un-ashamedly, to market The Stones as the natural successors to The Beatles in every way, and this included the conformity of identical stage clothes. It was completely accidental that The Stones scruffy wild bunch image was exploited through something as simple as them wanting to wear their own street clothes on stage and televi-sion. Flabbergasted stage managers would continually be harassing the band to hurry to their dressing rooms and change minutes before going on stage, only to be amazed by the sullen reply that they were in fact wearing their stage clothes.

Oldham at first furiously protested at the band's foolhardy arrogance until the press began picking up on their appearance with articles describing their image as stupefying and unique, with some magazines going so far as to list every item of clothing worn. This ignited his capitalising instincts and he quickly changed his views. No longer were The Stones simply successors to The Beatles. They were the opposition. Everything about The Stones from now on would be an exact contradiction of the Liver-pool moptops. Ironically, it was The Beatles' home town that provided the backdrop for The Stones' biggest internal bust-up to date when the group played The Cavern Club. It was here that it was discovered that Brian was taking an extra £5 a week. He was caught out by chance when Keith overheard a boasting Brian telling the manager of the club that he would soon be staying at better hotels than the others because he was the leader and made more than the others in the band. The whole group was furious, especially Keith who considered that to be the end of Brian's spell as leader of The Stones. He had held serious reservations anyway for some time and had made his feelings known on several occasions. One such occasion was at the Southend Odeon. Brian had eaten Keith's roast chicken dinner, for which Keith obliged Brian with a seriously blacked eye.

Returning to London and to Edith Grove after staying in even the cheapest hotels on the road was a depressing prospect and one that proved too much for Mick and Keith. They told Brian they wouldn't be going back. Instead they intended to move in with Andrew. Linda took pity on Brian, unhappy and alone at Edith Grove, and invited him back to her parents' home in Windsor. "My parents wanted to meet him anyway, so I invited him to dinner. Brian dressed up really nice, clean shirt and tie, very smart. He was so polite, impeccable manners, I found him very soft and gentle. He treated me like a lady and my parents thought he was wonderful. So after that he came a few more times to dinner and he loved my parents so much he kind of stayed."

It was time for the all important follow-up single to *Come On* and the band had been planning for weeks, rehearsing whenever possible between gigs. Once again a shortlist had been drawn up after running through almost the entire American Chess and Checker R&B catalogues. The group went to Decca's West Hampstead studios and recorded cover versions of *Fortune Teller* and *Poisoned Ivy* but these were discovered as too well known. They were withdrawn from Decca's pressing plant and schedule a month before the release date. The Stones returned to the recording studio, this time at studio 51 in Newport Street, and had another attempt at finding the right formula, but the sessions produced nothing but a frustrated, exhausted and non-productive tension.

Andrew left the studio and paced Soho streets, racking his brains for inspiration. He finally found it in Jermyn Street in the shape of John Lennon and Paul McCartney. The pair had just left a Variety Club awards presentation lunch where they had received a songwriters award. The two Beatles spotted Oldham and sauntered over to him, only to hear about the unhappy manager's dilemma. Lennon offered a simple but generous solution to The Stones' problem. He said the band could record a number they had written for their forthcoming album. Oldham couldn't believe his ears. He rushed the two Beatles back to the studio where all six Stones were staring blankly at their instruments.

The song recorded and released on November the 1st was *I Wanna Be Your Man* and after a quick run through The Stones had it down pat, with Brian's bottleneck guitar playing giving the record an authentic Chicago blues feel that was completely unheard of on a British pop disc at the time. A Beatles song done in the Rolling Stones style just couldn't fail. The 'B' side was an improvised mickey-take of Booker-T and the MGs instrumental hit *Green Onions* called *Stoned* which featured Mick occasionally uttering the words, 'stoned outta my mind.'

The song was credited to the band under the pseudonym of Nanker Phelge in memory of their Edith Grove flatmate. For this Oldham set up a publishing company in lightning time after a suggestion from Brian that all songwriting royalties should be shared evenly by the band. It was called Nanker Phelge Publishing. This company was to handle all future songwriting and recordings of The Stones, with the proceeds to be split six ways. Stu's share was set aside for Oldham himself. The Stones continued gigging right up until the end of 1963 with only one day off on Boxing Day, ending the year with a New Year's Eve date at The Drill Hall Ballroom, Lincoln. After the gig, Brian and Stu decided to pay a midnight visit to the town's eerie, darkened and deserted cathedral. While the pair stood motionless in the pitch darkness, staring up at its ancient spire, one long sustained note from the pulpit's organ wailed out into the night, breaking the deathly silence. Stu turned on his heels in a flash, ready to vacate the scene only to spot Brian completely unmoved by the experience, his eyes glazed and a wild and awkward grin plastered across his face. "Happy New Year," thought Stu.

5

Sweet Li'l Innocent Brian

The Stones kicked straight into the first day of 1964 with an appearance on the very first edition of the BBC's *Top of the Pops* before embarking on another nationwide tour of Great Britain two days later.

The Stones arrived at the Manchester TV studios several hours before they were to record their three and a half minute spot and retired to the studios' canteen where Brian and Keith got into a bitter argument with the Liverpool beat group, The Swinging Blue Jeans. The argument flared up between Brian and The Blue Jeans singer, Ray Ennis, and ended with Keith throwing a full tray of tea mugs at and over The Stones' chart rivals, followed by Brian swinging and raining punches down upon the stunned Northerners. BBC security men managed to separate the warring factions, although confessing that they had not a clue who belonged to which group, in time to go on stage. Witnesses to the pop punch-up included The Dave Clark Five, Dusty Springfield and The Hollies – all set to appear on the same show. After the show an unknowing BBC researcher asked Brian his opinion on the rumoured North/South divide and the competition between London/Liverpool bands, to which he replied to the hapless TV journalist, "We are on very friendly terms with all the northern beat groups. There's a mutual admiration between us all."

The Stones' second tour of England started at the Glenlyn Ballroom, Forest Hill, London and once again Brian was accompanied by Linda.

He had now taken to driving himself and Linda separately to

reachable destinations in Linda's parents' Vauxhall saloon. "Brian wanted his own thing, he wanted to be separate from the band, have his own space. The others would all be cramped up in the back of Stu's van while Brian would arrive in my parents' car. This was more to do with the whole band not wanting to travel with Brian. It was a really nice car but Brian always bumped it nearly every time coming home from gigs, tired and full of beer. There was always a stop sign or a parked car, never a major accident, just bumps."

The Stones toured consistently for the next few months with barely two days off in a row. On the first leg of the tour, The Stones shared equal billing with the all-girl American group, The Ronnettes, whose manager and producer was Philadelphia's infamous, Phil Spector, Andrew Oldham's very own role model, and to whom Spector had sent a very blunt and to the point telegram simply saying "Leave my girls alone!" A dire warning that both parties ignored to their later-reported mutual satisfaction. Ronnie Bennett, the lead singer of The Ronnettes, later married Spector in 1967 and divorced him in 1974.

On the 26th April The Stones released their first LP, uncomplicatedly entitled *The Rolling Stones*, which shot straight to the number-one spot in the UK charts. The album was testament to the band's by now nationwide notoriety as the album jacket featured a dark and moody close-up portrait of the group, by then socially aspirant photographer David Bailey. The cover bore just a white bordered photograph, with no graphics or title, except the Decca record-company logo in the top right-hand corner. This was a risky and pioneering step on the part of Decca records, implying that The Rolling Stones themselves were bigger than the music they created.

Brian continued to stay at the Lawrences' Windsor home, returning whenever possible from tour dates that brought him into the area. On one such night he returned and to his surprise found they had given the house a name. As he walked up the path he was greeted with a varnished wooden tree-bark plaque bearing the legend "Rolling Stone". Linda was snowed under with notes and postcards sent from Brian on that tour, and because of the close relationship, Linda's parents had almost adopted Brian. News from Brian came from exotic corners of Britain, such as Birkenhead and Southsea and he brought them back presents such as a poodle called Pip, a large sun-shaped clock, and perfume for Linda's mother. Harkening back to his childhood, he also presented the Lawrences with a pet goat called Billy G, which he refrained from dying blue, but delighted in walking around the streets of Windsor on a lead. This was a strange act for anyone else but Brian, and was later lampooned by his old friend Dick Taylor, now guitarist with The Pretty Things, in the promotion film for their hit single *Come and See Me*.

Brian's uncanny knack of complicating his personal life by combining it with his professional career was becoming an intrinsic part of his complex character. He had already embarked on a first-class route to alienation within the band by his increasing hostility towards Mick and his constant ill-treatment of Stu. Added to this was his insistence that Linda accompany him to gigs until the countless and obvious temptations of life on the road proved too much of a lure for the young rock and rolling bachelor and brought about a re-think and change in his attitude. Linda, interviewed in a 1964 edition of *16 Magazine* gave her interpretation of Brian's change of heart when she said, "In spite of Brian's long hair, we look very smart when we go out together. He used to take me to all The Stones concerts, but," and Linda looks a little sad when she says this, "now they are famous there's such a crush backstage that Brian considers it dangerous so I rarely go to the shows at all now." So it came as no surprise that when the triumphant tour hurtled through his home town of Cheltenham, Brian was alone.

Brian and the rest of The Stones were booked into the Savoy Hotel, Cheltenham, which days before their arrival had been literally besieged by fans. The band made it out the back of the hotel and into Stu's van miraculously unnoticed, and avoided the gathered mob at the theatre through Stu's inventive ploy of backing the van right up to the stage doors. Stu stayed with the van during The Stones' two performances as past experience had taught him that serious memento-wanting fans thought nothing of relieving it of wing mirrors, aerials, door handles and even a tyre on one occasion.

Once inside the safety of the dressing room Brian heard a knock on the door; it was Pat: "I had got in with one of the firemen I knew in Cheltenham. Linda wasn't around, like she had been before, always hovering in the background. It was very emotional. After the gig Brian came home to see Mark and it really upset him to bounce the little one on his knee. We met the following day, before the band had to leave, and spent the morning together, just walking and talking and visiting all our old haunts. We both knew that our feelings for each other were so volatile that it would be impossible for us to stay together as a couple, but we both knew that what we felt for each other was a bond that could never be broken, and to this day, so long after his death, the bond is as strong as ever."

The endless round of Odeon Theatres and ballroom appearances continued at a relentless pace for the band for the next few months – each one as frantic and near riot-prone as the last – a fearsome pace that didn't let up as third single time for the band and Oldham lit up their calendars. The thought of many unfruitful hours of demo-ing unfitting and unsuitable R&B classics and rarities weighed them all down heavily. Oldham realised that if The Stones' success was to continue following their latest hit and number-one album, their steadfast R&B catalogue needed a healthy shot of commercialism. He had grown tired of ransacking the sheet-music departments of record stores and publishers in every town they visited in his crusade to unearth suitable material for the band, of which he found there was precious little.

Once again Oldham looked to The Beatles for guidance, to the Lennon and McCartney songwriting set-up, whose own compositions had taken the Mersey-beaters to new heights of acceptance and stardom. He returned to the flat and through the locked door of the kitchen, where he housed two increasingly hostile Stones in the shape of Mick and Keith, and gave them an ultimatum: "The Beatles write their own songs, so you write me some songs or I'll leave you in there!" Oldham, quick to cover all angles of The Beatles' success story, also recognised the emerging potential of the third quiet Beatle, George Harrison, as a gifted and original songsmith, and a few weeks later was to draw a parallel with Brian, whom he considered The Stones' own third-ranker.

The first fruits of the enforced songwriting partnership of Jagger and Richards were a clutch of clumsy, sweet, romantic and overly sentimental ballads that were totally unsuitable or unusable for showbiz stalwarts like The Bachelors, The Seekers or the warbling blarney of Val Doonican, let alone The Rolling Stones, while Brian's efforts resulted in nothing at all. But Oldham did salvage one melodic oddity from the bunch, a Jagger/Richards composition entitled *It Should Be You* which he managed to convince a newly signed Decca singing hopeful, the smouldering and moodily named George Bean, to cover; both song and artist were never heard of again. This was followed by another managerial coup, the release of the Jagger/Richards loosely arranged love song entitled *My Only Girl*, which Oldham had cajoled American singer Gene Pitney into releasing. Pitney, at the time, was enjoying his first flush of success in Great Britain and had met Oldham and The Stones at a run-through of the TV show *Thank Your Lucky Stars* and got on well with them all. He told the *Daily Mirror*, "When I first saw The Rolling Stones I didn't know whether to say hello or bark, but once I got to know them they were great."

Oldham was interested in expanding his publishing operation and had had his eye on Pitney for some time. Offering him the song was a way of breaking the ice. Pitney drove back to London with the band after the show and ended the journey with Oldham as his PR man and the Jagger/Richards song, retitled *The Girl Belongs to Yesterday*, as a future new single.

Although Brian had hit a blank with his songwriting, he was still the most progressive and inventive musician within The Stones. It was something he had already come to realise but it wasn't about to be encouraged by Oldham, Mick or Keith. He considered that the new material that the three were concocting together was utter sell-out rubbish, and, compared to what the band had been playing night after night, went totally against what they had set out to represent: a true Blues and R&B band. This was a view that pre-loyalty days Jagger and Richards had shared with equal conviction, but now the tight three-man unit of Mick, Keith and Andrew that had formulated their new direction, ignored Brian's protests by going out of their way to make it quite clear that his opinions were neither practical or wanted. Brian could deal with his being shut out in the cold so long as the songs they produced were as weak and as watered down as their first attempts. This was to change with the release and success of subsequent Jagger/Richards material. It was the early days of a whole new conflict.

On the 5th July 1964 The Stones left England's shores for their first concert tour of the United States. A whirlwind, whistle-stop promotional event playing only twelve dates in support of their third US single *Not Fade Away*, following hot on the heels of the first-wave British invasion that had confronted America's youth with wholesome and toothsome Limey pop acts like Herman's Hermits, The Searchers and Gerry and the Pacemakers. The Stones were an easy marketing commodity although their records showed constant bad placing in the US Billboard top 100. The band flew to New York's Kennedy airport on flight 505 to a screaming welcoming committee that was by no means of Beatles proportions, but reassuring nonetheless, and set the modest but enthusiastic tone of the visit. The US authorities on the contrary were not as pleasant or as pleased with the visiting Englishmen abroad and subjected each Stone to a humiliating health check before allowing them through immigration, while having every item of luggage seized and searched by airport officials who shouted taunts of "Get your hair cut". An equally unimpressed Brian commented contemptuously that America seemed like a bigger version of Balham.

Oldham knew that establishing the songwriting element within the band was as essential to The Stones' future success as it had been for The Beatles. In fact it was now the main objective. The band needed commercially viable pop songs, *Sixteen, Boyfriend,* and *Jackie*-friendly material – a complete turnaround from the earthy Chicago Blues sound that had given rise to the band's tremendous, but early, popularity. Brian and Andrew clashed almost daily over the band's new choice of direction. The whole band, as well as Oldham, knew that Brian wasn't about to take so blatant a policy change lying down. Brian was a musicians' musician and not one to sell out easily to any form of commercialism, however materially rewarding, if it was at the expense of his musical integrity. However, complaining long and hard about each new release was difficult, as with every consecutive original single and album track the band became more popular and successful and gave Brian endless opportunities to wallow in an unrefusable and inexaustable gluttonous feast of the female sex; this he indulged in at a level that befitted his excessive nature but it left him completely at odds with himself, and made it impossible to justify his own resistance to such a winning formula.

The wheels were beginning to roll. Mick and Keith moving in with Andrew was more than a home-based convenience. It had been a well planned and calculated move on the manager's part to break the front-line Stones' domestic set-up. It had been a risky move as it was breaking up The Stones' instrumental core of Brian and Keith in favour of creating a songwriting partnership of Mick and Keith without knowing if they were capable of turning out anything like a humble tune – they had tossed off a Rice Crispies commercial without too much trouble but that wasn't much to go by – let alone a hit song.

It was a gamble that could have severely backfired. As it was, the move paid off handsomely. Andrew had his two Stones' songwriting team living under his roof in the heart of London and a domesticated and uncomplaining, rock-steady and reliable rhythm section on hand at a moment's notice – all of which left a capricious Brian stuck out in the wilds of Windsor walking his goat.

As Brian sat in the spacious front room of Linda's parents' home watching the frolicking poodle Pip bounce about happily, he quietly pondered the quandary that faced him within his band. He sat there in silence for some time until his concentration was broken by Linda, who entered and sat down beside him, and mustering all the courage she could find in her young body gingerly informed him that she was pregnant. Brian, an old hand by now at receiving such news, was well accustomed to such situations and prepared for the wrath to come. He expected at best a massive hysterical scene resulting in Linda's parents throwing him out into the street, but the blow-up never came, in fact the opposite, Linda's parents were both supportive and understanding. They had looked forward for some time to their eldest daughter settling down with a home and family of her own. All this unforeseen mishap did was to bring the now obvious wedding plans a little closer.

Brian was speechless. "My parents loved Brian and would do anything for him," Linda said. "My mum did his washing and ironing and my brother lent him clean shirts. Brian took to my family in a big way because it was the opposite to what his own upbringing and family life had been like. He had real straight parents, very different from us, we were all out in the open."

Brian suggested an abortion.

Despite Linda's parents' supportive level-headed and easygoing approach to the news, they were adamant about one thing:

Brian must inform his parents. Brian and Linda took off for Chel-tenham. "We were almost a mile away from his parents' home when he suddenly had this terrible asthma attack. He just couldn't face them, he was scared stiff. We went through the whole visit and didn't mention a thing, which was made all the more difficult when Brian's mother got out some old photographs of him and it slipped out that Brian had got a girl pregnant at school when he was about fifteen. They were still very upset about it. It didn't bother me. I didn't have that sort of prejudice."

Brian eventually chose to tell his parents by letter. "They thought it was terrible because I was pregnant. They wrote me back a very nasty letter which I've still got. They refused to accept it was true."

Linda, depressed by Brian's parents reaction, began to question her decision of going through with the birth, and discussed Brian's earlier proposition of an abortion. The two went for a con-sultation with the doctor, who asked the couple if they were in love. Brian and Linda both said yes and the doctor refused to have any more to do with it.

As The Stones went from strength to strength on the unstop-pable crest of the Jagger/Richards songwriting wave, Brian's inferiority complex began to get the better of him. He retreated to Windsor and tried to force songs to happen in his head. Linda supported and encouraged him, but to no avail. "He would really try hard to write something and his face would light up when anything would come into his mind. He was always writing little poems and trying to put them to music."

Brian felt that his efforts were nowhere near as good as the catchy hit material of Mick and Keith, so he never showed them to the band. This affected his confidence badly, and as it dimi-nished, Mick and Keith's grew.

Brian tried to compensate for his lack of lyrical output by con-centrating on his playing. He collaborated with Andrew Oldham on some instrumental material along with the help of former Shadows bass man Jet Harris, whom Brian had met when he had supported The Stones on their third English tour.

Harris had already enjoyed a string of instrumental hits in his own right since his dismissal from The Shadows. He told the *New Musical Express* that he planned to release an original Brian Jones composition as a forthcoming single, but Harris, whose fight against chronic drink addiction was about to fail, never released the disc, leaving Brian with plans to release the song himself. However, these never saw the light of day either. Brian abandoned his solo aspirations and songwriting and turned his attentions to projecting his image. He enhanced his already eye-catching appearance by bleaching his golden blond hair to almost peroxide white. His own stage persona, he felt, gave him the position of strength that he lacked in the studio although in his own mind he knew that he was the best musician in the band. His tremendous personal attraction to women was undeniable and this was to be his new approach as he was receiving more fanmail than Mick Jagger and Keith Richards put together. "There was tons of it," Linda remembers. "Brian would be sitting there reading it and saying to me, 'Do you think Mick got more than me this week?'"

Despite his newly heightened appearance, Brian could not disguise the anxieties that were starting to weigh heavily on him. He developed large, deep-sunken bags under his eyes. As the stress of his lifestyle mounted, so his asthma attacks worsened and he began carrying around a miniaturized inhaler at all times. He also began missing gigs, complaining of mental and physical exhaustion. Jagger's curt diagnosis of Brian was hypochondria.

The growing friction within the group also had an adverse affect on Jones. No one can be quite sure when the battle for the soul of the band began but Linda felt that Brian was very aware of the power play being orchestrated by Andrew, Mick and Keith. Silly snipes at Brian in the studio were becoming commonplace, vindictive and spiteful. Oldham would leave Brian alone in a sound booth for hours on end. The hapless Stone believed that he was being recorded. When he emerged from the booth he would find an empty studio and that his mike had been switched off. Even if his playing was recorded it would often be wiped from particular tracks. Not surprisingly, Brian Jones began avoiding recording sessions.

"He was much more mature that the others which made it harder for him to understand their attitude," said Pat Andrews. "He had control right up until this point, but being so strong-minded, he clashed with Andrew immediately and Brian instinctively knew he had lost power. Up until then he had confidence in himself and his music. Had they taken a little bit more time with each other, they might have got on well, but they were all too young. Brian's attitude changed completely by the time they went to America. He had resigned himself to the fact that it was too hard a fight to win and came back to me a totally different person." One reason for Brian's apparent disinterest was a typically intense relationship he had started some months earlier with a girl called Dawn Malloy.

On top of that, Brian's life was about to get that little bit more complicated when, on 23rd July, Linda gave birth to a baby boy. Brian, in a fit of awful inspiration, reversed the names of his first child and called his second Julian Mark. Understandably his action sent fur flying in a particular household in Cheltenham. Not that Brian had any time to worry about Pat Andrews' raging temper. At the same time as Linda was delivering his second son, Dawn Malloy informed him that she was pregnant. Julian Mark, not yet out of the hospital, was about to have a little brother or sister.

Meanwhile, plans for The Stones' second, and first 'major', tour of the USA had been underway for some time. Their first album had been released in America under the slogan, "England's newest hit makers," and reached the number 11 spot in the US top 20. American *Vogue* magazine ran a full-length article on the band with the titillating intro, "The Rolling Stones are different to The Beatles, more terrifying, the effect is sex."

Gered Mankowitz, a young freelance-photographer friend of Oldham, was hired to cover the tour. "I had already photographed Marianne Faithful for her manager, Tony Calder, who was trying to get her a record deal and he rung me saying that Andrew had seen the pictures and liked them, and would I like to accompany The Stones on their tour of the USA. I thought he was kidding because The Stones were, like, the biggest band. In a sense bigger than The Beatles, because The Beatles were Establishment. People forgot that they didn't get radical for years. The Stones were the most rebellious, the most exciting, raunchy, dangerous band there was. Except that they were in the top ten. So to an up and coming freelance photographer it was tantamount to saying 'Do you want to be given an awful lot of money?'"

The Stones flew straight to New York and played two shows at the Academy of Music, followed by an appearance on the massively popular *Ed Sullivan Show*. The show was broadcast from coast to coast. As The Stones played, the live audience got carried away and invaded the stage, intent on tearing it down for souvenirs. Pandemonium ensued. Sullivan later said in a statement to the press, "I promise you they'll never be back on our show . . . I didn't see The Rolling Stones until the day of the broadcast. They were recommended to me by my scouts in England. I was shocked myself when I saw them. Now The Dave Clark Five are nice fellows, they are gentlemen. It took me seventeen years to build this show and I'm not going to have it destroyed in a matter of weeks." The Rolling Stones reappeared on the *Ed Sullivan Show* just seven months after Sullivan's outburst.

The Stones criss-crossed the States playing fifteen shows in 21 days, as well as incorporating studio sessions at RCA in Hollywood and a further TV spot on the TAMI pop show in Santa Monica which had them topping the bill over America's musical institutions such as The Beach Boys, Smokey Robinson and James Brown, the latter vowing to the overawed and nervous band that his performance was going to make them wish they hadn't left England.

The Stones then played six shows in California supported by west-coasters The Byrds, the Dylan-inspired band whose entire image aped the look of Brian to the extent of employing a non-drummer in Michael Clarke. He had only been employed on the strength of his uncanny resemblance to the troubled Stone. He had never hit a drum in his life. Brian positively glowed with pride at their first meeting. Every night, he would stand in the wings watching their show, fully enjoying the narcissistic thrill of their performance.

Gered Mankowitz said, "The energy of these shows The Stones played amazed me. The hysteria of the audience, the sheer police presence and security people, it was madness and the authorities didn't know how to handle it at all. The things that some of these girls threw on to stage were amazing. They threw their panties and bras at them, especially at Brian and Mick with messages and invitations to parties or offers of an extremely rude nature by the sweetest of young girls. Brian loved America and went completely overboard on these tours leaving his 'father and prospective husband' worries firmly at home in Windsor. The fans really came to see Brian. There was this really famous banner that read 'Sweet Innocent Little Brian'. That's how they perceived him. I think some teenage magazine made up the slogan but honestly, can you imagine anyone less sweet and innocent?"

"He was his own worst enemy," Gered continued, "a liability. He would be at the hotel face-down asleep in his food, walking out of limousines in traffic jams and generally behaving very badly. I saw all that and sensed people's reactions to it. He got out of a car once, in Dallas I think, in the middle of this jam, and we were on, like, this massive flyover and he just opens the door and disappears for two or three nights in the middle of the tour."

Despite his errant behaviour, it was on this tour that Brian met and struck up a friendship with Bob Dylan.

"Brian rang my room and asked me down and there was Bob Dylan," Mankowitz recalls. "I was really taken aback. They were going out somewhere together and there was this skinny little guy in this blue suit and dark sunglasses. Bob Dylan in a bright blue mohair suit, very distressing! I wanted him to be blowing in the wind in jeans and that but he wasn't."

The infamous Pamela Des Barres, the one-time queen of LA's groupie scene, reveals in her biography, *A Confession of a Groupie*, how she began her career as a full-time sweetheart of rock. It was as a thrill-seeking teenager that she crept up to Brian's rented bungalow during The Stones' stay in LA.

"I went round the back of his bungalow to peek in the window at the beautiful Brian, who was cavorting with two scantily clad ladies of Spanish descent. While I watched, some teenyboppers banged on the front door, begging him to come out and give them autographs. He threw open the door in his underwear, holding a broom as some kind of weapon, and shouted, 'If you don't get the hell out of here, I'll drag you in here and fuck you!' They all ran squealing into the moonlight."

Brian stepped up his own tour tempo, leaving a trail of debris in his wake as he enjoyed the varied pleasures of life on the road to the full. Yet, throughout all the debauchery, he still maintained regular contact with Linda. The cards and letters would arrive from Hollywood, Chicago, New York, in fact every port of call.

"I got them all," she confirms. "He was saying he loved me but he was taking some very strange stuff, psychedelic drugs, and drinking a lot. He was changing in attitude. Andrew and everyone were saying, 'Oh, think of the publicity, Brian, if you get married – your career would be finished', making Brian feel very insecure. He already was and it didn't help us any!"

The furious pace The Stones' machine was keeping made little allowance for stable home hours or a private life. Their itinerary was running a good six months ahead of them, with two shows a night being commonplace and as many radio or TV appearances a day. Linda was resigned to seeing precious little of Brian. She was busy learning to be a mother and felt that their understanding of each other's roles would keep their relationship strong. Brian didn't.

The pressures of fatherhood and family ties had no room in his environment. They were incompatible. Andrew had been right in one sense. A quiet suburban family-man image wasn't what the public expected of a Rolling Stone. Nor was it what he wanted for himself. A vast new world was now open to him, a pop star's paradise of wine, women and song. Brian returned from America and told Linda he was moving out.

He found a new flat at number 7, Elm Park Garden Mews, Chelsea. Linda was heartbroken. She tried desperately to get Brian to change his mind. Her entreaties fell on stony ground. "He said, 'I don't think so because I am going to die before I reach thirty.' Anyway, I got cold shivers, it was as if he had seen a doctor that had told him he had a terminal illness."

Ronney Monney, a close friend of both Linda and Brian's, said "Brian knew he was walking out on the great love of his life. Linda was the only person he ever really loved because she was the only person who would give him anything for nothing. She was his shining light amongst so much shit."

Brian was now experimenting openly with drugs, meeting with dealers in London clubs and pubs, disappearing to the toilets and swallowing handfuls of pills and tablets which he then washed down with bottles of booze. As Brian's enormous amphetamine and drink intake soared, his asthmatic complications developed serious medical side effects.

His vulnerability to illness had already caused him to miss several gigs in the past. Claiming an allergy to one of his many prescribed pills or medicines, if he did show up for concerts or recording sessions, he would be covered in unsightly red blotches. He would be breathing heavily and his mood was always one of great depression.

The pressure of stage work, touring and his repeated attacks, combined with his heavy drink and drug binging, were affecting his performance. The unpredictability of his attacks scared him and this in turn would precipitate enormous emotional trauma, leaving him completely exhausted and drained after each gig. A number of times he was hospitalised. Lying in bed, he would plot the best way to replenish his supply of pills. Once he had gained a supply of what were fast becoming his constant companions, he would pop them with a complete disregard of the dosage instructions.

The Stones left for the US and their third American tour on the 29th April 1965, once again accompanied by Gered Mankowitz. "You have to accept that Brian took drugs and consequently there were character changes," he states.

"There was always something he couldn't handle. He just got worse and worse. I didn't see him on a day to day basis but when I was on tour with them I did see him a lot and he would go through incredible changes. He would behave in a curious and strange way which could be quite amusing from a distance.

"Like the time when the hotel had this little boating marina. They would put a limited amount of petrol in your boat and you were supposed to play about between the buoys and no further. Brian just takes off straight out to sea with everybody watching him phutting off into the distance and the coastguards having to tow him back in, tripping.

"He did everying to excess. But the really funny thing about it was he was very resilient in spite of his binges and being so often in such a state. I don't know if he was particularly strong physically and that was what kept him going, but he could take whatever it was. He never used to know and he would be over the top, and them somehow, after two or three days of that, it was like it never happened."

In May, Brian was served with affiliation orders from both Pat and Linda, seeking paternity rights from Brian over their respective sons. Pat alleged breach of marriage, enticement and association for Mark Julian. Linda sought an affiliation for Julian Mark, a lump sum and a final settlement.

Brian told his friend, RM writer, Peter Jones, "No one would choose to live the life I live." Pat Andrews comments, "I would never have gone public about Mark until I read it in the papers about Linda and their calling the baby Julian Mark."

By mid-1965 the tight relationship between Mick, Keith and

Andrew had turned into an unrelenting daily source of torment to Brian. Despite his other mounting problems, this saddened and frustrated him immensely. In his weak mental and physical state, Brian was in no shape to fight Andrew's massive influence over the group. Instead, he withdrew and left himself wide open to be set up time and time again.

As far as Brian was concerned, Oldham's mania for publicity was detrimental to the band. Oldham would always publicise the most trivial incidents relating to the group and this, Brian felt, made The Stones look like complete morons. Unbeknown to him, this was a view that Eric Easton was fast subscribing to.

Whispers started circulating that all was not well within The Stones' office. There was quite some substance to them. Eric Easton, for one, was beginning to feel undervalued. He felt that his managerial role was continually being undermined by his junior half.

Andrew's insistence on conducting and consulting with Mick and Keith alone in the privacy of their shared flat, ensured that Oldham's visits to the West End offices were less and less frequent. Left alone, Easton started to get suspicious and resentful. Their mutual association was upset. Battle lines were being drawn up.

This breakdown in communications led the pair into arguing over money and every other Stones-related matter. The age gap between them, although not a problem at the beginning, had now become a significant wedge between them.

It left the youthful Andrew affiliated with Mick and Keith whilst Eric was now viewed as a relic, no longer in tune with current trends, his strategies and suggestions for the group laughed off as totally out of date and redundant. In return, Eric felt that Andrew had just used his experience, maturity and connections within the business for his own personal gratification and gain. Easton viewed such clandestine acts with hatred.

Brian sensed the Oldham/Easton collaboration was heading for a fighting finish and, sure enough, the final bell started ringing for Easton in July 1965, when Andrew met a man called Alan Klein and Easton's demise became inevitable.

Alan Klein was born in Newark, USA, on 18th December 1931. His mother had died when he was two years old and his father, a butcher, put him and two of his three sisters into an orthodox

Jewish orphanage for ten years until he was financially able to take care of them.

After a brief spell in the army, Klein started work for a newspaper distributor in New Jersey while attending an evening class in accountancy. He then landed an accountant's position with a New York law company, eventually starting his own music-publishing business, handling the song rights for an all-girl singing group called The Shirelles.

His first taste of the music business was enough to influence his transition from book-keeper to manager. To that end, Klein made the shrewd move of signing soul-singers Sam Cooke and Bobby Vinton to management deals. The partnerships were successful.

Klein's driving ambition and boundless energy reaped him a small fortune and a rapidly expanding empire while his reputation as a tough-talking, no-nonsense dealer earned him a notoriety that preceded him across the Atlantic. In 1964, the wily New Yorker took the opportunity presented by a London vacation to drop in on the offices of The Beatles.

It was there that he cheekily suggested to manager Brian Epstein that he should be given the job of financial manager to The Beatles in return for allowing his client, Sam Cooke, to be used as a support act for The Fab Four on their forthcoming US tour.

Andrew had met Klein and his lawyer, Marty Machat, at a Columbia Records Convention in Miami. Oldham hired Machat on his own behalf before moving in on Klein who, Oldham felt, was essential in securing a better deal for himself and The Stones.

Oldham appointed him his personal, exclusive business manager. This left Oldham free from everyday Stones' business and able to pursue external personal and creative activities, while retaining responsibility for the band's recorded output and publicity. Klein agreed to the deal on one condition, a condition Oldham was only too glad to agree to. Eric Easton had to go.

Easton received a telegram from Klein that informed him he was no longer wanted by either Oldham or The Stones. Furthermore, Klein and Oldham were prepared to buy him out. Easton, too long in the game to be intimidated by a young 21-year-old egomaniac and a heavy-handed New York calculator, promptly started legal proceedings as Oldham quickly left the country.

Brian was quite unhappy about this management reshuffle. He

made it clear that he felt the deals had been undertaken without proper band consultation. However, his protests to Mick and Keith received short shrift. They simply reminded Brian of his exact same manoeuvres on their behalf a mere two years earlier. Two days after he had officially become their manager, Brian shrugged his acceptance of Klein at a formal meeting at the London Hilton Hotel.

Despite Brian's reservations over his new boss, Klein's first round of hard-hitting negotiations produced dividends and secured Brian and the rest of the Stones a substantially better record and royalty deal with Decca, putting considerably more money in their pockets than ever before. The true mechanics of Klein's dealings wouldn't come to light until much later so for the time being it seemed as if everyone was to benefit.

Brian, in his characteristically flamboyant manner, immediately went out and bought from George Harrison, at a reasonable price, a Rolls Royce Silver Cloud with tinted windows. Taking full advantage of the mystical Beatle's first period of material-possession rejection, it was, Brian said, "a car befitting the leader of The Rolling Stones".

The Stones played the London Palladium on 1st August 1965, their first show in the capital for nearly six months. Their two shows incited scenes of mass hysteria and the biggest police presence they had yet encountered this side of the Atlantic. Brian emerged clad in virgin white from head to foot to steal the show effortlessly with his huge mop of bleached blond hair dancing brilliantly in the spotlight. He also adjusted his amp volume to a level that completely obliterated Jagger's vocals throughout the shows. It was the band's last gig before they took a well earned three-week break.

Brian, with time on his hands and Linda's paternity order hanging over his head, thought up a tricky but workable solution to a delicate problem. He invited Linda on holiday. Freed from the pressures of being a Rolling Stone, they could talk things over, under relaxed and pleasant circumstances. Linda was happy to agree and the pair flew to Morocco.

"That trip was marvellous to start with," Linda recalls. "It was as if he was trying to make me independent, have an experience. Before this I had only ever been to Canada when I was younger. But it was in Morocco where I first met Brian's new friends, his entourage, his hangers-on."

Brian's new circle of friends included people like Robert Fraser, the Mayfair art-dealer; Christopher Gibbs, a young sculptor and antique collector; and Donald Cammell, a director; along with a young French model named ZouZou.

She invited Linda along on a modelling shoot in Tangier. Linda innocently accepted thinking that ZouZou was trying to be friendly. She returned to Brian in tears claiming over-friendly advances from the model's direction. "I was so upset," she recalls, "because I still loved Brian and I thought he had brought us here to get us back together." Brian returned to England ahead of Linda, leaving her to return with Robert Fraser.

Once back in the UK, the couple split up for good, Linda settling for a one-off, out of court payment for her and their son Julian. Brian made a statement before going back on the road with The Stones that he had now cut off all association with Linda and had paid a lump sum for the maintenance of the child.

Brian didn't need to look far for new female company. With the news that Linda planned to move with Julian to America in order to open a boutique in Hollywood using the money Brian had given her, he began seeing ZouZou.

The French model spoke little to no English. Brian spoke no French at all, so conversations were sparse, but this suited him. Brian was happy to be free from responsibilities and able to play the field once again. He wasn't interested in a serious relationship and said so to the press, revealing in the process his chauvinistic attitude towards the fairer sex.

"I haven't tied myself down with a girl yet," he reported. "After all, how many girls could I find who would make my tea, cook my meals, tidy my house and talk intellectually to me while I sat watching with my feet up?"

Well, that was ZouZou out for a start. Their language barrier saw to that. "It took such a long time to say just one thing to each other," Brian morosely commented after they had split up.

Meanwhile, The Stones' fifth single, *(I Can't Get No) Satisfaction*, had shot to number one and the band played a short series of gigs in West Germany, beginning at the Munsterland Hall in Munster.

Three days later, backstage at a gig in Munich, Brian was introduced to a young German/Italian model called Anita Pallenberg, a stunningly beautiful cat-like creature of 19. Brian fell for her instantly. "I decided to kidnap Brian," Pallenberg stated.

"It sounds ridiculous but they even made a film about it, about kidnapping a popstar (*Privilege*) starring Paul Jones. This was the original story. Brian seemed to be the most sexually flexible. I knew I could just talk to him. As a matter of fact when I met him I was his groupie really. I got backstage with a photographer, I told him I just wanted to meet them. I had some Amyl Nitrate and a piece of hash.

"I asked Brian if he wanted a joint and he said yes, so he asked me back to his hotel and he cried all night. He was so upset about Mick and Keith still, saying they had teamed up on him. I felt so sorry for him. Brian was fantastic, he had everything going for him, but he was just too complicated."

Brian threw himself head-first into a relationship with Anita. For the next few months, the couple hopped about Europe, re-dezvousing at every Stones gig. With Anita at his side Brian's confidence gradually returned. Weighing up his assets, he realised that despite the internal strife, he was still by far the most popular Stone. He also had the most stunning girlfriend and the flashiest car. But it wasn't nearly enough. Bitter frustration still clawed away at his insides because of his demise in stature within the band. His inability to write gave Jagger and Richards the start on him. He had to get back on top at any cost.

After finishing their German tour, The Stones played England before flying out to Canada for the start of a mammoth US tour, Anita waving Brian goodbye at Heathrow.

Mankowitz, now the band's official photographer, flew out with them. "There was a real need that the band seemed to recognise that every time they played in America, it was really crucial. They had quite a lot of business problems going on and were in continuous danger of being stopped by local police because of crowd control.

"Crowd control was pretty primitive and the fans were very passionate. Mick was a master at whipping them up so there was this tremendous tension and the band exploited it brilliantly by stopping gigs and there would be this big disappointment. But in terms of PR it was probably quite good . . . the band was doing very well and everyone wanted to make sure they toured there again and again. They knew then they were going to become very very famous."

On every US visit, Brian continued his friendship with Bob

Dylan. On one occasion, the pair, accompanied by Dylan's guitarist Robbie Robertson, got together in Brian's hotel room and jammed by candlelight, getting stoned until Brian knocked over the candle and set fire to the room.

The Stones were now on a prolific run and enjoying the heights of constant success. They had scored two number-one singles and a number-one album in a matter of months and sold out every show on both sides of the Atlantic. Yet, for some, this had been achieved in spite of Brian, not because of him.

"That's what added to a lot of the resentment that built up," Mankowitz confirms, "because Mick and Keith knew that the band were capable of great things, great performances, success, and Brian wasn't going to be part of it. His self-destructive impulses would get in the way and they must have resented that, Brian shambling around drunk on the stage playing *Popeye the Sailor Man* instead of *Satisfaction*.

"It was a weird phenomena, a great musician, and he is letting the side down, but his impact was undeniable. Mick being so visually aware must have known that Brian looked great. They all looked pretty good but Brian had particular flair, more visual flair than any of them. He was a focal point, enormously popular with the fans, at least on a par with Mick, if not more. They loved him, they thought he was wonderful and he loved it and he looked fantastic all the time.

"This skinny little cat with these blond locks, unbelievable, with a wicked smile. They thought him extraordinary. So, you're in this band and you've got this guy who had got all this going for him. The band is going from success to success and you feel whatever else that you are huge, you're there, the second-biggest rock band in the world.

"The world is at your feet – things aren't going smoothly because they never do, and this little guy is fucking up. Now how do you feel about it? You don't feel great because he is fucking up, he can't play notes properly, so they're stuck with him, they can't sack him, they can't replace him and they can't do without him. Its a crazy situation, but the guy's increasingly becoming a liability."

6

The Road To Morocco

Brian began the new year by facing Pat's paternity court proceedings. He was found guilty in his absence and ordered to pay costs of £2 and ten shillings per week.

In April, The Stones released their fourth LP, their first complete originally penned album. It was entitled *Aftermath* and went straight to number one. The album's fourteen tracks as usual bore no songwriting credits for Jones but his confidence-enhancing involvement with Anita had renewed his lapsed musical integrity and his instrumental supremacy was stamped on every track.

On *Aftermath* Brian excelled himself, playing a dozen or more instruments with an enviable fluency. His range included everything from the conventional to the exotic and on to the downright ridiculous. Harpsichord, dulcimer, sitar and marimbas, as well as a child's plastic banjo, were all incorporated brilliantly and innovatively into the music, illustrating perfectly Brian's uncanny and adventurous field of vision.

Peter Jones, who reviewed the album and was present with Brian on several trips to the studio, said, "Brian started out as a much better guitarist than Keith but Keith had more of a natural feel, whereas Brian was capable of getting exactly the same sound and feel he wanted out of any instrument. *Paint it Black* was an obvious example. Brian played the sitar like he played rhythm guitar. It probably made George Harrison cringe but it worked brilliantly."

Even Brian's backing vocals were uncharacteristically up-front and pronounced, most notably on tracks like *It's Not Easy* and *Goin' Home*.

Yet, even during this creative burst of energy, Brian, after contributing, shaping and even saving certain tracks from obvious disaster, would sit back, rest on his laurels and get stoned.

"He was so clever musically," Peter Jones asserts, "that he thought, this is easy, I don't have to worry about it. He knew he could make things more interesting, more fulfilling and rewarding without really trying and he would rely on this and just stretch it out."

Keith Altham, who was writing for the *New Musical Express* during the making of *Aftermath*, interviewed Brian several times. He said, "It was almost a natural feel he had for picking up instruments and playing them immediately but he was limited in what he could do. As soon as he found out he could play a few bits and pieces on it he didn't have the discipline or the concentration to stick at it and take it any further. Just like the latest plaything, pick it up, play it, put it down and forget it, which was a bit like how he was with people."

Brian moved house once again, this time to number one, Courtfield Road, South Kensington. His Elm Park mews flat had been receiving the regular and unfavourable interest of the local constabulary. The problem had arisen due to the flat's close proximity to the home of a well-known London society doctor who listed amongst his private patients a large number of suspected drug-users.

Although Brian's exceptionally unhealthy intake of such substances was on the whole legally prescribed, he was still using a large quantity that was not. Several visits to his home by his doctor neighbour had subsequently aroused police suspicions. Brian's Chelsea neighbours had also tipped the law off. Their reasons were purely selfish.

Although they found Brian to be unfailingly polite and charming at all times, they were anxious to put an end to the annoying all night and day vigil kept up outside Brian's door by numbers of teenage girls. Reading the signs, Brian moved Anita into his new Courtfield Road home, a huge and spacious flat just off the Gloucester Road in SW7.

With the help of Christopher Gibbs, the couple decorated the flat's huge thirty-foot high rooms using a Moroccan theme. It was

Brian's homage to the country that had so strongly gripped his imagination. The walls were hung with original, intricately embroidered Arabic rugs and the floors were piled high with cushions arranged around a centre piece hookah, giving the impression of entering the interior of a Bedouin tent.

There was a minstrels' gallery that ran round the top of the rooms. It was made of carved wood and exotic instruments hung from it. The gallery was only accessible by climbing a rope ladder which led to a trap door. The door opened up to a stairway which in turn led to an attic. Brian felt it was the first real home since moving from Cheltenham.

Installed in his new home with Anita, Brian abandoned his wild boy about town image for that of the much happier homebodied 'host'. He busied himself with entertaining his new circle of socialite friends and acquaintances who were constantly 'just passing by'. Even visiting bands from across the Atlantic, like The Byrds, Bob Dylan and Sonny and Cher beat a path to his West London door.

For anyone who considered themselves anyone, Brian's house became the key London meeting place to stay at. His hospitality was faultless and his parties endless, so much so in fact, that his high-society profile in town was suddenly questioned. *Rave* magazine even ran an article which asked the question: "Where is Brian Jones?" A more in-depth investigation would have revealed that Oldham's latest technique of only booking interviews with Mick and Keith was keeping Brian out of the headlines.

One person who knew where Brian was was Dawn Malloy. She was only weeks away from bringing his fifth illegitimate child into the world. Naturally, she had been in contact with The Stones' office and looked set to follow the examples of Pat and Linda by dragging Brian back to court (at least in name). The news eventually filtered back to the office that Dawn had given birth to a baby boy and was now seeking a paternity settlement from Brian. He, in turn, had locked himself away in his West London tent, trying to avoid the entire issue by simply ignoring the matter and leaving the legalities to Andrew and Klein.

Andrew got Dawn to sign a legally binding contract to the effect that Brian would pay her a lump sum and she, in turn, would relinquish all further rights and claims on the Rolling Stone. Dawn received £700 and signed the documents witnessed by Mick Jagger. Andrew deducted the money from Brian's account and the matter was forgotten.

Brian then decided to take another trip to Tangier, this time with Anita, Christopher Gibbs and his newly appointed chauffeur Tom Keylock.

Brian had discovered Morocco on the recommendation of his friend, the young Etonian Robert Fraser, the wealthy London art gallery owner and heir to the House of Fraser fortune. People like Fraser – wealthy, upmarket individuals – were now typical of The Stones' inner circle of friends and associates, mainly attracted to the band by Brian. Tangier in turn was the fashionable and exclusive location for such international rich young things and had been since the late 1950s (although Bob and Bing passed through much earlier).

It had a well deserved reputation for easy-going licentiousness, which remained intact, even after it had lost its international free-port status. This has much to do with the fact that Moroccans are not Arabs. They speak Arabic and hold Islam as their official language but are in fact descended from the Moors, with smatterings from ancient Carthage and Phoenicia, Greece and Rome.

With its long-established trade links with the rest of Africa, Morocco has developed a culture all of its own, vibrant, strange and dangerous, at least to the impressionable westerner. This was a view held by Brion Gysin, the artist and poet who arrived in Tangier for a short break in 1953 and was so instantly smitten, he never left.

Brian was as entranced and affected as Gysin had been and after only one trip referred to the country as his spiritual home. He would wander around the crowded marketplaces and bazaars with Christopher and Anita, learning to haggle whilst hoarding trinkets, jewellery, kaftans and copper wares by the trunkful.

"He had this brilliant gift," enthused Gibbs. "If he went into a marketplace where there were all these black villagers playing with various instruments, he would pick any one of them out and somehow communicate what he wanted. Then he would get hold of the instrument and somehow make it do what it was supposed to do, any type of weird instrument. Or he would go into a junk shop and do the very same thing. He was very charming".

Brian would spend the entire day wandering around the markets, soaking up the rich atmosphere created in part by the heady

April 7th 1967. A hectic matinee at Rome's Palasport. The hysterical audience included Gina Lollobrigida, Jane Fonda and Brigitte Bardot. (Rex Features)

En route to Marrakesh, April 1967 (Excel Productions)

Left: Sightseeing in Morocco. Brian was being kept busy while Keith Richards and Anita made their escape. Note Brian's poor attempt at travelling incognito. (Excel Productions) *Right:* Brian and his portable tape machine.

Brian and Anita at the Hotel in Marrakesh the day before they split up. (Excel Productions)

The photographer Michael Cooper joins Keith Richards, Brian Jones and Bill Wyman as they leave Heathrow for New York. (Associated Press)

The London Palladium 1967 (ATV)

Olympic Studios 1967

New York 1967. On the way to the photo session for the *Satanic Majesties* album cover. (Brian Jones Fan Club)

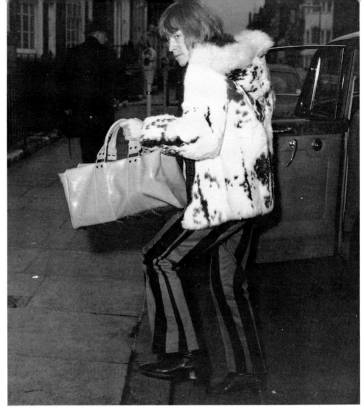

Entering the Harley Street Nursing Home (Hulton Deutsch)

Brian's room at The Priory Nursing Home at Roehampton (Hulton Deutsch)

Brian after being arrested at Courtfield Rd, March 1968 (Hulton Deutsch)

Tom Keylock and Frank Thorogood at Redlands in 1967

(Left to right) Tom Keylock, Brian Jones, Jackie, Suki Porter and Fred Trowbridge during a b
in the court sessions, 26th September 1957.

November 1967. Freed from the Scrubs
on bail, Brian and solicitor Peter Howard
stop off for a much-needed drink at the
White Horse in Longford, Middlesex.

aroma of hashish and incense burning in little battered metal bowls on every trader's stall. Hypnotic and melodic music would filter through the crowds as Brian sipped mint tea and watched the local musicians, from tribes like the G'nou, converge on the market square.

The G'nou can trace their ancestry back to West Africa and had originally arrived in Morocco as slave-traders' booty. Gibbs introduced Brian to them and their music, and took him to the village of Joujouka, a tiny settlement hidden away in the foothills of the Rif mountains. Here, the master musicians played an even more intoxicating blend of music than they had heard in the marketplaces of Tangier, all of it played on centuries-old hand-carved pipes, flutes and drums.

"It's a place that has a great deal of live music happening all the time and Brian loved that," Gibbs recalls. "It went on all day and Brian was always interested in it because there wasn't that sort of thing happening in London of course. Morocco had such varied music, steeped in tradition, and these villagers would get together and play instruments and they all had a song to sing. Brian was just so into that."

The combination of music and drugs, so freely available and so openly used, together with the abundance of eager and willing Berber women, with their intoxicating tattooed breasts and genitalia showing intricate patterns and symbols in blue, selling themselves for sex with a brazenness that bordered on self-contempt, added up to paradise for Brian.

The group of travellers booked into the Hotel Minzai back in Tangier. "We had this suite in the hotel with a beautiful view overlooking the sea," continued Gibbs, "and we got back there and Brian started bickering with Anita. They ended up having a fight and Brian tried to thump Anita. He missed and hit a window frame – he hadn't seen it, a large wrought-iron frame – busting his wrist up very badly. So we took him to the Clinique Californie, which was a sort of Moroccan nursing home, and dumped him there in pain, feeling very sorry for himself while Anita and I carried on with the holiday.

"Then Anita and I met this famous dope-dealer called Achmed, whose nickname was Hanifer which meant 'the farter'. He dealt in everything, jewellery and dope. When Brian got out of the clinic, we introduced him to Achmed and of course they got on really well."

Brian, even with his wrist in plaster, continued his and Anita's previous arguments. The rows were now becoming more heated than before and far more intense.

"They were at each other non-stop, squabbling and bickering everywhere they went," Gibbs confirms. "Brian, Anita and I hung around with Achmed from them on, smoking these great quantities of hash and Brian saying we must get some of this stuff back to England."

In fact, Achmed hid half a kilo of the finest Moroccan hash in the bases of two ornamental candlestick-holders. Brian paid for both items and then told Christopher to send them back to England via his newly opened antiques shop in London.

"Brian reasoned that it was safe that way as no one would question the fact they they were not genuine antiques. I liked Brian very much but he was maddening, one of the most selfish people I have ever met in my life. He never gave a thought to anybody else. He was like a very selfish child."

Brion Gysin, an old friend of Gibbs, introduced the group to a villager called Hanri who lived in Jajouka. A painter by trade, as a boy he had taken part in the village's music rituals and rites dedicated to the 'Great God Pan'. Hanri had danced the key role, symbolising the wild figure of Pan himself.

"Brian was very keen on that because it was the most important role during all their festivals," Gibbs recalled. "Pan was the sort of god-like spirit that it all revolved around. Hanri was a tremendous hustler and the village needed money to build proper irrigation and a school for the children. He was really into the idea of all these rich white people bringing money to his village which was completely isolated – a donkey ride for hours along several miles of track, no roads to it, a very primitive place. Brian was very taken with the idea of building a school out there so the children would be educated and eventually find jobs.

"They were all fascinated by him and made all these mosque collages of him, of his face with seeds and beads. There are probably a few still knocking about down there. Gysin had opened a restaurant in Tangier and was very involved with the writer William Burroughs at the time," Gibbs continues.

"Together they had invented this thing called the Dream Machine which was this thing that had two revolving cylinders with holes pierced in them and lights behind them. You looked through the cylinders, the lights made patterns and you were meant to start dreaming. Well . . . Brion Gysin thought the invention would raise money for the village and he got various people interested enough to invest money in it. He got Helena Rubenstein to put money up and Robert Fraser, and everyone was going to go back to Joujouka. Brian wasn't sure about the Dream Machine but he was going along for the music, as that was his thing. However, after a couple of days he had to return to England on Rolling Stones business but he promised he would be back."

The Stones were now preparing to release their very first 'Greatest Hits' compilation entitled *Big Hits, High Tide and Green Grass*. Brian and Anita continued to wage the war they had started in Tangier, the battle made all the worse by Marianne Faithful's shock revelation that she had slept with Brian upon his return from Morocco.

Towards the end of 1966, *Time* magazine ran an article entitled 'Swinging London'. London had come alive in an explosion of fashion, music and style. England had won the World Cup (for the first and only time) at Wembley and the austere post-War years were finally a memory. It had taken the country over 15 years to begin its economic recovery from World War Two, a conflict they had nominally won and, compared with the immediate post-War period of left-over rationing, archaic industries and the angst of the loss of an empire, any improvement, any change, was welcomed.

The one thing that characterized the 1960s was the desire to look good. The way things were packaged and presented became as important as the product itself; colourful, bright, bold, loud and most of all exciting. This was what the public wanted, especially the young. For the first time teenagers were recognised as an emerging economic force, not just as a transitory stage between childhood and adulthood.

They had the money and they wanted to spend it. With a near-unquenchable appetite for something new, this spawned a wave of equally young entrepreneurs who catered for them. From clothes to music, there was everything for the aspiring Twiggy or young boy who sat in his teenage, lamplit bedroom, miming to his favourite band and modelling himself on its members. Together they paraded up and down the Kings Road on a Saturday afternoon, filling their Union Jack carrier-bags from boutiques like 'I Was Lord Kitchener's Valet', Granny Takes A Trip and Lord John, buying their miniskirts from Mary Quant and their boots from Biba.

The weekend still started with *Ready Steady Go* and Cathy McGowan but now you also raced to the Bat Cave, opened Channel D and got Lost in Space. Television had a huge impact on people, influencing audiences with deliberately American-style presentation. Consumerism was being established in Britain for the first time. 'We're Backing Britain,' was the slogan, as was, 'Put a tiger in your tank,' and 'Beanz meanz Heinz'.

Pirate radio was defying the government by broadcasting the latest underground sounds from outside the established three-mile limit, signalling the start of the protest era. Young people were demanding more freedom, buoyed no doubt by the ever-increasing use of drugs such as LSD and hash which expanded the mind and unlocked the door to a lifestyle never before imagined. The myth that drugs like opium, cocaine or hash were mere playthings of the rich or the intelligentsia was shattered by their widespread usage. The drug paraphernalia of the 1960s had a message and that was that everybody could have some fun, so tune in, turn on and drop out.

The Rolling Stones were the embodiment of this awareness and lifestyle and looked set to lead the way into 1967 by selling over a million more records than The Beatles throughout the previous year. They certainly had the following and there wasn't a hope in hell's chance they would receive any MBEs.

The planned release of *Big Hits (High Tide, Green Grass)* meant that the short return to musical form that Brian had shown, especially during the recording of *Aftermath*, wasn't going to be given the chance to continue or flourish. Even the finishing touches to the band's eleventh single *Have You Seen Your Mother Baby* was being taken care of by Mick, Keith and Andrew, who had flown out to RCA in America without the rest of the band.

The great divide continued and was showing more clearly in each of The Stones' individual bank accounts. Brian, Bill and Charlie were beginning to feel Klein's economic pinch whereas Mick was spending time looking at several townhouses in London. Brian boosted his flagging bank account by joining a modelling agency and accepting assignments from trendy fashion-designers and magazines. The necessity of becoming the first moonlighting Rolling Stone obviously rankled with him and the gap widened even further.

Meanwhile, the job of organising various photo sessions for the cover of The Stones' compilation was left to Andrew. He contacted various photographers to work on shots of the band in order to compile a colour booklet that was to accompany the album. Oldham finally settled on Gered Mankovitz, Jerrold Schatzberg and Guy Webster to do the pictures.

Brian, with no immediate recording requirements, once again made the most of his physical appearance, gaining visual prominence on all of the sessions. Capitalizing on his natural photogenic quality and his command of fashion, Brian dramatically displayed his plaster-clad wrist in front of the fisheye-lens shot for the front cover, dressed in an outrageous red and black striped suit. The photograph used for the back of the sleeve had him staring into the camera at close range as the rest of The Stones filed in line behind him. His contrasting mop of pure white hair and black turtleneck sweater dominated the lens.

Gered Mankowitz's work on the booklet made up the bulk of the record's packaging. It showed the band, captured in Olympic Studios, looking pale, weary and fatigued but still sartorially elegant.

"Their clothes," says Mankowitz, "were just like any others, High Street clothes, anyone could have them – but they were the extreme of it. Brian was very into checked trousers and rollneck sweaters and white shoes. Pretty weird look. I know people that would pay an absolute fortune for some of Brian's shoes. You cannot look at those pictures without focusing on Brian first. He stood out, either because he looked different or he looked fantastic, or he was being plain difficult, hiding, lurking or reading a newspaper. I was trying to give equal presence to the whole band, trying to give Charlie some presence and Bill even. It all started with not wanting to make Mick the centre of attention. At the time I was trying to make the band five people. That session in Masons Yard was the most successful and prolific I did. There's a shot with Brian standing on a brick and the others are below him, so he looks like he is standing apart. And the 'Out of Your Head' shot where he is right in the foreground, it just turned out that way."

In January 1967, Klein's office announced to the world that The Stones were expected to gross in excess of £20 million in the coming year. The figure, he said, was made up chiefly from record royalties, personal appearances and box-office takings from two proposed films he had planned for the band.

Brian was singled out as the obvious star of these two new projects and a starting date was set for November 1966, but the only real contact Brian had with the film industry was when he accompanied Anita to Munich for the start of filming *A Degree of Murder* or *Mord and Totshlag*, a film in which she had landed the leading role. Brian had been commissioned to compose the film's musical score by its director, Volker Schlondorff.

In keeping with Brian's impulsive nature, he had thrown himself head-first into his relationship with Anita without a moment's thought. Ironically enough, it had begun in Munich almost a year before, a relationship that was as volatile and stormy as it was passionate and loving. Anita influenced Brian greatly and cultivated the already dandified image of the most stylish Stone, giving him a dangerous edge.

While shooting photos in Germany, to be used for publicity and posters for *A Degree of Murder*, Anita got Brian to dress up in an old Nazi SS uniform, complete with swastika, insignia and jackboots she had found in a surplus store in Munich.

The pair, who had cut their hair in identical styles, adopted various poses. Anita was dressed from head to toe in catburglar black and Brian in his menacing, recycled stormtrooper outfit, reclined and cavorted amidst the dismembered bodies of children's dolls that lay scattered at their feet. Other pictures showed Brian standing to attention, his booted foot firmly grinding the chest of a prostrate doll.

The pictures went mainly unnoticed when they appeared in the German newspapers, but in England it was a different story. The violent images outraged many. Brian answered his critics by feebly claiming that the shots were in fact an anti-Nazi protest and it was a coincidence that he just happened to be in Germany at the time.

Anita, it seemed, could always extract the response she required from Brian, easily and without question. In strict contrast, Andrew Loog Oldham had encountered militant resistance from the word go. Anita started to encourage Brian to wear her clothes, costume jewellery and make-up. Together they would go shopping in women's boutiques and the ladies' departments of London's most fashionable stores, buying chiffon blouses, women's hats, silk scarves, bracelets and trinkets, setting a style that pre-empted pop-star glamour. He was a prototype for many to follow.

Brian, as do many women, considered clothing to be one of the strongest forms of self-expression. It was a statement, and one he relished using to the full, cross-dressing and blurring the edges between male and female but somehow remaining entirely masculine (although Brian did ask Anita on one occasion to dress him up fully in the style of French vocalist Francoise Hardy in readiness for sex). It was this image that Brian is probably best remembered for and certainly its effect had been immediate right from the beginning. As Small Faces drummer Kenney Jones who worked with Brian on the soundtrack of *A Degree Of Murder* testified: "He stood out from all the others by the way he dressed which was a million miles away from how we looked: a bunch of mods. I remember I was shocked when I finally spoke to him. I had expected him to be girlish, which was how he looked. What really took me back a step was the fact that he was the very opposite. He had this very deep posh voice and was surprisingly manly. It wasn't how I'd imagined him at all."

Brian and Anita were like Siamese twins, inseparable lookalikes, and when she fell out with her German director halfway through filming, she flew back to Heathrow into the waiting arms of Brian. Both the German and English press immediately predicted marriage. Brian rebuffed such a prediction and said he considered marriage for him, at this particular moment, a mistake.

1967, the year The Stones were expected to make their £20 million, began with yet another spot on their old favourite, *The Ed Sullivan Show*. It was arranged to plug the band's new single *Let's Spend the Night Together*. Wary of the song's lyrics, the show's producers insisted that The Stones compromise and change the chorus line to 'Let's spend some time together'. Rather weakly, the rebels of rock agreed.

Yet they were still finding time to hit the headlines. On the 22nd January, two days after the release of their sixth album, *Between the Buttons*, the band caused an uproar by appearing on the massively popular *Sunday Night at the Palladium* TV show. The show was something of a British institution and was well known for inviting all the show's acts on to a revolving stage for the grand finale. When The Stones refused to appear in this section (probably in a bid to reassert their street credentials in the light of the *Ed Sullivan Show* débâble), the desired, outraged headlines duly followed. All press, they say, is good press.

As Oldham immersed himself more and more in his own external affairs, he hired a publicist, Les Perrin, an ex-Fleet Street reporter and publicity man, to ease his Stone-related chores. Brian was more than a little peeved at the way interviews following the Palladium incident had only featured Mick, and he arranged, via Perrin, a series of interviews for himself.

These interview requests were closely vetted by both Andrew and Klein at The Stones' office; they only gave the go-ahead for Brian to talk to the music papers when it was felt he couldn't do any more damage following his Nazi escapade.

Brian spoke to the *New Musical Express*, intelligently and coherently, about the barriers his band were demolishing. He said, "Our generation is growing up with us and they believe in the same things we do. They have moved with us, like the hippies in New York; they all think like us and question some of the basic immoralities in present-day society; the war in Vietnam, the persecution of homosexuals, the illegality of abortion and drug-taking. We believe there can be no evolution without revolution. I realise there are other inequalities – the ratio between affluence and reward for work done is all wrong."

Though happy to see his views in print once again, Brian still suspected the office of adopting a policy of a Brian Jones blackout. Consequently, Brian set about courting the tabloids himself, feeling he had more than made up for his indiscretions and had plenty to say.

A couple of nights later at Blazes nightclub in Kensington, Brian was sharing his table with two attractive girls when he was approached by two men. They introduced themselves and asked to join him and his party. Brian welcomed them to the table. Once sitting, the two strangers began talking openly about Brian's and other performers' involvement with drugs.

Chatting for hours, and plying him with drinks, they encouraged Brian to show them just what it was all about. Brian happily obliged, taking from his pocket his usual handfuls of assorted tablets and a quantity of speed which he swallowed greedily in a "nothing to it" fashion.

Brian then excused himself and went to the bar where he was spotted by the visiting American musician, Frank Zappa, who tapped him on the shoulder in order to congratulate him on the success of *Between the Buttons*. Brian spun around and belched in his face before returning to his now empty table with a round of drinks.

On 5th February the *News of the World* published extracts from that night's conversation in the first part of a series covering the lurid drug-taking exploits of pop stars. The articles were headlined 'Pop Stars and Drugs' and featured a photograph of Mick Jagger opposite another of the Denny Laine-led group The Moody Blues. Both had arrows pointing to them with captions that read, "Left, The Moody Blues Group rented a house in Roehampton, a Thames suburb of London where parties became known as the Roehampton Raves", "Mick Jagger, right, of The Rolling Stones, was a visitor to the house. He also admitted to our investigators that he had sampled LSD."

The article went on to say, "He told us, 'I don't go much on it (LSD), now the cats (fans) have taken it up it'll just get a dirty name. I remember the first time I took it, it was on tour with Bo Diddley." During the time we were at Blazes club in Kensington, London, Jagger took about six Benzedrine tablets. 'I just wouldn't keep awake in places like this if I didn't have them.' Later at Blazes, Jagger showed a companion and two girls a small piece of hash (marijuana) and invited them to his flat for 'a smoke'."

Brian recognised the conversation and realised the two men had been reporters who had mistaken him for Mick Jagger. It was a crushing double blow for Brian. It was one thing being mistaken for Mick, but to be mistaken for Mick and make banner headlines was quite another. The whole affair, Brian sensed, was set to have far greater repercussions than a simple *News of the World* cockeyed expose.

Jagger was stunned and incensed by the article and took the opportunity presented by a live appearance on the Eamonn Andrews talk show to announce that he was going to sue the newspaper for printing such a blatant lie.

The *News of the World* quickly recognised their mistake and, fearing a claim that could cost a fortune, became just as incensed as Jagger. They knew full well that what they were claiming was on the whole true. They had just got their identities wrong.

Jagger's libel action, however, meant that the paper was now prevented from publishing any further revelations pertaining to the case. Plans for a follow-up were now scuppered, unless any other incriminating evidence fell inadvertently into their hands. If that happened, it would enable the paper to successfully refute Jagger's claims and continue with their crusade.

In a mood of revenge, the newspaper put their reporter Trevor Kempson on the case. Kempson prided himself on his investigative journalism. He had made his mark as a freelancer in his home town of Reading by uncovering the identities and whereabouts of the Great Train Robbers. This had earned him a star place on the *News of the World* in 1966.

"There was no doubt it was a pride and personal thing now," said Kempson. "The paper was embarrassed at not recognising Jagger from Jones and they knew that they had been right about their report in the first place. If only they had got someone that knew which Stone was which, there wouldn't have been a lawsuit to face. They wanted to get The Stones badly and the best way to get to them was to get someone on the inside, which was easy. They in turn had contacted me at the paper and told me what was what, that there was going to be a party some of The Stones were having down in Sussex (Redlands) and we were tipped off to that. It was someone who worked closely with the band and he told us there was supposedly drugs being taken down there."

The *News of the World* contacted Scotland Yard, who alerted the West Sussex police. They quickly secured a warrant and at 7.55 p.m. on 12th February, the police raided Redlands, Keith's secluded hideaway. Christopher Gibbs, one of Keith's guests on the night of the bust, said that he had gone along with Michael Cooper, Mick and Marianne and Robert Fraser.

"Robert had this sort of Moroccan manservant called Ali Mohammed," he said. "George Harrison and Patti Boyd had been there but had gone home and Brian had been up all night fighting with Anita over the soundtrack for her film, so he didn't go down at all."

The group also included a young Kings Road hippy called

Nicky Kramer and a 27-year-old Canadian who went by the curious nickname of the Acid King (David Schneidermann). The police took away various implements and substances ranging for hand-carved wooden pipes, cigarette butts, a glass phial and a polythene bag containing one tablet confiscated from Fraser. As they were leaving they gave Keith a dire warning that if there were any traces of drugs or if dangerous drugs were found to have been used on the premises, he would be held responsible.

Just as the police left, the phone rang. It was Brian ringing to inform his stunned group of pals that he and Anita had made it up and were on their way.

The bust made a mockery of Jagger's writ against the *News of the World* and the stage was set for an interesting and high-profile court case that might as well have been held in a public square in the shadow of the gallows. It was England's very first music and drug related trial and the outraged Establishment was baying for The Stones' blood. In fact, there was a very real possibility that Jagger, Richards and Fraser (the only ones subsequently charged) would, in fact, go to jail.

Keith made plans to escape the frenzied media attention and hired Brian's chauffeur, Tom Keylock, to drive him to France for a short break. Brian suggested that he and Anita join them and extend the trip through France and Spain and down to Morocco.

The plan was put into action and Keith, accompanied by Brian and Anita set off with Keylock towards Paris in Keith's Bentley. They were later joined in France by a woman called Deborah Dixon, the girlfriend of Brian's friend, Robert Cammell. The group's intention was for them to converge at the Hotel Minzah in Tangier, where they would be met by Mick and Marianne, Robert Fraser and Christopher Gibbs.

The group set off from London and crossed the channel to France without incident until Brian and Anita got to the Spanish border. Brian had overdosed in the back of the car and was rushed to a Spanish hospital for emergency treatment. The hospital insisted on incarcerating Brian for several days and he was adamant that the group continue their journey without them.

Leaving him in his hospital bed on his 25th birthday, Anita and Deborah rendezvoused with Keith and Tom in Barcelona, checking in for the night at a hotel where a telegram was already awaiting them. It was from Brian. It seemed he had made a miraculous recovery and was now demanding Anita's return. Anita ignored the message and in the morning the group pressed on without Deborah, who felt the atmosphere between Keith and Anita was freezing her out. She flew back to France.

Brian sent another telegram to the hotel but this either arrived too late or met with the same fate as the first. Anita, free from Brian's demanding and oppressive complexities, found she was enjoying her time with Keith and the two, driven by Keylock, savoured a further five nights of anonymity, staying in remote little towns in and around Marbella before Anita finally returned to Brian's bedside. Keith and Tom carried on to Gibraltar, crossed over to North Africa and Tangier. Brian and Anita flew back to London where he underwent further tests before they too finally flew to Morocco.

The moment he saw them together, Brian instinctively knew that there had been some liaison between Anita and Keith. The quick glances and body language between the pair spoke volumes. Brian said nothing, choosing to blot the thought from his mind by indulging in an orgy of drink and drugs, wandering around the markets of Tangier in a stoned and paranoid trance.

Christopher Gibbs had booked into a different hotel from the Stones party and watched helplessly as the disorientated Brian's self-esteem hit rock bottom. "I wanted to go to Morocco to relax, so I was staying separately," he explains.

"I didn't want to be tied to him because everything would have revolved around him and I wanted to lead my own life. He was so paranoid now about everyone. He was questioning everyone's motives – especially foreigners (other holidaymakers) and villagers. I'd say to him, 'Brian, they've never heard of you, they are just having a holiday or they live here, they don't know you,' but he'd be saying 'No, no, no, no, no . . .'

"We took him out and rented this dilapidated house on the edge of Marrakesh – very nice with a big overgrown garden and hundreds of peacocks in it. Robert Fraser arranged it while Anita was off with Keith. Micky Brown, who was married to Brian's friend Tara Brown, who had only recently died, came with us. Tom Keylock was supposed to be looking after Brian, because somebody had to. Someone had to get him up, dress him and make sure he was alright, but Keylock wasn't interested, he wasn't very chummy. Everyone was very edgy then."

Brion Gysin had arranged to take the whole entourage up into the mountains and the entire gang met up the next morning around the hotel swimming pool. Brian remained in a paralytically stoned state, preventing him from even getting out of bed. Anita decided to travel with the others.

Achmed the Hanifer was on hand to dish out the necessities for the trip, and trip they did, dropping acid and heading across the desert towards the snow-capped mountains in the distance. Not suprisingly the journey was eventually abandoned because the acid took over and the group, amidst a freak thunderstorm, headed back to Marrakesh.

On their return Anita went to find Brian at the rented house. She discovered him rolling about with two naked, tattooed Berber whores. Brian lovingly informed Anita that they wanted her to join them. Anita was disgusted at the prospect and turned to leave, at which point Brian's violent streak erupted. He once again lashed out at the shocked and terrified girl, berating her severely as the naked prostitutes stood and watched.

Anita fled back to the hotel and to Keith. Mick, who had been entertaining the photographer Cecil Beaton at a nearby restaurant over dinner, returned to find the bruised and bewildered Anita swimming in the hotel pool and being comforted by Keith under the watchful scrutiny of Keylock the chauffeur.

Gysin, who was staying in a house close to the hotel, received a message the next day from Keylock asking him to go along to the Minzah Hotel. Gysin was met by Keylock who explained that a whole planeload of reporters sent by the *News of The World*, intent on persecuting The Stones, had just touched down in Marrakesh.

Gysin sensed an urgency in the burly driver's actions and felt a litle uneasy in his presence. Keylock bore down on him and continued, "The Stones are strong and The Stones will win, but we do have a weak link. You know who it is: Brian. He talks his bloody head off to reporters and tells them everything. Brian must be kept away from them for his own good and ours."

Keylock told Gysin to find Brian and take him to the marketplace, where he could tape the local musicians. This was something which Gysin had promised Brian since they had first met. Keylock gave precise instructions to bring him back no sooner than 6 p.m.

Then Keylock patted Gysin on the back and, finishing with a smile, said, "There's a good chap." Although the request was put to him in very polite terms, he couldn't help but feel he was carrying out strict orders, and woe betide him if they weren't carried out to the letter.

Gysin took Brian, as instructed, to a place called the Djemaa el Fna and introduced him to a group of musicians. They also met a couple of self-proclaimed mystical holymen who went by the arcane name of the "Hash Head" brothers. The group sat huddled together on a rug ready for the musicians to begin. They had started smoking handfuls of hash which they pulled on through the brothers' elaborately decorated pipe. Matted hair, rotten teeth, beads and coins hung from the instrument and Brian had to possess it. He then proceeded to puff heavily on the pipe until, as Gysin reported, "His eyes stood out on stalks like a stoned snail and his lungs nearly burst."

When Gysin thought Brian had smoked his fill he dragged the comatose Stone to his feet and ushered him towards another friend's house in order for Brian to sleep. But Brian had different plans. Instead, much to Gysin's amazement, Brian stumbled off towards the hotel clutching the brothers' pipe. Gysin returned home. Meanwhile, Brian reached the hotel lobby only to find the entire party had left. He broke down, and phoned Gysin, sobbing uncontrollably down the phone to him, his only compatriot left in a strange land. Gysin, fearing the worst, rushed over to the hotel and instructed the desk to call a doctor, recognising Brian was out of control and heading for an attack or even a seizure. A doctor arrived and sedated Brian. The pair of them got him into bed. Gysin stayed until the sedative took effect and Brian fell asleep.

7

Gimme Shelter

Although everyone had checked out of the hotel together, they had not all returned directly to London. Keith and Anita hid out together like a pair of fugitives in Marrakesh. They were looked after by Tom Keylock. Mick and Marianne flew to Ireland to escape the growing turmoil and backbiting. They then added to Brian's misery by inviting Keith and Anita to join them. Brian left Marrakesh alone and flew to Paris where he stayed with Donald Cammel for short time, licking his wounds before returning to England to wait for Anita.

He met Anita at the airport. She arrived alone (Keith was being driven back by Keylock), and he took her back to Courtfield Road where a bitter row ensued. The result was that Anita left in tears, vowing never to return. Brian refused to believe her, confident that he would eventually win her back. Nothing seemed more unlikely.

Brian had already been cut out of the heart of The Stones but with Anita he had been fighting back. Now, with her gone, his resolve to get back on top faded. Instead, a feeling of real desertion and loneliness set in, dominating all his actions and thoughts. Brian summed up his feelings when he bitterly told his friend, Dave Thomson, the sometime press photographer, "First they took my music, then they took my band and now they've taken my love."

Heartbroken and humiliated at his loss of Anita to, of all people, someone in his own band, Brian, tired, stressed-out and hurt, sought comfort and peace once gain in his other world, the world of drugs. He stepped up his intake, surpassing his past dependency tenfold. Yet Brian was not to be allowed the luxury of coming to terms with his inner traumas in familiar home surroundings. It was business as usual for the band with another gruelling European tour ready to roll. It was a decidedly uneasy group that took to the stage on the tour's opening night. Brian and Keith stood poles apart, rigidly glued to the spot, staring straight ahead to avoid even a tiny glance at one another. Jagger meanwhile, tried for all his worth not to notice as the friction mounted, dancing back and forth between his two flanking guitarists, counting down his set list until he could at last take a bow and thankfully get out of the hall. The tense atmosphere continued throughout the tour, unrelenting and exhausting for all concerned until the nervewracked and exhausted band arrived back in Britain weeks later.

In what may be seen as a small act of revenge, Brian began seeing a girl called Linda Keith, who, prior to the trip to Morocco, had been Keith's girlfriend. It was Linda who first introduced Brian to a casual acquaintenance of hers, a wild-looking black afro-haired guitarist from Seattle named Jimi Hendrix. She had also been inadvertently instrumental in Hendrix's earliest dealings with his eventual manager, Chris Chandler, the bass-playing Animal.

Linda had accompanied The Stones and The Animals on a trip to the US in 1966. One night, she had accompanied Brian and Keith to The Cafe Wha, a seedy backstreet dive in Greenwich Village, New York, where the three had sat mesmerised as the young, left-handed virtuoso known as Jimi Hendrix had laid waste to his audience. Days later Linda revisited the cafe, this time accompanied by Chandler who, disenchanted with his life as an Animal, was on the look out for pastures new. Linda suggested to Chandler that managing new acts could aid his departure from playing, and, if so, then young Jimi was the best place to start.

Having already made Jimi's acquaintance, Linda set about securing the guitarist's attention with more than just a business proposition. Her overtures to Jimi triggered the end of her liaison with Richards. It was finally extinguished when she repeated her suggestions to Hendrix some months later following his triumphant introduction to England.

Over those months, Hendrix formed a firm friendship with Brian and witnessed first-hand the complete erosion of Jones's self-respect on his many subsequent visits to London. Hendrix respected Brian both as a person and as a musician and, as a foreigner and outsider in a strange land, felt an empathy for him as the beleaguered Stone became further isolated from his former friends and colleagues. The two musicians became very close.

Hendrix called Brian his blood brother and their nights out on the town became regular excursions whenever Hendrix was in London.

Brian's involvement with Linda would have rounded out a bizarre and incestuous swop nicely if it had not been for the fact that Linda still wanted Keith, and Brian, Anita. But then nothing was running smoothly for Brian any more. Even so, Brian and Anita drove to the country for a break, before flying off to Cannes for the film festival, where one of the German entries was *A Degree of Murder*, the film he and Anita had worked on. It was a trip that he was not looking forward to.

Once in the South of France, Brian deperately tried to repair his relationship with Anita while Keith hovered darkly in the background. Maturely resigned to "what will be, will be", Keith left them to their arguments and returned hours later to find Anita waiting for him and the news that a very dejected Brian had departed. He and Anita were finished for good. She was now Keith Richards' girl.

On his return to London, Brian removed all traces of Anita from his Courtfield Road home and, resuming his frenzied and chaotic lifestyle once again, installed two new girl lodgers in her place.

On the 10th May, Mick, Keith and Robert Fraser appeared at Chichester Crown Court in Sussex following the drug raid at Redlands, where they elected to be tried by jury. All three were bound over on a hundred pounds' bail and ordered to appear again at the West Sussex Quarter Sessions on 27th June.

Trevor Kempson, who covered the court appearance for the *News of the World*, said, "The one the paper was really after, now thinking that was it for Jagger and Richards, was Brian Jones."

Sure enough just as Mick and Keith were leaving Chichester Crown Courthouse, Brian and his friend Prince Stanislaus Klossowski were being driven towards Kensington police station after being arrested by Detective Sergeant Norman Pilcher of Scotland

Yard at number one, Courtfield Road on suspicion of possessing illegal and dangerous drugs. They were held overnight and subsequently charged with the unlawful possession of dangerous drugs and ordered to appear at Marlborough Street Magistrates Court the following day.

Brian arrived at the court in his Rolls Royce, driven by his newly appointed chauffeur, Brian Palastanga, and emerged dressed in a relatively sober, dark blue suit and polka-dot tie, hiding behind a pair of dark glasses. Amid screams from over a hundred girls, he and Prince Stanislaus entered the building, where the three-minute hearing left them remanded on £250 bail each and the case adjourned until 2nd June. Brian sent his seldom-seen parents a telegram which read, "Please don't worry. Don't jump to nasty conclusions and don't judge me too harshly. All my love. Brian."

The rest of the Stones breathed a sigh of relief at the news that Brian's lawyer had advised him to have no further contact with them until his next appearance in court. The frosty and unbearable silence between Keith and Brian had made working as a band almost impossible. Brian paid a visit to Olympic Studios on the night of his release and sat in with The Beatles. They had taken to recording there, and Brian sang backing vocals on a track the band were working on entitled *Baby, You're a Rich Man*. As he recorded his part, Brian was watched by a pensive Mick Jagger who had also popped in. Neither one of them spoke to each other.

As the long weeks of isolation and worry stretched out ahead of Brian, serving to accelerate his already advanced state of decline, the rest of the dispersed and depressed Stones managed the occasional trip to the studio in his absence. They were due to start work on a follow-up studio album to the *Big Hits (High Tide, Green Grass)* collection. The weeks between trials were, unsurprisingly, non-productive, feeding Andrew and Klein's worries that the end for The Stones looked a definite possibility. Without any recording commitments Brian took up an invitation to sit in with The Beatles on a session at a studio in London's Kingsway. It was the third time he had been asked to contribute to a Beatles recording. The first time he provided the unessential but appreciated handclaps on *Yellow Submarine*. When The Beatles next recorded at Olympic, Paul McCartney had originally asked Brian along, assuming he would turn up and contribute some guitar to a track they were working on entitled *You Know My Name, Look Up My Number*.

Brian arrived at the studio on 8th June complete with an alto saxophone and recorded through the night, playing shakily but, as McCartney later said, "Exactly in the style they wanted".

Brian, in addition to his flirtation with Linda, was now enjoying the comforting support of another young blonde named Suki Potier. Suki had been close to Brian's friend Tara Brown and was involved in the car crash that had killed him some months before. Suki was a fashion model whose striking good looks bore more than a passing resemblance to Anita. "We both needed somebody at that time," she says. "I hadn't recovered from losing Tara, something that also upset Brian terribly, and he was heartbroken over Anita."

Suki moved in with Brian at Courtfield Road and was horrified at the dilapidated surroundings of the once elegantly adorned flat. Plates of half eaten takeaway meals were stacked precariously on the tables and in the sink. Wardrobe doors were smashed and splintered mirrors gaped open, hanging off their hinges as clothes, magazines and books lay strewn across the floors. There was a huge Nazi flag draped fully over an armchair while more than a hundred albums lay in a pathetic pile, sleeveless and stacked in a corner.

Christopher Gibbs, who had originally advised Brian on his furniture and fittings, said, "He was living in complete chaos. He had hundreds of beautiful clothes, but these were left lying about all over the floor, either burnt or covered in food. All ruined and filthy, and there'd be thousands and thousands of pounds' worth of the stuff. There were dozens of instruments that were smashed and hadn't been repaired; they were scattered everywhere. It was a terrible mess, but it was the same wherever he went. When he left the mews flat it was disgusting. He didn't live like normal people. He didn't go to bed at night and get up in the morning, he got up when he felt like it and went to bed when he felt like it. It didn't have anything to do with when the buses were running, or the banks were open, or even if there was any daylight. Everyone had to revolve around him. He would arrive at a restaurant just as it was closing with eight or ten people in it, at about 12.45 and he would be surprised when they had nothing on the menu and he would make a fuss about it."

Brian and Suki did not stay at Courtfield Road for long. Brian had become obsessed with the thought that the police and press had mounted a definite persecution plan and were intent on harassing him and eventually putting him behind bars. He felt the flat wasn't safe and was sure his phone was bugged, repeatedly grabbing the receiver and screaming abuse into it. Police and ambulances were repeatedly called to his flat and broke in each time following numerous hoax phonecalls to the Chelsea police station. The calls variously alleged that Brian had been taken ill, was committing suicide and in danger. Break-ins, fires and prowlers were also reported. The calls, police said, were made by someone claiming to work for The Stones.

In a worried mood and at his wits' end, Brian called an impromptu press conference which he conducted from the balcony of the flat, wrapped in a silk kimono. He complained to journalists of the hoax calls and the daily police presence outside his home. He spoke about the unmarked vehicles which were manned by plainclothes officers. He also chastised the media's intrusion into his private life. Later on, Brian began fearing reprisals for his public claims and so he made plans to visit America.

There was a perfect opportunity to do so.

Three days of music, peace and love was how the Monterey International Pop Festival (a non-profit-making event to be held in San Francisco) was billed. It was the official start of the summer of love and Brian's destination on 16th June. He had been invited to America by his friend Jimi Hendrix to just hang out and relax in order to take his mind off his drug bust. Hendrix also wanted to introduce his new band, The Experience, for the first time to his homeland.

Brian met up with Hendrix and his group, drummer Mitch Mitchell and bass-player Noel Redding, at Heathrow airport. Redding made the mistake of sitting next to Brian on the plane throughout the thirteen-hour flight to California and accepting Brian's offer of some LSD. He spent the entire flight totally wired, glistening with sweat and gripping the seat for dear life as the effect of the drug took a strange hold. Redding recalled Brian's contorted face grinning madly, flashing in and out of his mind. Still, at least there the bewildered bass-player received a clearer, personal insight into his band-leader's music and lyrics. It was, thanks to Brian, Redding's first dealing with drugs.

When they arrived at Monterey Brian wandered around the festival campsite swathed in a breathtaking display of silk and lace finery, wrapped in a gold and pink fringed lame cloak, bedecked with Moroccan jewellery, necklaces, scarves, beads and bells, including a crystal swastika and crucifix. He meandered amongst the hippie's campfires and tents with Andy Warhol, like a medieval prince bestowing his goodwill on his following, who had dubbed him His Majesty for the event.

For three days, Brian held court and dropped acid with the West Coast hippy hierarchy. This included The Byrds, David Crosby, The Grateful Dead's Jerry Garcia, John Phillips of The Mamas and Papas, who hosted the event and whose brainchild – along with ex-Beatles publicist Derek Taylor, producer Lou Addler and music-manager Alan Pariser – the festival had been, Buffalo Springfield, The Jefferson Airplane and Big Brother and the Holding Company, whose singer was the young Janis Joplin. After a particularly wild session of substance abuse with actors Dennis Hopper and Peter Fonda, on the last day of the festival Brian ambled slowly on to the stage and in a weak and strained voice introduced as his friend and "fellow countryman of yours, The Jimi Hendrix Experience," leaving to the sound of Jimi's opening chords to *Sgt Pepper's Lonely Hearts Club Band*, a tribute to the just-released barrier-breaking new album by The Beatles of the same name.

When Brian returned from Monterey, he was physically whacked, mentally drained and disorientated. He dared not return to Courtfield Road for fear of further police action. He was still convinced that he was the subject of their surveillance. Instead, he moved into the Royal Gardens Hotel in Kensington, accompanied by Suki and Brian Palastanga. Once at the hotel, Brian felt the first effects of an inevitable comedown, and not wishing to ride out the storm, sent Palastanga out to score him some more drugs. Pushing a wad of notes into the driver's hand, Palastanga returned with a large quantity of hash which he handed to Brian. By now, he had surrounded himself with a gathering of assorted hangers-on, all of whom disappeared with him into his suite.

Brian Palastanga, who had booked into the adjacent room, waited patiently for his boss's next request. After several hours the door flew open and Brian charged in screaming and shouting,

"I've had enough! I'm going to end it all!" According to Palastanga, Brian was wild-eyed and clearly out of his mind. He rushed straight to the window and struggled with its catch, all the while screaming at the stunned chauffeur that he was going to kill himself. Palastanga leapt from the bed and grappled the delirious guitarist to the floor, sitting on him until he at last calmed down and eventually passed out. When he came to and was informed about his actions, he and Suki became convinced that Brian was heading towards a complete breakdown.

Still, that didn't stop Brian breaking his lawyer's advice. On 22nd June, he met up with the rest of The Stones at Olympic Studios. Although he was clearly under the influence of drugs, Brian was able to perform with the band on several tracks, adding his usual dabblings and trappings to the overtly psychedelic-sounding new material. Amazingly, the injuries that Brian had suffered from his attack on Anita in Morocco had not healed and nor would they for the rest of his life. Because of this, Brian considered his guitar-playing suffered and was below par on these sessions. He insisted on fiddling with a variety of other instruments that lay around the studio, adding snippets and phrases of orchestral harp, mellotron, Indian drums, flutes and recorders to finished takes. He completed the session propped up in a sound-booth by a dozen pillows, unable to stand but still playing. The sessions continued and Brian, although deteriorating visibly as time passed, managed to appear on most tracks, aided by the support of studio amps, chairs and cushions.

In truth, Brian considered the band's latest endeavours their biggest mistake to date. He labelled the music Jagger and Richards' folly, a second-rate *Sergeant Pepper* and commercial crap, warning the band that so serious a departure from the blues was a colossal error.

On 25th June, after a long day at Olympic, Brian, along with Mick, Marianne and Keith, went to the EMI studios in Abbey Road in order to attend the BBC's live broadcast for the *Our World* programme. This was an ambitious attempt to bring the populations of the five continents together through music.

The show was beamed out to places as far off as Cape Kennedy, Montreal and Morocco and watched by an estimated audience of 400 million people. The English offering was a performance by The Beatles with their message for the world – *All You Need Is Love*.

Two days later, on 27th June, the Jagger/Richards/Fraser trial started at the West Sussex Quarter Sessions, presided over by Mr Leslie Block, a Sussex landowner, dairy-farmer and Justice of the Peace. Block found himself conducting the most sensational trial since the scandalous case of Christine Keeler in 1963. From June 27th to 29th the sleepy coastal town of Chichester was turned into a three-ring circus with beautiful summer weather, hotdog and ice-cream stalls, balloon-sellers and a funfair creating a party-like atmosphere normally only seen at state visits.

Michael Havers QC, a future Attorney-General, represented both Mick and Keith while the revellers outside the courthouse sported T-shirts saying, "Free The Stones". Robert Fraser's barrister was William Denny, while the prosecuting counsel in all three cases was Malcolm Morris QC.

Having been charged with the illegal possession of amphetamines, Mick Jagger's was the first case heard. Havers had to convince the jury that Mick had got the four tablets on prescription from a doctor, albeit on a verbal basis. Dr Raymond Firth of Knightsbridge had been Jagger's doctor since 1965. He testified that Mick had asked him about some tablets he had bought in Europe to help him cope with stress. As the conversation was held over the phone, the doctor assumed that they were amphetamines and gave Jagger permission to go on taking the pills, but only in an emergency. In Dr Firth's opinion it was a valid prescription. Judge Block conferred with his fellow magistrates, two farmers and a newsagent, and instructed the jury that the evidence presented was not a defence to the charge. The jury retired for six minutes before returning the verdict of guilty.

Robert Fraser had, on his counsel's advice, pleaded guilty and Denny went to great pains to stress Fraser's titanic struggle against heroin addiction. Sentence for Fraser was deferred until the end of Richards' trial. Jagger and Fraser were then handcuffed to prison officers and taken to spend the night in Lewes prison.

After a humble prison breakfast, Jagger and Fraser were again handcuffed and taken back to the court. At Chichester they were put into a holding cell to await sentencing. Up above in the gallery, the packed court waited in silent anticipation. The jury was about to be given the full account of the raid on Redlands. The prosecution, Malcolm Morris, implied that not only were drugs taken but a full-blown sex orgy was also in process. Mentions of 'nudity' and a 'fur rug' sent the packed press bench into a frenzy, scribbling feverishly in their notepads.

Woman Detective Constable Rosemary Slade, a police witness for the prosecution, testified that "Miss X", as Marianne Faithful was referred to, was "completely naked" when the raiding party arrived. Woman Detective Constable Evelyn Fuller described how Marianne "deliberately let the rug fall" when she was searched. Banner headlines screamed "Naked Girl at Stones Party" to the nation the next day.

Keith Richards was next in the witness box. He told the court of "a wicked conspiracy" and denied allowing his premises to be used for the smoking of cannabis, causing Judge Block, in his summing up, to all but instruct the jury to convict Keith. It took the jury little more than an hour to reach the unanimous verdict of guilty.

Gasps of "No" rang out from the public gallery as the trio stood in the dock for sentencing. They heard Judge Block say, "Keith Richards, the offence for which you have very properly been convicted carries a maximum sentence imposed by Parliament of up to ten years." At this point there was a huge uproar from the gallery. After he had calmed it down, Judge Block continued. "That is a view of the seriousness of the offence. You will go to prison for one year. You will also pay £500 towards the costs of the prosecution." Block sentenced Robert Fraser to six months' imprisonment and a £200 fine. Finally, he sentenced Jagger to three months in prison and a £200 fine. The three were led away and as news reached the crowd outside, all they could hear were shouts of "Shame".

A decoy van fought its way through the crowds at the back of the court as Jagger, Richards and Fraser were hustled into a squad car waiting at the front of the building. Outside Chichester, they were transferred to a police van and driven to London where their first stop was Brixton Prison, Mick's place of abode for the next three months while Keith and Robert Fraser were bound for Wormwood Scrubs.

As soon as sentencing was completed, Michael Havers requested and got a certificate of leave for both Jagger and Richards to appeal their convictions and sentences. The preliminary hearing was set for the next day.

With agreement from the prosecutor Morris not to oppose bail,

Michael Havers stood before Lord Justice Diplock in the Appeal Court in London. After 25 minutes the two Stones were granted bail of £5000 each, along with further sureties of £2000 each. Robert Fraser didn't fare as well. His application was turned down.

That same day, at the ingenious suggestion of Palastanga, Jones had been booked into the Royal Kensington Gardens Hotel just to keep him away from the spotlight and out of trouble. The hotel was the perfect hideaway as it was under seige from thousands of Monkees fans who had gathered to welcome the visiting pop sensations from America.

As the hotel was virtually inpregnable it was the perfect location in which to hide Jones. He was ensconced in a room on the very floor that The Monkees inhabited. Mickey Dolenz, the band's drummer, was amazed to find the bemused Stone wandering about the corridors of the fortress-style hotel. He talked at length with Brian and that night, in protest at the treatment being dished out to The Stones, Dolenz's group donned black armbands throughout their sold-out concerts at London's Wembley Empire Pool.

History has not recorded how Jones felt about the public downfall of Jagger and Richards. But his descent into his own private hell continued unabated. Suki couldn't stand by and watch Brian's decay continue any longer. After a heartrending talk, she convinced Brian to begin consulting a psychiatrist.

The couple visited Harley Street doctor, Dr Lennard Henry, whose recommendation was for Brian, on 3rd July, to admit himself into health clinic in Hampshire. Brian signed in as Mr L. Howlett, but after only 48 hours, on the advice of the clinic, he discharged himself. He returned to Dr Henry to seek the further specialised treatment that he considered beyond their scope of professionalism or cure. Lennard Henry considered residential treatment the only option.

Brian had brought himself to the brink of breaking point by the combination of his disaffection within the band, a failed love affair with Anita, severe drug and alcohol abuse and the stress of having lived his life in the public eye for so many years. On 6th July, Brian was admitted to the Priory Nursing Home in Roehampton, the hospital's location disturbingly close to Redlands, Keith Richards' house that was at the centre of the recent *News of*

The World revelations. Naturally, such a close proximity to the building fuelled Brian's paranoiac fears.

Brian booked in using the pseudonym of Mr L. Howlett again. He was introduced to a Dr Anthony Flood who, he was informed, would take care of all of his admission procedures.

Brian, who had arrived in the company of Suki, Brian Palastanga and a whole group of friends, told the doctor he would not be staying unless he was allocated a double room, preferably with a double bed for him and Suki, as well as rooms for all his guests.

Dr Flood refused all of Brian's requests and realised his case with Brian had obviously already begun. He notes, "I feel that this insistence on having a girl there with him wasn't entirely because he wanted a friend to be close, to be holding his hand because he was terrified. He needed to exhibit his sexual prowess in a state of desperation."

Two of the three attendant psychiatrists considered that Brian was suffering from paranoia. It was the correct diagnosis, but they could never have known that in Brian's case it was a paranoia, however drug-induced, that was based on reality. This is borne out by the *News of the World*'s Trevor Kempson, who said, "Of course Brian was being set up, all through 1967 and later in 1968. First the police would be tipped off that Brian was holding drugs and a few minutes later the tip-off would come to me. I think that what happened was that someone in The Stones' organisation also wanted him out of the way."

In addition, Brian Palastanga had informed Brian, while in the Priory, that he had heard of a plot, organised by the police, to plant more drugs in his flat. They would simply await his return and find them both. Brian was devastated. He begged Dr Flood to let him out for the evening in order to clear the flat of all his belongings, insisting that the band needed him in the studio for a recording session. The doctor reluctantly agreed, on the condition that he was back by midnight.

Suki cleared the Courtfield Road flat of most of Brian's things and checked herself and Brian into the London Hilton, using the same name of Mr and Mrs Howlett. Brian returned to the Priory at seven the next morning, drugged, drunk and unable to stand. Helping himself to the contents of the ward's medical cabinet he swallowed a handful of sleeping pills and slept. Dr Flood began his patient's diagnosis anew, stressing that Brian didn't live in the real world any more. "Brian resented being ordinary or dressing normally. He never wanted to be a part of the world in which he lived and when anything interfered his reaction was to buy it off or pretend it didn't exist. He had the money so he could be different from 99.9 per cent of the population. He could be what he wanted to be so long as he didn't step outside of what is a funny corridor, a milky way upon only which Brian Jones walked."

Suki commuted between the London Hilton and another hotel near to the clinic at Richmond Hill until Dr Flood considered Brian was stable enough to leave on 24th July. Following his discharge, the couple went to stay at Christopher Gibbs' house in London. "I was very fond of him," Gibbs explains, "but he is not the sort of person you want to come and stay. He just appeared after leaving the clinic. I was very relaxed, very easy come easy go and liked staying up all night too, but I wasn't expecting him and he turned up and said, 'Can I hang out here for a few days?' He wasn't really house-trained and would leave cigarettes burning on all the furniture, on an antique book that you valued and I would complain but the next minute he'd have burned a hole in the mattress or the floor, or anything. God it was so difficult not to hit him. I had to eventually tell him to make another plan. I may make him sound impossible, and he was, but actually he was very charming too. I was very fond of him but he was pretty incoherent, rambling on and on about things. It was like someone thinking out loud."

Brian and Suki flew to Marbella for three weeks to stay with Nicki Browne at her villa, before returning and briefly residing in a hotel at Maidenhead. Brian's plan was to lie low before meeting up with the rest of The Stones in order to record the final phases of their next LP, the sleeve of which was to be shot by The Stones' new chief photographer, Michael Cooper. Cooper's arrival on the scene marked the departure of Andrew Oldham, who had been conspicuous by his absence during the band's recent trials and tribulations, never more so than when his ex-flatmates Mick and Keith arrived together at the High Court of Appeals on a cloudless sunny day on 31st July.

Queues of schoolgirls snaked back through Fleet Street. Their arrival stimulated wild cheering from the huge crowd. Somebody shouted at Jagger, "How does it feel to be free?" "Lovely," came the reply. Keith had contracted a dose of chicken pox and was given permission to wait in an isolated room as Lord Chief Justice Parker quashed his conviction and sentence. The three appeal judges agreed that the evidence against him was flimsy and that the original judge had failed to point this out to the jury.

Mick Jagger's conviction was upheld but the prison sentence was set aside in favour of one year's conditional discharge. Lord Parker explained, "That means you will have to be of good behaviour for twelve months. If in that time you do commit another offence, you will not only be punished for that offence but you will be brought back and punished for this one also. You are, whether you like it or not, the idol of a large number of young people in this country. Being in that position, you have very grave responsibilities. If you do come to be punished, it is only natural that those responsibilities should carry higher penalites."

The band's next move was to sort out their management. Oldham had long since distanced himself from the band's activities and, not suprisingly, had experienced a shift of attitude from the group towards him because of it. The group's displeasure mainly stemmed from Oldham's virtual snubbing of the band when things got tough.

"Andrew had lost his grip over the band," Mankowitz reflected. "It couldn't have been any clearer that the band had outgrown him. The final split happened at a session at the Olympic Studios when Mick and Keith brought Michael along and walked up to Andrew and said, 'He is doing the cover.' Nothing could have been plainer. For the first time Andrew was being told by the band what to do. I wasn't phased out, neither was Andrew, we were being replaced. It was a clean split between The Stones and their manager, and my alliance was to Andrew because he had brought me into The Stones and they wanted independence."

Keith Altham viewed Oldham's departure more in keeping with the trend sweeping the music scene at the time. "What had happened by that time is that managers like Andrew, who tended to be simpatico with the band, had got out of their depth. They had done as much as they could in terms of building the image, keeping the personality situation together, but they couldn't really handle the legal side, merchandising and profits that were now coming in from those places. They didn't know what to do. They had no comparative situation to go by and they didn't have the right background. Klein did. He was tough. He knew these people had got bad deals in the record companies and he went in and said, 'Listen, either you do this, or I am taking them out,' and they paid because they knew they were getting huge profits, disproportionate to the amount that the players and artists were actually getting, and that was the key to his success.

"He wasn't a great mental genius or anything. He had a good sense of accountancy, he was ruthless in his own way and he was, like, American-tough.

"Klein was a business manager, Klein was an accountant, the kind of manager that Oldham wasn't. I mean, you start to talk about Epstein, Kit Lambert and Andrew, they were all fans really. They all had flair, Epstein, Lambert and Stigwood, tremendous flair. But it only worked until the real money started rolling in, and then it was a whole different ballgame."

In September, The Stones flew to New York to meet with Klein in order to inform him of Oldham's departure and to organise the photo session with Cooper. It was agreed that Klein would assume all responsibilites: management and production. His team flew across the Atlantic and set up offices in London's Maddox Street.

Brian flew back separately from the other Stones, travelling with Michael Cooper, who journeyed back under the title of the Rolling Stones' road manager. The pair arrived at Heathrow, Brian looking as splendid as ever in a fur waistcoat and plum-coloured woman's floppy hat, complete with a huge blinking 3-D eye pendant. They were immediately seized by airport police and officials and grilled for several hours. Before being allowed to go, they and their luggage were thoroughly searched.

Brian was adamant he was never going back to Courtfield Road. The memories and fears the place conjured up were too painful and disturbing for him to ever imagine living there again. He and Suki rented a new flat at number 17, Chesham Street, in Belgravia, and ordered their remaining items from Courtfield Road to be put into storage.

Brian had only been back on English soil and settled into his new address for a matter of days before he was paid another visit by the very police officer who had arrested him, Detective Sergeant Norman Pilcher. As Pilcher waited outside, Brian contacted his lawyers immediately and refused the police entry until they were present. He was then taken to their office and interrogated by detectives who claimed they were investigating a murder inquiry. The victim, they alleged, was a frequent visitor to the same clubs as Brian and had been seen with Brian on the night of his death.

This flimsy and threadbare connection was eventually completely dismissed but highlighted further the ridiculous lengths the police were prepared to go to in pursuit of their prey.

On 30th October Brian appeared at the Inner London Sessions for trial on the drugs charge from the previous June. Arriving in his silver Rolls Royce and dressed formally in a pinstriped suit, white shirt and tie, he pleaded guilty to the possession of cannabis. His willingness to do so persuaded police to amazingly overlook the small matter of the cocaine and methedrine also found in the raid. Brian admitted responsibility for any cannabis smoked earlier on his premises, thereby nobly letting his companion Prince Stanislas Klossowski off the hook with an order to pay 75 guineas towards his legal costs.

James Comyn QC, Brian's eminent counsel, pleaded for mercy and offered a variety of mitigating circumstances, ranging from the fact that Brian had never taken any hard drugs, except LSD, and had never been in serious trouble before. He also gave a solemn promise that Brian would never touch cannabis again.

Dr Henry gave evidence concerning Brian's disturbed mental state to support Comyn's pleas that he shouldn't be sent to prison.

The psychiatrist asserted, "It would completely destroy his mental health, he would go into a psychotic depression, he might even attempt to injure himself."

In the witness box Brian was as repentant as his QC had asked him to be. Questioning him on the stand he asked, "Is it your intention to have nothing more to do with drugs?" Brian, in a pale whisper answered, "That is my precise intention. They have only brought me trouble and disrupted my career and I hope this will be an example to anyone who is tempted to try them."

It was a heartfelt statement, but one that fell on the deaf ears of Mr R.E. Seaton, the chairman of the Court. At the beginning of the trial he had spoken to the press of his determination to stamp out what he referred to as "a growing canker in this country", and after a short adjournment, Brian was sentenced to prison terms of nine months and three months to run concurrently. He was also ordered to pay 10 and 50 guineas in costs. Pandemonium broke out in the public gallery as Comyn gave notice of appeal and asked if Brian could have bail. "No," was Mr Seaton's reply.

Brian was bundled into a grey prison van, driven past his Rolls Royce and on to Wormwood Scrubs to begin his sentence.

The prison staff gleefully awaited the celebrity's arrival. They had recently seen Mick and Keith slip through their fingers. Meanwhile, the inmates, thinking Brian was gay, planned a malicious welcome, shouting obscenities from their cells as he arrived and threatening to cut off his hair.

Brian was shown to his cell and the door slammed shut behind him.

The next day both his doctor and counsel appeared before a High Court Judge in the privacy of his chambers and pleaded for bail on medical grounds. It was granted on condition that Brian undergo an independent examination by a psychiatrist appointed by the court, and a surety of £750 was paid. Within the hour a warder handed Brian his clothes and told him he was free to go.

Brian, in an effort to stay one jump ahead of the law and driven by his paranoia and suspicions, swapped cars, trading in his Rolls Royce Silver Cloud for a newer model in blue. But after only a couple of days of its purchase, to his horror, he and Palastanga were flashed down by the police after leaving a London club. Two uniformed police officers ordered both of them out of the car while it was thoroughly searched.

Brian narrowly avoided arrest as the drugs in his possession had been wrapped in silver paper and hastily shoved into the driver's mouth. After letting them go, Brian and Palastanga continued their journey along the Embankment. Suddenly Brian ordered the driver to stop the car.

As they got out, Brian ran to the river wall and screamed he was going to jump into the Thames. Not for the first time, the harassed chauffeur managed to pull Brian back from an attempt on his own life. After getting him back in the car, he drove straight to the Priory clinic, where he deposited Brian.

Brian continued visiting the clinic as an out-patient until on 12th December his appeal came before Lord Chief Justice Parker in the Court of Criminal Appeal in Fleet Street. On the same day The Stones had cleverly coincided the release of their seventh and long-awaited album, *Their Satanic Majesties Request*. The title was a satirical play on words and a sardonic assessment of the three main Stones' fragile liberties.

The independent psychiatric report, asked for by the Court of Appeal, had been prepared by Dr Walter Neustatter and was presented in Brian's defence. Neustatter came highly recommended, having been described by Dr Flood as "having done more for forensic psychiatry than any other ten psychiatrists put together".

His report clearly pointed out that Brian was an intelligent and sensitive individual but it went on to say, "Mr Jones' thought processes do reveal some weakening of his reality ties as a result of intense free-floating anxiety. He currently tends to feel very threatened by the world about him as a result of his increasingly inadequate control of aggressive instinctual impulses."

The report continued, "Mr Jones' sexual problems are closely interrelated to his difficulties of aggression – that is, he experiences very intense anxiety surrounding phallic and sadistic sexuality because of his implicit aggressive strivings."

In Dr Neustatter's opinion this anxiety prevented any mature heterosexual adjustment and verged on an Oedipus complex. Neustatter's conclusions confirmed Dr Henry's view that imprisonment would lead to a complete mental breakdown and probably suicide.

Lord Chief Justice Parker also agreed with the team of psychiatrists and Brian's nine-month sentence was set aside. He was fined £1000 and put on probation for three years provided he continued to receive psychiatric treatment. Leaving the court Brian mumbled to a throng of reporters, "I want to be left alone to get on with my life," before being whisked away in his Rolls Royce.

The evening papers reported the case with the usual banner headlines; this time it was "The Mind of Brian Jones".

He celebrated his release with a drink and drug taking binge that had him hospitalised again within two days, and with a toothache to boot.

Dr Flood discharged Brian after he had spent the night at the clinic and had two teeth removed. He expressed the opinion that Brian needed time to relax and recommended Brian take a long holiday. By now, Brian had lost the services of his much put-upon chauffeur Brian Palastanga who had quit just prior to his appeal trial. Brian was now under the watchful eye of another Stones-appointed wheelman, John Corey. Corey picked Brian up from the Priory. Brian, with his usual tact and diplomacy, flew out to Ceylon in the company of Linda Keith, leaving a shattered Suki, distraught and just a little annoyed. Brian returned weeks later and moved Linda into the Chesham Street flat which Suki, in his absence, had wisely vacated.

The couple started a round of regular socialising. They were seen most nights drinking and partying at all of Brian's London haunts. They also attended a press reception for the band Grape-fruit, along with (much to Linda's glee) Jimi Hendrix. At the party, Brian now heavily bearded and potbellied, was photo-graphed laughing happily with Mick and Jimi and talked for the first time in months about his commitment to the band. He even defended their abysmal *Satanic* album. A period of calm seemed to have descended upon his life and he began attending Stones sessions once again. In fact, Brian's prediction that their *Satanic Majesties* album would be greeted as a commercial and critical failure had proved devastatingly accurate.

He clearly saw that The Stones needed to pull themselves to-gether musically and he seized the opportunity to lead the way in the studio. Brian envisaged shaping and evolving heavier and rockier riffs in a bid to return The Stones' sound to its pre-psyche-delic and pop glory, something that even Jagger and Richards realised was essential. Even so, they resented Brian's smug "I told you so" attitude. The pair, creatively dry, made way for Brian's ideas but were determined not to let this newfound confi-dence enable a climb-back to power. Neither, it seems, was anyone else.

As Brian returned home from the studio in the early hours of a March morning, he found his Chesham Street front door demol-ished by a welcoming party led by a cheerful and smiling DS Pilcher and at least a dozen uniformed officers. They searched the premises, found nothing and left. (In 1973 DS Pilcher was arrested and charged on corruption and blackmailing offences.)

To add to his woes, Linda had finally realised that Brian's strengths did not lie in loyalty to one partner. After ignoring his claim that he had slept with sixty-four women in one month, the truth was finally brought home to her when she saw him cavort-ing with another woman at a famous London nightspot.

Devastated, she tried to commit suicide by swallowing the contents of a bottle of sleeping tablets. Her naked body was found after the police had received a mysterious phonecall from someone within the Stones' circle. The newspapers had another field day and continued the familiar theme in two-inch banner headlines, "Naked Stones Girl in Drug Drama".

Brian was immediately evicted by his landlord, who gave him half an hour to clear out, even going so far as to ask the police to forcibly remove Brian from his property. Immensely enjoying the attention, the landlord turned to reporters and said, "Although Mr Jones's belongings are still here we don't want him back!"

Brian, looking genuinely shocked and disturbed, said later that the flat was in fact rented to his chauffeur and he only used it when in town. He was trying in vain to give the impression that Linda was in fact the girlfriend of John Corey.

Linda recovered in hospital and, resenting Brian's public disowning of her and the relegation of their relationship to acquaintance status, refused to have any more to do with him or The Stones. Brian found himself, once again, arm in arm with Suki.

Following his eviction from two other hotels, one for attacking a member of staff with a plate of chips and the other for purposely flooding the rooms, Brian moved temporarily into the Imperial Hotel in Queens Gate, London before moving yet again to a rented flat on the third floor of Royal Avenue House, Kings Road.

Brian's intention was to find a permanent address out of London and to that end he and Suki would drive out into the countryside for days on end, to places like Cornwall, Sussex and the Cotswolds, looking at property: houses, farms and cottages.

They eventually found and settled on a house in Sussex called Cotchford.

Once again, Brian had stopped visiting the studio almost completely except for a brief visit in order to record his guitar part for the band's next single *Jumping Jack Flash*. Instead, he intended to devote his time to a life of leisure, enjoying long rides in the country, planning further trips to Morocco, and much to the annoyance of the office staff, going on impulse-spending sprees that had already amassed double-decker buses, a tram and a horsedrawn charabanc.

Jo Bergman, who worked in the Stones' office, had to deal with the countless enquiries and delivery notes that resulted from Brian's "shopping" and often had to fend off irate suppliers by persuading them that they had been a victim of a hoax perpetuated by a bogus Brian Jones. Brian's biggest purchase to date came from a visit to the funfair at Battersea Park where he spotted a particular attraction called "The Waltzer". He spent some time happily whirling round and round on it before ordering his chauffeur to buy it so he could eventually install it in his house in the country. The happy fairground-owner let Brian spend the rest of the day going on all the rides free of charge.

Brian then put further escapades on hold long enough to join the band on a surprise, and by now rare, appearance, playing live at the *New Musical Express* Poll Winners concert at the Empire Pool, Wembley, where they were to receive the award for best R&B band. It was the group's first public appearance in England for nearly two years and it was to be Brian's last.

Brian continued to stay at the Kings Road flat while the owners of his newly acquired Sussex property finalised all the details.

On the morning of 20th May, as the early light filtered through the windows of Brian's bedroom, he was awakened by a loud pounding on his front door. He sat there listening as the knocking continued and realised only too well what it meant.

Brian reached for the phone and dialled the Rolling Stones' PR man, Les Perrin, just as the door crashed open. Jo Bergman had already been mysteriously informed of impending trouble and reached Royal Avenue House before 9 a.m., to be greeted at the door by a jolly policeman.

Once inside she saw three of the policeman's colleagues standing over a huddled-up Brian, holding a piece of cannabis they had allegedly found in a ball of wool. The dismayed and shaking Brian could only say, "Oh no, this can't happen again." He was taken to Chelsea police station where he was formally charged before appearing later the same day at Marlborough Street Magistrates Court. He arrived unshaven and deathly white, dressed in a disarray of mismatched clothes he had thrown on during his arrest. He was charged with possessing a quantity of cannabis and released on £2000 bail pending trial before the Inner London Sessions, the setting of his last brush with authority.

Brian was front-page news yet again as the papers gleefully reported, "Rolling Stone Arrested". Trevor Kempson claims that

Fleet Street had been ready to run the story for weeks. The head-line was already set up but no one was sure who it would be, hence the Rolling Stone title. There had been a tip-off that there was going to be a raid and it was most likely that it was going to be Brian.

Brian, accompanied by Suki, was driven away from the court in a hired car supplied by the office. The driver was told by Brian to take him to the Priory Nursing Home as he didn't feel well. There he received a visit from Linda Lawrence, who had read of his arrest in the evening papers. She felt that seeing his son Julian would be a help to him. Suki made her excuses and left Brian holding the baby in his arms.

The rest of the band decided that the best course of action now was to get Brian out of town. He was taken to Sussex to hide out at Redlands while Keith holidayed abroad with Anita. Brian was put under the strict supervision of Tom Keylock, whose orders were to keep him at Redlands until Brian's case was heard on 11th June. This shortsighted and insensitive decision by the Stones' organisation was an example of how little regard was given to his feelings. Brian hadn't forgotten the role Keylock had played so callously in Morocco and was none too happy at spending his time cooped up in the country, virtually under lock and key, with someone who so obviously despised him.

The mutual feelings between the two only antagonised the situation further. Brian complained bitterly to the Stones' office that Keylock was treating him like a prisoner and in turn Keylock maintained he was only doing a job and it was in Brian Jones's in-terest. In defiance of everyone, Brian flew to Tangier together with Suki and Christopher Gibbs.

"He was obsessed with the thought of going to jail and his re-lationship with Suki was suffering," Gibbs recalled. "They were squabbling all the time. I was in my room one evening, cooling off after a particularly hot day, when Brian rushed in in a panic, say-ing, 'Quick, quick, come to my room.' He was really hysterical. So I went with him to his room and the whole place was a mess. Smashed mirrors, smashed glass, smashed everything, and Suki was lying on the bed, unconscious and bleeding. Brian was say-ing, 'What are we gonna do about this?'

"He had given her the most terrible beating for one reason or another. I said, 'No, Brian, what are you going to do about this?

You phone a doctor now.' He was completely off the wall by now, saying, 'No, I can't do that.' So I had to do it. Anyway, I managed to get a doctor and ambulance and they turned up with Suki still unconscious, while Brian was pretending he had nothing whatsoever do with it. He then said to me, 'You go with her to the hospital, man. I think I'll just hang around here.' I was furious. I grabbed him. 'You won't just hang around here, now get in there,' and I pushed him head-first into the ambulance. The Moroccans are very good, no questions asked sort of thing, but Brian really didn't want anything to do with it all. He was totally irresponsible."

While Suki recovered, Brian and Christopher visited the tiny village of Joujouka once more. Brian wanted to record the musicians and borrowed some tape machines from Brion Gysin. Unfortunately they were faulty and the mission was abandoned.

They returned to England, Brian to face trial and Suki to receive further medical treatment.

Brian, accompanied by Tom Keylock, went to court where he pleaded not guilty and elected to be tried by jury. He was granted unrestricted bail and the trial was set for 26th September. Dodging the crowd outside, Keylock drove Brian and Suki back to Redlands, stopping off at the clinic once more to pick up some medication for Brian, which he needed to take with him on another short break to Spain and Morocco.

Brian returned to Morocco again with the ever-faithful Suki and sound-engineer George Chkiantz. He was determined to record Joujouka's Rites of Pan festival and for two days and nights the intrepid group camped out on a hillside smoking marijuana and witnessing scenes very few Europeans had seen.

The Pan Rites were part of a festival of music and dancing that has not changed in centuries. Brian and Chkiantz started recording at sundown and continued into the early hours of the morning when the isolated village was bathed in an unearthly light and the children danced in a shameless and primitive manner.

At noon the next day the festival started up again. As sunset approached, the musicians finished playing and put down their instruments. Two of them passed Brian and Suki carrying a snow-white goat which was to be the evening meal. Brian turned to Suki and said in a whisper, "That's me," and pointed to the goat's blond fringe. Spellbound, he continued to watch and again said, "That's me," as the goat was slaughtered on the ground before them.

An important part of the evening ritual was for the guest of honour, Brian, to pay homage to Pan by wrapping himself in a freshly skinned pelt and absorbing the blood and warmth of the animal. Luckily Brian had been warned beforehand and disappeared at the precise moment, but this angered the villagers, something which sent him into a paranoid panic that lasted for days. He now feared that he was cursed.

Back in Tangier, after the festival, Brian was in self-destruct mode again. He stood on the balcony yelling, "Salaam aleikhum," which he had been told meant "Good morning", to everyone who passed underneath. For those who answered back, he would should "Hi", but for those who didn't, Brian would scream "Cunt".

After a whole morning of this, Brian asked George, "What's good morning in Arabic?" George, slightly mystified, replied, "You've been saying it all morning, it's salaam aleikhum." Brian said, "No. Phone room service, I'm sure I've got it wrong."

According to George, Brian was very insistent about it and kept saying, "It's alright. Just phone them. I must know."

George then recalls, "Brian fell over – he suddenly went completely paralysed and fell over like a statue. Fortunately, he didn't go over the balcony. He just hit his head. I was quite alarmed, but Suki said, 'Brian does this every night. Just throw a blanket over him and leave him there.'"

The group flew back to London and on 26th September Brian arrived at the Inner Sessions at Marylebone Street Magistrates Court dressed smartly in a single-breasted dark suit but looking pale and tired with huge circles under his eyes. The public gallery was, as usual, packed with teenage girls while the cramped press bench eagerly anticipated the errant Rolling Stone getting his "just desserts".

When asked to plead to the charge of unlawfully possessing cannabis, Brian, his face deathly white and his voice trembling, whispered in a barely audible tone, "Not guilty." He gave his address as Redlands, West Wittering, Sussex while the jury of ten men and two women listened keenly to his account of the "bust".

Brian's defence was that if he had known of the existence of any drugs he would have been able to dispose of them as the police knocked. He went on to point out that he didn't have any knowledge of a ball of wool. "When the ball of wool was shown to me I was absolutely shattered," he testified. "I felt everything swim. I don't knit. I don't darn socks and I don't have a girlfriend who darns socks. Last year the Lord Chief Justice made it clear to me what would happen if I were ever convicted on this sort of charge. Last year's affair made me very frightened of the drug."

Brian's psychiatrist, Dr Anthony Flood, was the first to give evidence after lunch. He said, "Nothing suggested to me that Jones was playing around with drugs. If I put a reefer by this young man, he would run a mile."

Then Michael Havers asked Brian about the effects of cannabis, to which he replied, "It heightens an experience." Brian's reply was almost lost as the whole court's attention swung in the direction of the door and Mick and Keith squashed into the public gallery alongside Keylock and Suki.

They had arrived in time to hear the summing-up for the jury by Chairman Reginald Seaton. He said that the burden of proof lay with the police and not Brian and that their case was circumstantial. The jury retired for 45 minutes and then delivered a verdict of guilty. Brian slumped back in his seat, burying his ashen face in his hands mumbling "No, no, no. It can't be true." Gasps from the public gallery greeted the announcement. Keith visibly trembled and Suki became hysterical.

Chairman Seaton, amidst the uproar, said, "I think this was a lapse and I don't want to interfere with the probation order that already applies to this man. I am going to fine you according to your means. You must keep clear of this stuff. You really must watch your step. You will be fined fifty pounds with one hundred guineas' costs. For goodness sake, don't get into trouble again or you really will be in serious trouble."

Hand in hand with Suki, the jubilant Brian left the court, stopping to pose for photographs with Mick and smiling at the assembled crowd of schoolgirls. Mick was asked his opinion on the case by a reporter and said, "We are very happy Brian didn't have to go to jail." Brian, holding on to Suki's hand, said, "It's wonderful to be free. Someone planted that drug in my flat but I don't know who. I will state to my death that I did not commit this offence."

Brian now seemed totally disinterested in his career as a Rolling Stone. His rare visits to the studio during the latter part of the recording of *Beggars Banquet* had stopped producing anything close to his earlier inspired ideas and he eventually stopped showing up altogether. Brian's contribution to the Stones' next project was also looking like producing a similar level of non-participation.

The Rolling Stones' *Rock and Roll Circus* was the title of the band's planned colour TV spectacular for world distribution in December. The group had hired a Big Top from Sir Robert Fossett's circus, complete with jugglers, acrobats, clowns and wild animals, in order to stage an event featuring the cream of British rock talent. The line-up included The Who, Eric Clapton, Jethro Tull, John Lennon assisted by Yoko, and, of course, The Rolling Stones.

On the day of shooting, Brian, dressed as a wizard, spent most of his time standing over a pile of rejected costumes, deciding what to put on next, before finally choosing a top hat with horns – all this in order to mumble his one memorable line, "Here come the clowns." He lamely strummed along with the band on a half-dozen new numbers from their forthcoming album, *Beggars Banquet*. The songs premiered included *Parachute Woman, You Can't Always Get What You Want* and *No Expectations*.

Jagger considered the whole performance below par and the film was shelved. It was Brian Jones's last appearance with the band he had formed and to this day it has never been released.

8

Through Cotchford's Past Darkly

Mrs Mary Hallett was born almost 80 years ago at Cotchford Farm, a beautiful sixteenth-century farmhouse a mile east of the tiny Sussex village of Hartfield. She still lives in Cotchford Lane today, in a charming secluded house hidden from view amidst clusters of trees and bushes, a stone's throw away from the very room in which she entered the world.

Mary's world is Cotchford Farm and Lane. One of eight children, she was brought up on Cotchford Farm and, in turn, raised her own family there. During that time, she has witnessed the one-time working arable farm, with its collection of labourer's cottages, turn into country-mansion retreats, occupied solely by those wealthy enough to enjoy such high living standards. "We shared the house in those days with another family until my mother moved us up along the lane," Mary says.

Her early happy memories of country life during the 1920s are indeed a book in themselves. Running to and fro from the local village, picking up the farmworker's wages, snitching horse and cart rides along winding lanes and even acting as an innocent go-between for an unscrupulous farmworker and the wife of a local publican, these were true adventures indeed for a little girl.

Set against the leafy rural backdrop of the Ashdown Forest, Mary's adolescence couldn't have been more idyllic. But tragedy was to play a big part in Mary's later life. Her first husband died after suffering for many years with meningitis. He was found slumped at the wheel of his Post Office van. He had been robbed whilst he lay dying. Mary's only son was knocked down and killed on a nearby road.

In 1924, a family called the Milnes moved into Cotchford Farm. They were the first of the rich families to descend on Cotchford Lane.

Mary watched for hours as builders and gardeners laboured away in the house and grounds transforming the once muddy paths and fields into green lawns and ornate walkways. The new owner, A.A. Milne, was a writer and Cotchford Lane was to become the setting for his best-loved work, *Winnie the Pooh*.

This is a collection of tales featuring an imaginary bear and his adventures with Christopher Robin, a character who was inspired and based on Milne's own son of the same name. The stories are filled with rabbits, an owl, a piglet and a certain bear, and anyone who has read those stories can't help but be filled with wonder when walking along these lanes and through the adjoining woods.

As you make the walk, it is impossible not to remember the scenes or recognise their illustrated versions, drawn so brilliantly by E.H. Sheppard in all of Milne's books. "100 Aker Wood", "The Six Pine Trees", "The Sandy Pit" and, most importantly, "Pooh Bridge", the old wooden bridge that crosses the stream where Christopher Robin raced Pooh-sticks, are all there, large as life.

Mary was used to seeing Christopher Robin playing happily in the Lane and grew very fond of him. She still has a fading painted portrait of the little boy hanging in her living room. It hangs alongside one of her boloved son.

"It was Milne's wife Daphine that did most of the original work in the gardens. It was her that had the sundial put in," Mary says, referring to the lawn's handsome centrepiece with its hand-carved figures of Milne's famous characters, Pooh Bear, Eeyore and Piglet dancing endlessly round and round it. Milne was to die in 1955 and Christopher Robin, strangely keen to escape his literary past, put Cotchford up for sale.

A year later Cotchford Farm was taken over by a wealthy young couple, Stewart and Margarita Taylor. Stewart was American and Margarita Spanish and they too carried out extensive alterations in and around the farm. The most bewildering of these, to Mary at least, was the installation of an outside swimming pool.

The English climate is renowned for dampening even the hardiest swimmer's enthusiasm. Nonetheless a swimming pool is a standard requirement for a wealthy young American, albeit in the heart of rural Sussex woodland.

Mary got to know the Taylors well and when Margarita fell ill she offered to clean for them. "They had a young daughter by then called Linda, and Margarita couldn't manage so I would go over in the morning to do the household chores. I ended up as housekeeper. It was a strange feeling to be back cleaning my old room some forty years on."

Mary stayed with the Taylors for 13 years until in 1968 the couple split and Margarita announced that she had sold the house and was moving back to Spain. "It was quite a shock but Margarita had drawn up a contract which said I would be able to stay on in my old job."

The Taylors had also made provisions for their other staff, most notably the gardener, Michael Martin. "I had already cleaned for the actor Richard Harris when he rented Cotchford from the Taylors whilst they holidayed abroad," Mary says. "So I was like a part of the furniture."

The identity of Cotchford's new owner wasn't disclosed other than the fact that he had agreed to Margarita's conditions and the jobs had been assured. Cotchford's newest master would be down to inspect the place the following morning.

Michael Martin the gardener had a clear memory of that morning. "We were in the garden, Les (Mary's second husband) and I," he says. "We hadn't been told who had bought the house right up to the last minute, when this Rolls Royce pulled into the drive. It had tinted windows so we still couldn't see who was in it. Then this dollybird got out and minced up the path to us and introduced herself as a secretary and told us we were now working for The Rolling Stones.

"Well, that was that, I decided there and then it won't be for long. I wouldn't mind working for The Beatles but I'm not working for The Rolling Stones."

Mary greeted the news with similar misgivings. Although not at all familiar with the pop-music world she, like Martin, had been fed a regular diet of Fleet Street horror stories concerning the band and she too felt a small sense of foreboding.

Brian's arrival at Cotchford that morning was to do little to dispel these initial feelings.

He emerged from his blue Rolls Royce, wearing multi-coloured trousers, his face buried in the collar of a large brown fur cape and hidden beneath a huge, floppy woman's hat. Flanked by Suki and his chauffeur, he was whisked past the intrigued gardener and disappeared inside the house without uttering a word.

"We still hadn't a clue who it was," says Martin. "He looked like a giant teddy bear!"

Mrs Hallett's recollection is equally clear. "The first time I went down was with Linda, who was about twelve then I suppose and I said, 'Who's that woman down the drive?' She went into hysterics laughing, saying, "That's Brian Jones of The Rolling Stones."

If these initial impressions of Brian had been alarming, Mary was soon to see him in a different light. "He was the most polite and kindest boy I've known. You couldn't have wished for a nicer boy, he was kindness itself."

Martin too soon warmed to his new employer. "He called me Artichoke because I grew vegetables in the gardens and always made sure he had plenty in the house, and if I had time I would cook for him, instead of his chauffeur, who Brian didn't seem to like."

Brian had bought Cotchford Farm in November 1968 for the sum of £35,000, initially intending it to be a weekend retreat and peaceful sanctuary where he could go to recover after raving it up all week in London. After only a couple of visits, however, he had permanently moved in. The slow and calm pace of life represented something of a return to his childhood. He was once again back in the clean air of the country.

Brian had finally tired of the constant changes of address. He no longer enjoyed his virtually nomadic lifestyle or the unstable domestic problems inherent in it. He had been the only Stone not to own his own home, the only one never featured in all those "Stones at Home" articles the numerous teen mags were wont to do. The others had wisely invested money in property. Jagger had bought Stargroves, a huge Elizabethan mansion house in Berkshire (once owned by Oliver Cromwell), Bill Wyman owned Gedding Hall, an equally impressive mansion in Suffolk, Charlie had bought an ancient Sussex manor house from Britain's attorney-general, Lord Shawcross, while Keith owned Redlands.

Cotchford brought Brian back in line with the rest of the band. He wanted desperately to be able to invite his parents down to a real house and show it off. He had often talked of how he was going to get his act together and settle down with a house in the country.

"I am a country boy at heart," he was fond of saying when talking endlessly about his plans to install some kind of normality into his life. He had other plans too that needed urgent consideration, plans that until now had been no more than wistful promises to himself. Cotchford was the realization of all this but it was much more. It was a safe and cosy hideaway where he could sit and think, hidden from view behind the very rows of pine trees and bushes that had originally inspired Milne's fictional world of Pooh.

Brian crammed the house with his impressive, priceless collection of antiques and trinkets, beautifully woven rugs, screens, hand-carved tables and ornaments. They adorned every inch of the low-beamed rooms, all amassed from his numerous sojourns to Morocco and the marketplaces of Tangiers, or from one of his regular visits to Christopher Gibbs's antique shop in London.

Brian cared little for the rest of the ancient farm's extraordinary history. The fact that William the Conqueror had stayed there bore little significance for him. It was the idea of living in the house at Pooh Corner that thrilled him. He liked nothing better than to excitedly drag guests around the grounds to show off the pool and the lifesize statue of Christopher Robin, leaving until last the sundial which he would point to and then read aloud its inscription: "This warm and sunny spot belongs to Pooh and here he wonders what to do".

"It's perfect," Brian would say. "It's exactly what I'm doing."

On other occasions, Brian would not be so contented and the dark destructive side of his character would return. For example there is a famous rumour that Milne buried the original manuscripts for his books under the sundial. When drunk, Brian often had to be dissuaded from taking a sledgehammer and smashing the sundial to check the validity of these rumours.

Like all of Cotchford's previous owners, Brian wanted changes made to the house. He ordered renovations and decorations to suit his personal taste, an idea he had got from Keith who had made extensive alterations to Redlands, turning the grand but rustic country mansion into a home more befitting a pop star of Rolling Stone calibre. Keith, at the insistence of Tom Keylock, had hired an old schoolfriend of his to carry out the work, a builder named Frank Thorogood. So when Keith suggested the same builder to Brian, it seemed a natural choice.

Thorogood was hired and within a couple of days, he put in an estimate of somewhere in the region of £10,000 for the alterations that Brian had planned. This quote was to cover work both within the house and its adjoinging acreage. Brian, who knew nothing of building work, accepted the quote. Thorogood, in turn, hired three workmen from nearby Chichester. Their names were Mo, Johnny and David, and, under the overall supervision of Tom Keylock, they set to work.

Thorogood, a Londoner, persuaded Brian that it would be a good idea if he lived in at Cotchford during the week and returned home at weekends, since driving back and forth from London would only prolong the work. Brian agreed to Thorogood's idea. There was a garage block set a little to the left of the main house which had a small flat above it. It had housed the Milnes' gardener years ago but had since remained empty, though Mrs Hallett had used it in the past to store some of the Taylors' belongings.

The flat was cleaned and made ready for Thorogood. Brian had only been living at Cotchford for a few days when Frank moved in with a companion. Thorogood, who had a wife living in London, was accompanied by his then girlfriend and mistress, Janet Lawson, a nurse from the nearby town. Brian was unhappy with the situation. He was new to the area and wanted desperately to fit in with his neighbours. He was determined not to upset them by encouraging blatant acts of infidelity. He knew only too well from his Cheltenham childhood how news travels in small towns.

Mrs Hallett remembers Brian's considerable concern over the situation, "It wasn't just Frank! Mo and Johnny practically moved straight in with Frank and they were the most unfaithful chaps that ever walked. They were all married. I've seen Mo sitting with a girl on his knee, cuddling her and talking to his wife on the phone and saying, 'I'll see you on such and such a day, I'm very busy at the moment.' Brian said to me one day, 'It doesn't matter what girls I have, I am a single boy but I don't agree with these men having girls.' He was very straight about it but he didn't know how to confront them."

Thorogood's long association with Keylock meant that the

builder was given trustee status. He was therefore awarded special priviledges.

Keylock had plenty of duties in mind for his old school pal and gave Thorogood the power to draw money from the Stones' London office to pay for the day to day living expenses of him and his men. These, in turn, would be charged to Jones's account. Frank was also to take over as Brian's unofficial minder and to report all of Jones's activities back to Keylock. Keylock had performed exactly the same task for Richards when Brian stayed at Redlands.

Brian suspected as much but was too insecure to do anything about it and, anyhow, in a strange way, he welcomed the company, however incompatible he and Frank's gang of builders were.

Mary says, "He hated being on his own. He would come up to my house if there was no one at the farm. He would come up to the house and have a moan about Frank or Mo. He was so glad of any company or someone to talk to that he would forget that they really worked for him. He could have given orders but he didn't want them to think of him in that way."

Determined to show the band that he could clean himself up, Brian was keeping his drug intake to a minimum, using only his legally prescribed sleeping tablets and tranquillizers. Having Frank around helped. If Thorogood was Keylock's deputy, there to keep an eye on the troublesome Stone, then Brian wasn't about to give him any ammunition. Not that he had to try too hard.

Jones's paranoia about being busted again made him too nervous for that. He wouldn't even let Suki so much as smoke a joint in the house. He was still drinking heavily but this was restricted to chilled wine and beer which he would sip constantly, sitting by the side of the pool, strumming a guitar or strolling through the grounds.

"No way man, I'm clean now. I'm a boozer again," he told his old friend Tony Sanchez one afternoon when he came to visit, with Brian gleefully refusing the offer of a customary toot of cocaine. Brian's efforts to endear himself to the local population were larely successful.

He never paraded his wealth in public nor flaunted his celebrity status. He was aware that most of the village were poorly paid farmworkers or labourers much older than himself with families to support. He knew swanning around town in his Rolls Royce waving hundreds of pounds under their noses was not the way to win them over.

Therefore he bought himself a Vespa scooter to buzz anonymously down to Hartfield, stopping daily at the local pub, The Haywagon, to drink with the regulars. Dennis Burke, one of the pub's barmen, who still lives in the village, remembers Brian mixing in happily with the clientele.

"He couldn't help but stand out because of his clothes," he says. (Brian had now adopted a curious mixture of Carnaby Street psychedelia and cow-shed chic.) "He never made much of the fact that he was a pop star. He would just pop in and down a few pints with the lads, mostly too many I thought. Many a time I saw him being helped on to his bike after a session. Some of the youngsters would fish in the stream behind his farm and take him their catch and earn themselves a few bob. He was a likeable sort."

"These are the 'real' people," Brian told Sanchez, going on to describe his new country neighbours as "down to earth folk just going about their business, doing real jobs, not like those bastards and junkies up in London!" He found it hard to believe just how far removed he had become from enjoying the simple pleasures of life.

Brian was clearly enjoying his role as country squire and villager, going for long walks down the lanes and across the fields, with his dog chasing wildly behind him. He was looking fitter than he had for a long time, and friends who visited Brian at Cotchford were amazed at the change in him.

"Brian definitely changed for the better after moving to the country," Suki said. Brian's newfound serenity, however, was to be shortlived. His precarious position within the band began to haunt him once again. Not that it was ever far from his mind.

"In the first few weeks he had managed to keep on top of it," Suki said, "then it hit him with a bang." To help him, Suki suggested that Brian take a break and get out of England for a while, go somewhere he could relax, away from the band completely. She pointed out that Keith and Anita, Mick and Marianne were holidaying in Peru. He would not be missing anything. It was the perfect time, Brian agreed. In January 1969 he and Suki flew to Ceylon. They returned to England on 12th January in order for

Brian's appeal to be heard in court. It was denied, leaving Brian with two convictions to his credit. Suki felt that Brian knew then that he was finally finished as a Rolling Stone. They had long since stopped inviting or even informing him of sessions and he hadn't seen or heard a word from them since the *Rock 'n Roll Circus* back in December.

Distraught at his increasing isolation, Brian started visiting his old haunts in London again, stumbling drunk from one club or party to another, surrounded once again by the selfsame junkies and hangers-on who mere weeks ago he had turned his back on for good. Suki knew he was settling back into that old routine and watched in horror as his slide gained momentum and his condition worsened after each drink-frenzied trip to the capital.

It was the side of Brian she knew only too well. "Once he started drinking heavily he just got worse and worse," she confirmed. "His temper returned. It was that vile aggressive part of him you just couldn't reason with." If this pattern continued it had to be at the expense of their relationship, and just how abruptly that came to an end depended on Brian. This less desirable part of Brian's nature was not confined to London. It was now evident in the village and pubs of Hartfield.

Within a matter of months of moving to Cotchford Farm the locals were clearly wishing he had chosen somewhere else to live out his childhood fantasies. His friendly few beers with the locals were now excessively maudlin or bad-tempered binges. On one occasion, he ended an evening's drinking at The Haywagon by crashing his scooter through the window of the shop opposite.

Brian's appearance seemed to deteriorate as quickly as his behaviour. He gained over a stone in weight and the bags under his eyes, which had always been an exaggerated feature, were now even heavier and darker, framed by a shaggy mass of raddled blond hair. He looked like a giant panda, pacing his cage as he slumped lethargically around the garden at Cotchford. He resembled, more potently, an elderly decaying Christopher Robin.

The strain of living with Brian was now intolerable for Suki. His violent paranoid mood swings were one thing to contend with, but being left stranded in the country for days on end while he raved in London was something completely different. She decided it was time to leave. "I wanted to split. I told him I'd come back when he wasn't a pop star any more." Suki's reasoning was lost on Brian. He saw her departure as an act of desertion, failing to recognise that it wasn't an easy decision for Suki.

She still loved Brian, but he was out of control, constantly accusing her of unfaithfulness and, in particular, of being over-friendly with Frank Thorogood. If she was to salvage anything of their relationship she needed to put some distance between them. Soon after, Suki moved out.

With the stability that Suki offered now gone, Brian's interest in the day to day running of Cotchford all but vanished. His accusations concerning Frank and Suki had hardly improved an already shaky relationship with the builder; he now avoided even the smallest confrontations.

So when Frank, tired of his cramped living conditions above the garage, calmly informed Brian he was moving into the house, Brian merely nodded. One night in the London club Blazes, Brian confided in his friends, including Tony Sanchez. He spoke about his fears of how he now saw his own home situation starting to mirror his predicament within the band: "Those builders aren't doing what they're meant to be doing," he complained bitterly.

"They act as if they own the place! As if I wasn't there. People just arrive saying they have come to fix this or that and they stick around for days." Yet Brian did nothing to discourage those liberties. Ever the grateful host, he was fast turning his new home into a magnet for the multitudes of starstruck social climbers and junkie ego-boosters that are attracted to the rich and famous.

They were all eager to join in on one of Brian's seemingly endless parties where huge outsized amplifiers would pump rock music out into the once peaceful Sussex valley. Eeyore would have been far from impressed. The neighbours certainly were not.

"The music rolled through the valley. It was dreadful," Mary Hallett says. "Like the end of the world was coming, it was awful! When I would go down in the morning, I would say to him, 'I think you scared quite a few people last night.' That would make him giggle and say, 'Why was that?' then he would thank me for pointing it out."

Mick and Keith had been kept informed via Keylock of Brian's recent carryings-on. They got in touch with Alexis Korner, the Stones' old mate and mentor. Alexis was still close to the band, especially to Brian. Mick and Keith explained to him the difficulties the band were having with Brian and how sick they considered him to be.

Korner was aware that there had been no contact between Brian and his old band-mates for some time, but felt, despite Brian's behaviour, they still seemed worried about him. Mick asked Alexis if he would visit Brian at Cotchford and try and pull him together, emphasizing that Alexis was someone that their wayward colleague would listen to. Alexis made Jagger no promises but agreed to see what he could do to help. A visit was planned for the following weekend. Korner wanted to make the visit seem like a purely social event to put Brian at ease.

Meanwhile, Michael Martin was attempting to get Brian to take a holiday but, without Suki to organise it, it was a futile gesture. "Brian set aside two weeks in order to plan somewhere to go," Martin explains. "I asked him a couple of times if he had thought of somewhere but he just kept saying he was still thinking. At the end of the two weeks he was still thinking!"

Korner decided to take his wife Bobbie and young daughter Sappho down to Cotchford. He hadn't seen Brian for some time and was looking forward to meeting up with his old friend. When he arrived at the house, Korner was greatly shocked by Brian's appearance. "He looked like a fat mummified Louis the Fourteenth" was how Korner described him. For his part, Brian was pleased to see the Korners and the group sat and talked for hours about his future plans.

"He was still drinking a lot and at one point fell asleep in mid-sentence," Korner recalls. "The conversation mainly revolved around music but Brian also talked at length about the bad feeling between himself and the builders. He was keen to point out the parts of the house that had supposedly been either refurbished or renovated. He would point to this part or that saying 'That cost me such and such.'" Korner noticed that these particular parts of the house were half finished or not touched at all.

It was late when the Korners left. Alexis told Brian he would get back to him in a·few days so they could talk some more and would ring to confirm a date. When Alexis called Brian later that week, as promised, he was disturbed to hear Brian speaking in almost a whisper and pleading for Alexis to visit. "Brian was saying that since my last visit someone had been locking him in the house." Alexis told Brian not to panic and said he would be down soon. He assumed that Brian was mislaying the keys himself. Mrs Hallett thought the same at first when Brian would turn up on her doorstep. "We would go out shopping and when we came back he would be sitting there waiting for us. He would be lost because there was no one in the house to let him in."

On his subsequent visit to Brian's, Alexis went alone and was relieved to find him in a happier state of mind and eager to talk. "He still retained vague plans about putting a new group together and I intended to encourage that," Alexis said. Korner had just formed a band called The New Church and the two musicians discussed the possibility of Brian joining. "At first I said yes but finally I had to say no. I didn't want the responsibility of taking care of Brian on the road, not in the condition he was in."

The New Church had a German tour lined up and Korner knew that taking Brian on the road could prove disastrous. Jones was still the most popular Stone in many parts of the Continent, but most notably in Germany, where the band had originally been billed as Brian Jones and the Rolling Stones. Alexis wasn't about to risk a low-key, low-budget tour with a high-risk, high-profile Stone and with little or no security! Alexis tried to explain his concern to Brian, taking great care not to damage his obviously fragile enthusiasm and commitment. He devised a plan whereby Alexis would help Brian form his own band, setting up rehearsals and auditioning musicians. They drew up a list of possible players and gave themselves a target of six months from the start of rehearsals to create a fully formed band, ready to work.

The musical climate was perfect for a band of Brian and Alexis' planning. Eric Clapton, since folding Cream, was busying himself with the formation of Blind Faith, the progressive rock band which incorporated the talents of Steve Winwood, Ginger Baker and Rick Grech.

Graham Nash had said goodbye to The Hollies, swapped the rain of Manchester for the sunshine of LA and, along with ex-Byrd David Crosby and Steven Stills from Buffalo Springfield, was busy putting the finishing touches to Crosby, Stills and Nash. Even Brian's old label-mate, Steve Marriott, who had tired of being a Small Face, had united with the face of 1968, ex-Herd singer Peter Frampton and Spooky Tooth bass-player Greg Ridley in the rock venture they were calling Humble Pie.

It was the start of the age that was later to be chronicled as the supergroup era. Brian still held strong links with the musical hierarchy on both sides of the Atlantic. It had always been to Brian's door that the likes of Dylan, Hendrix and the Byrds made a beeline on their visits to England. Alexis could see Brian having no problem finding people to play with.

Brian's music room at Cotchford was turned into a rehearsal studio, and filled out with two organs, guitars, amps and a drumkit. Brian set about contacting the various musicians he and Alexis had chosen. Steve Marriott was one of the first Brian spoke to. "We were rehearsing not far from Brian's house when he heard that me and Peter were putting a band together," Marriott recalled. "Brian rang me and said he would like to come down and have a play. We thought great! We were all really into the idea of him joining the band. He was a nice bloke and a great player when he was together."

Brian also contacted Jimi Hendrix's drummer Mitch Mitchell, Vinegar Joe singer Elkie Brooks, drummer Micky Waller, Walker Brother Gary Leeds, record-producer Jimmy Miller and none other than John Lennon, all of whom expressed interest.

Brian was excited but mainly relieved by his friends' support. It was the boost to his musical confidence he needed. Alexis was happy with Brian's progress but was blissfully unaware that he was in fact paving the way for Brian's departure from The Rolling Stones. By encouraging these new-band plans, Korner was in turn making Mick, Keith and Klein's job of sacking Brian a lot easier. When Alexis excitedly reported he had got Brian playing again, once for 14 hours solid and on his own songs, they knew that the time had come to move.

9

Death At Pooh Corner

When the grim-faced trio of Charlie Watts, Keith Richards and Mick Jagger arrived at Cotchford Farm on that warm June night, Brian Jones instinctively knew that he was no longer in The Rolling Stones. He had gone through the scene so many times in his mind that the awkward meeting seemed to unfold before him like an act from a well rehearsed play. When the group finally left, Brian Jones felt a mixture of panic and relief. Financially, however, his future seemed assured. The group had offered him a generous one-off payment of £100,000 to be followed by a yearly payment of £20,000, for as long as the group existed.

When Alexis heard the news of Brian's sacking, he was concerned for his old friend. Fearful that his dismissal would crush him completely and undo all their weeks of good work, he and Bobbie went to see Brian the following day. They were amazed to see how calmly Brian had taken it. Instead of finding him, as they had expected, in a state of mourning, Brian was in a good frame of mind. He was chirpy and eager to rehearse. He was also sober. Alexis believed him when he said he hadn't felt so good in years. If anything Brian's departure from The Stones only seemed to strengthen his resolve to get his own band on the road.

"It was like a giant weight had been lifted from his shoulders," Brian's friend, journalist Peter Jones, said after seeing him in London a couple of nights later. "'We're going to be bigger than anyone would believe,' Brian told me. He talked about his new-group plans, he was excited and saying how he wanted to go back to real rock and roll and cut out all that commercial crap The Stones put out."

Brian had arranged a meeting with Jones after being reassured by the Stones' secretary, Shirley Arnold, that the full facilities of the Stones' office in terms of press and promotion were still at his disposal. He was told not to hesitate to ask if he needed anything. For Brian, who would need to maintain a high profile now he was separated from The Stones, this was a stroke of good luck.

That night, Brian had dinner with Maurice Gibb and his wife Lulu. They were happy to see the revitalized Brian and reported, "He joined us for dinner along with Cynthia Lennon and Twiggy. He was certainly happier than we'd seen him in a long time."

As rehearsals got under way, and the likes of John Mayall, Mitch Mitchell and Steve Winwood pulled up at the farm, Brian's confidence soared. When they weren't jamming or playing, Brian either locked himself away in his small oak-beamed studio or walked through the gardens of Cotchford blowing loudly on his saxophone, a habit that greatly annoyed Michael Martin. "He would come out and blow the bloody thing for hours on end. It used to drive me mad."

Bolstered by the support of Alexis and his fellow musicians, Brian was feeling strong and decisive. This seemed to unsettle his part-time builder and house guest, Frank. Brian knew he had turned a blind eye to the builder's antics for too long. Thorogood, Mo, Johnny and Corey were still sauntering back and forth to Cotchford and acting like they owned the place. Brian would receive his promised £100,000 in a few weeks' time and if he was to regain control over his estate he knew he had to get his house in order first.

It was a jubilant Brian that opened the door to Mrs Hallett a couple of days later. "We're alright now," he told her. "My money is coming through from America." "I remember it clearly," she says. "It was the same day there was a story in the paper about Mick Jagger. The *News of the World* were running an article about Jagger's recent drugs bust in London. Mick and Marianne Faithful had been arrested at their house in Cheyne Walk and charged with possession of a quarter of an ounce of hash and a quantity of heroin by the very officer, Detective Sergeant Norman Pilcher, and his team of detectives that had done such a splendid job on Brian. "Brian was laughing like a drain when he heard the news on the radio." 'Someone must have put poor ole Mick up,' he said to me. 'Mick wouldn't keep any drugs in his house.' Then Brian's mood changed all of a sudden. He started to look very scared and said, "It has really quite worried me. Mrs Hallett, have you got any brandy?" He didn't have any drink left in the house. I remembered that I had a bottle at home. I fetched it for him and it calmed him down. He offered me a drop but it was too early in the morning. He poured it for me anyway, only he poured out a full half-pint mug!"

Keylock was still visiting Cotchford, checking up on his men's progress, like a general inspecting his troops. But the troops were restless. In the wake of Brian's departure from The Stones, John Corey, Brian's chauffeur and minder, had been deployed elsewhere by the group's London office, sending a clear message to the workmen that a budgeting operation was in progress. Keylock found he was constantly reassuring the jittery builders that their wages were assured. However, in the light of recent events, more cutbacks would have to be made.

It was on one of Keylock's visits to the front line that Michael Martin overheard Frank telling Tom that Mrs Hallett should go. Mrs Hallett had made no secret of the fact that she didn't like Keylock or any of the builders and wasted little time in telling them so at every opportunity. "I knew that they weren't real builders, more like jacks of all trades!"

By now, Mary was close to Brian. She had become a surrogate mother figure and confidante to him. He had even installed her phone so that he could call her at all times of the day and night, and he payed every bill. "Shall I tell you what I think it was," she explained. "My son was killed when he was twenty-three by a car and just after that Brian moved in and he was around a similar age. In a way he gave me back something which I had lost." The builders had contemptuously recognised this and treated her as such. But now she became an irritant to them and they clashed on a daily basis. Now that money was tight, Thorogood saw her as superfluous to Brian's needs and an unnecessary drain on resources. Keylock took charge of the situation and a bizarre series of petty confrontations ensued.

"They didn't like me around. It unnerved them," she stated. "If they saw me coming down the path I would hear them say, 'Quick, Mrs Hallett is coming.' I used to know they were up to no good as they wouldn't half be shifting." Mary's wages were then mysteriously cut and she asked Brian why. It was the first Brian had heard of it and he was outraged. Ringing the accountants in London, Brian put the problem right and Mary's money returned to normal. "They wanted to get rid of me, but Brian wouldn't hear of it. I had to get permission from the office in London for anything I needed for the house and was told I was spending too much money on feeding the cats." Brian had inherited three cats from the Taylors when they sold him Cotchford but that number had multiplied to nine over the following months. "I used to get their food plus one pint of milk a day and I was told it was too much and to get a cheaper brand. Well, the builders were awful to those cats, they knocked them about and kicked them across the room. I told Brian and he said he would put a stop to it, but they still carried on. So I took them all home to live with me. I hadn't liked what was going on, but I felt I couldn't say very much because it wasn't my place to. It was really none of my business, but I would watch them just help themselves to everything, go in to Brian's cupboards and take things off the shelves, put them in their bags and off they would go. So many things would disappear.

"One morning when I was at the sink Mo came up and stood really close. He started being very rude and rubbing himself against me, so I turned round quick as you like and emptied a packet of Flash down his trousers. I kept away for a while after that."

This constant provocation was making the already tense atmosphere at the farm unbearable for everyone. Michael Martin reasoned, "Up until this point Brian had been too easy-going and had not paid enough attention to what was going on. He started to have his say but he sort of still half trusted them. He couldn't see that things were getting well out of hand. They were taking outrageous liberties with him. Mo threatened to fill me in if I made a fuss about what I saw them doing." Despite these threats Martin felt he had to alert Brian, but Martin had underestimated Brian's level of perception and the fact that he was already wising up fast. Brian had actually installed an intercom system in the house which he had rigged up to speakers in his bedroom where he could listen in on the builders' daily commentary.

Since breaking up with Suki, Brian had now met another leggy blonde Pallenberg lookalike, a 22-year-old Swedish model called Anna Vohlin, who in June moved into Cotchford. Brian's relationship with Anna was nothing like as intense as it had been with Suki. It had started out as a casual fling, a one-night stand, until Keylock strongly protested about his involvement with her. This puzzled and amused Brian who typically reacted by keeping her around.

Brian's rekindled interest in playing meant that Anna was spending less time with him than she was with the rest of his entourage. She was effectively becoming just another house guest. This suited Brian although he still harboured nagging doubts over Suki and Frank.

He knew from experience that Frank and Mo had high sexual appetites which were matched only by their low sexual morals. Keeping Anna at a reasonable and safe distance made sure he avoided any similar suspicions and scenes. Especially as Frank, in addition to Janet (who it transpires had more of an interest in Keylock than Frank), was now enjoying the favours of Jackie Fitzsimmons, a minicab-driver he knew from Hornsey, North London. Jackie had become something of a personal chauffeur to Thorogood. He justified her regular intrusions at Cotchford by her filling in for the redeployed Corey as Brian's occasional driver. Meanwhile both Mo and Johnny were keeping their deeds despicably dirty, most recently by taking a fancy to the girlfriend of a carpet-fitter from London, and locking her in an upstairs bedroom using the novel method of banging six-inch nails through the doorpost. Not that Anna helped much in dampening the men's ardour. "That Anna," Mrs Hallett said, "she didn't make Brian happy. She would wander around the house in front of the builders in one of those crochet string-vest type of dresses, which you could see right through, and the little devil never wore anything underneath."

Then, another woman entered Brian's chaste life. Ever since Andrew Oldham had purposely set out to create an image for The Stones that directly rivalled that of The Beatles, teenagers, both boys and girls, had stood firmly on one side of the fence or the other. You were either a Stones fan or a Beatles fan, but never both. Each band had their fanatical diehard followers. They were the fans that slept outside under the porches and hedges of group members' houses, all night and in all weathers, or waited in the car parks of Olympic and Abbey Road Studios in the faint hope of catching a fleeting glimpse of their idols. The Beatles had the hardcore "Apple Scruffs", the Stones had simply Stones fans. But they all had their favourite.

Helen Spittal (now Helen Colby)'s favourite was Brian Jones. Spittal was a slight 16-year-old, auburn-haired girl from Hampton Court. All the Stones knew Helen. They had seen her sitting disappointedly ouside Olympic Studios a hundred times, waiting for Brian. "It was harder to get to see Brian because he didn't turn up to all the sessions. Mick and Charlie would come out to me and cheer me up by saying Brian would be down tomorrow."

Through Helen's constant vigil at both the studios and the Stones' offices she became firm friends with Shirley Arnold, who began passing the schoolgirl's notes and letters on to Brian personally, and, in time, his replies back to her. "Then one night Charlie came out at Olympic and said, 'It's your lucky night tonight. Brian is coming down.'" Although they had never met, Brian recognised Helen immediately and warmly scolded her for being out so late. It was the beginning of a special relationship that Helen still cherishes to this day. "He became like a big brother to me. He was always asking me about my school work and friends and made sure that I got home early if he saw me out waiting at the studio."

It was Brian's affection for Helen that moved Shirley to allow her special treatment and privileges, like access to video-tapings and *Top of the Pops* appearances, as well as being privy to insider Stones information and tour dates. Ever since buying Cotchford, Brian had been promising to take Helen down to the house for a visit. "About a week after Brian had left The Stones Shirley rang me and said Brian had asked if I would like to go down and visit him at Cotchford." Helen took the train from London and was met by a minicab from East Grinstead Cab Company at Haywards Heath station, which took her the rest of the way. Brian was standing in the driveway with his collie dog, Emily, when the cab arrived. She didn't think twice when Brian declared he had no money and Frank paid the driver. Happily embracing, they went into the house.

Brian took Helen on a guided tour around the house and gardens before introducing her to Anna and settling down beside the pool with a bottle of chilled white wine. There Brian told her

147

about the tapes he was making in his studio with Alexis and how he wanted his new band to sound like Credence Clearwater Revival. "He was telling me about the people he was going to be playing with and took me upstairs to play me the single *Proud Mary*." Then Brian's mood changed and he whispered to Helen while looking out of the window at Frank. "He pointed to Frank and told me he was supposed to be a builder, but he never did anything. He said he was lazy. I said, 'Why don't you sack him?' and he just mumbled. I watched Frank after that because Brian kept on about him and he did absolutely nothing all day. There were no signs of construction work going on at all. He was just wandering around like part of the scenery."

Helen couldn't help noticing that Brian wasn't looking in the best of health. His weight had continued to creep up steadily, his hair was lank and his face looked tired and blotchy. Despite this, he still agreed to Helen photographing him several times in the grounds of Cotchford, dressed in his trademark hooped black and white matelot shirt (which he had stolen years ago from Dick Taylor) striped red and blue trousers and canvas beach shoes with no socks. He allowed the photos to be taken on the condition that the pictures never left her possession, after which they returned to the house for dinner.

Anna had cooked a roast chicken and fresh vegetables picked from the garden. When the food was ready the two girls sat down at the table and waited for Brian. "Brian said he wasn't eating because he wanted to lose weight," and instead poured himself another of his usual half-pint measures of wine. "I told him if he wanted to lose weight he should stop drinking like he did and eat proper meals. He had been drinking every minute of the day without seeming at all drunk and it was then that I realised what everyone had been saying was true. He was an alcoholic."

After dinner Brian and Helen retired to the house's spacious L-shaped living room while Anna made some coffee, which Brian also refused, preferring instead to open another bottle of wine. After watching *Top of the Pops*, conversation once again turned to Brian's future plans. Helen asked if he would be going to the Stones' planned free gig in Hyde Park in a fortnight's time. He laughed out loud and said, "I'd probably be the only one they would charge to get in." Brian's comment had puzzled Helen. "I didn't understand what he meant because up till that point I believed Brian had left The Stones of his own free will. He hadn't wanted to tell me he had been sacked, to protect me from the truth. He never once let on. He just asked me if I thought he should go and then he started talking about Anita, saying she was pregnant and she would be there and it wouldn't be right. You could see the hurt in his eyes."

A loud knock on the door interrupted Helen's thoughts and she watched as Anna went to answer it. She opened it to a pretty young girl who both she and Brian's dogs obviously knew well. "Brian's dogs went mad over her, jumping up at her, making an awful fuss." It was Jackie, Thorogood's alternative cab-driving mistress, who had arrived from London. She handed Brian a little bottle of pills which Brian was keen to show Helen were on pre-scription. Anna laughed and told her how Brian had tipped out her luggage and inspected every item the day she had come to stay at Cotchford in case someone was setting him up.

Brian could not afford to wait any longer in getting rid of Frank and the others. He still had not received any of the promised pay-ment from the Stones' office and his bills were mounting up at an alarming rate. Not that this deterred the builders from charging even the smallest of their daily essentials and materials to his badly depleted account. The daily necessities and tools of the trade were now including vital cases of beer and spirits which they would either pick up in the village themselves or have ship-ped to Cotchford using Brian's cab account.

In desperation, Brian turned to Tony Sanchez and asked him to work for him in the vain hope that maybe he could call a halt to the madness. Brian gave Sanchez an astonishing update on the diabolical extremes to which Frank and his men were now going. They had started hiding his scooter and even gone so far as to order duplicate sets of furniture for themselves, which he had been charged for too.

Brian told Sanchez he had questioned Frank about the incident but had been rudely told not to be so petty. "They think I am a millionaire or something but I am not," he went on to explain.

The builders still assumed Brian was spaced out and that it was all going unnoticed. "I'm not blind," he said defiantly. "I've got a good idea who ripped me off and how much for." Sanchez had to turn down Brian's offer. He cared for Brian but Tony's loyalties rested with Keith. Brian shrugged and fixed a steely glare in the direction of Thorogood.

According to Michael Martin, Frank and the others were now in no fit state to be working. "They were just pulling the place apart and not putting it back together again. They would start drinking at about midday every day, starting off with a few beers, then wine, then it would be anything goes. Brian was very uptight himself and would have a beer and that would be that for another day."

Martin, in addition to his gardening interests, was a deeply religious man who gave a bible class a couple of times a week in the nearby village of Crowborough.

"Brian started talking to me about the Bible and he asked me if he could come along and talk to my class. He wanted to tell them how unhappy he was and warn the younger ones not to do the things he had done in life, not to take his example. To my knowledge he was reading the Bible every day. He had this huge leather-bound Bible that he knew back to front."

The 2nd July 1969 started in the usual manner for Mary Hallett. She had gone down to Cotchford in the early morning to clean, starting in the living room on the previous night's debris and making her walk around the house. Brian was asleep with Anna in his upstairs bedroom and the builders were sitting round the table in a side room off the kitchen finishing breakfast. Mary reached this room at the end of her round of chores. "I'd only got that one last room to do before I finished so I said, 'Well, you chaps, it's out of here because I want to come in.' 'Oh, we aren't moving,' they told me and they all stayed stuck at the table, so I started to clean around them. I would have been there all day if I had waited for them to move." Mary began mopping the floor. The room had a stone floor.

"I got the mop as wet as I could because I meant them to get wet in order to make them move. It soaked them. They were really annoyed with me and started calling me all sorts of names. Well, I let off at them, I was swearing like a trooper when all of a sudden there were these peals of laughter from upstairs. Brian had the intercom switched on, listening in, and he had gone into hysterics, roaring with laughter."

Brian told Mary to expect people coming down later that day in order to prepare her for the extra mess the following day, and to put her mind at rest concerning strangers approaching the house.

"I would keep watch on the house for Brian because from

where my window was I could see right out across the river and all along where he couldn't see. If I saw anyone suspicious walking towards the house I used to ring him and tell him so he could be ready for them."

Mary also noticed that Brian's asthma was particularly bad that day. "He had a job speaking to me."

Mo and Johnny had left the house and after talking briefly with Keylock, who had spent the night there, busied themselves by manoeuvring a huge wooden beam that had been delivered and propped up in the driveway through to the garden. "It's big enough to crucify Jesus Christ and his twelve apostles," Mo who had been left in charge (Thorogood had gone to London on business) was saying aloud for the benefit of Michael Martin who was working near by.

Martin ignored the builder's baiting and continued with his work only to have his concentration further interrupted by the arrival at the gate of a familiar face: Suki Poitier. She was followed, at around five o'clock, by a group of young girls. They wandered freely in the garden and in and out of the house, while music blared from Brian's upstairs windows and a dozen cars blocked the drive.

Martin stopped work in the garden and got ready to leave for his class. Thorogood had returned and he and his men had downed tools and were now mingling happily with the guests who, he noticed, were a mixture of local people and Londoners.

Suki, who had turned up intent on speaking to Brian, was involved in deep conversation with Anna. She had returned to the farm a couple of times in the past since leaving Brian, mostly to collect belongings but always with an eye to reconciliation.

Martin gave the scene little thought as he slammed the door of his mini-van and pulled out into the lane. It was, after all, a normal day at Cotchford.

The Hallett household had known better than to expect a restful night. Dusk was approaching and the Cotchford revellers showed little sign of quietening down.

Pauline Hallett, Mary's teenage daughter, couldn't sleep. The acoustics of Cotchford Lane made the party sound as if it was bring thrown in her own back garden. Les and Mary were wide awake, resigned to the fact that Brian's get-together was going to be a long one. Suddenly, the sounds of good-natured partying changed. Mary listened. "There was a terrific lot of screaming coming from down there, awful screaming noises and then car doors slamming and engines going and cars screeching away. I sent Les out to see what was going on, and these cars were off down the lane and then there was silence. The next thing I heard was a funny crackling noise which I couldn't understand, so I got up again to look out of the window."

Early the next morning, Michael Martin's phone rang. It was a friend who told him to tune into the radio. The morning news programme was running a news flash which remains vivid in Michael Martin's memory. It said, "Police believe the body of a man found dead at a house in Sussex early today was a member of The Rolling Stones pop group."

Mrs Hallett had not heard the radio that morning and she left for work at nine as normal. She was stopped midway down the lane by Tom Keylock who grabbed her by the arm and ushered her quickly down the farmhouse path. It was then that she heard, for the second time, the same crackling noise she had heard the previous night. But now she was able to identify the source of the alien crackle. It was police walkie-talkies.

Crowds of photographers and reporters were swarming in and around the grounds, hustling and jostling with each other for a better position and angle. They hadn't seen Mary. Tom had made sure of that. As soon as she was safely inside the house, he went outside to the gate to talk to the crowd who surged towards him.

Mary went through into the kitchen to where Anna was sitting. She didn't need to ask her where Brian was. One look at the girl's ashen face spoke enough. The two women were joined by Frank, who stared at Mary menacingly and told her, "Say nothing to nobody about anything." "He said if I was asked any questions I was to say that I didn't know."

Keylock returned to the house and pulled Frank to one side. He instructed the builder to take hold of Anna and smuggle her out of the back door and up through the orchard to where a car was waiting. He said to Frank, "No one will spot you. There are no reporters that way."

After Frank had led the shaken and pale Anna away, Mary was left alone. She sat quietly in the kitchen and ignored as best she could the persistent tappings on the windows and the popping of flashbulbs.

152

Mary's thoughts were interrupted by the phone ringing. It was Thorogood asking for Keylock to pick him up from East Grinstead police station where he had gone, after leaving Anna, to give a statement concerning the previous night's events. There he had told detectives that he and Miss Janet Lawson were spending a quiet evening alone at the flat when at around 10.30 there was a knock on the door. He answered it to Brian Jones who asked if he and Janet wanted to join him and Anna down by the pool for an evening drink. It was a warm night so Frank agreed to follow shortly. He noticed that Brian appeared slightly the worse for drink and was slurring his words.

When Frank and Janet reached the pool both Brian and Anna were sitting on the wooden bench at the shallow end. They were surrounded by an array of bottles, brandy, vodka and whisky, which they sipped constantly. Brian had already consumed over half a bottle of brandy and was periodically swallowing little black pills. At about 11.30 Brian suggested a swim, to which both girls protested, arguing he was in no shape to go into the water. Frank went with Brian into the house to change, followed by Anna. Returning to the pool all three dived into the water, which was very warm – kept at its customary 90 degrees. After a few minutes Anna got out and went back to the house with Janet, who was a non-swimmer. Frank stayed with Brian for a further 10-15 minutes before he himself went back to the house for a cigarette. This left Brian swimming alone. Janet passed Frank in the doorway and the next thing he heard was the girl shouting for help. He and Anna rushed out into the garden to the water's edge and saw Brian lying face-down at the deep end of the pool. Frank and Anna jumped in and made three attempts to reach him before getting a good enough grip to enable Frank to pull him to the surface. There all three lifted Brian out. Janet used her nursing training to adminster artificial respiration. Anna applied the kiss of life and said she was sure she felt Brian's hand grip hers. But then there was no other movement. Frank's statement made no mention of a party.

The next morning, Mary's body-clock woke her as usual and, after breakfast, she got ready for work, leaving her house at 9 a.m. She closed the gate behind her and stepped out into the lane. It was a warm sunny morning and Cotchford Lane was its quiet and peaceful self once again. Mary walked the short distance between the two houses in an almost trance-like state, her eyes fixed on a thick stream of smoke rising above the treetops. She turned right into the farm's gravel drive and saw a low-sided truck that was parked adjacent to the house. She had never seen it before. Frank and Mo were busy loading it with boxes and crates.

Following the trail of smoke, Mary went through the house and out into the garden to where Tom Keylock and Michael Martin were standing guard over a huge bonfire. Keylock had obviously spent the night at the house.

Mary recollects, "Michael Martin had got there before me and he told me they had got the huge bonfire started and they they were burning all of Brian's things, I don't know why." Michael Martin was equally dismayed by Keylock's actions, but dutifully carried out the bulky minder's orders.

Piles of Brian's clothes, damp as if left out overnight, were bundled together by the side of the fire. Martin threw each item on to the fire, one at a time, as instructed, and watched them smoulder in silence. He was interrupted by Thorogood who appeared by his side carrying piles of Brian's books which he instructed Martin to burn as well. Martin was near the end of this dubious task when Thorogood, in one last attempt to aggravate the religious gardener, produced Brian's leather-bound Bible and tossed it on to the flames before callously walking away.

"I managed to rescue it as soon as I could," Martin recalled. After this he was left alone in the garden for several hours while Mary made her way around the house as usual. Going from room to room, she noticed many of Brian's valuable possessions were missing. Cupboard doors gaped open and shelves were cleared. As she inspected further, the truck in the driveway began to pull away.

Mary hurried to the front door and watched the heavily laden vehicle disappear down the lane. She turned to go back into the house, but something caught her attention and she stopped. Something else was missing. "The builders had loaded up the lorry with the front gate and the garden's iron railing and made off with them."

The police returned to the house a little after midday to talk to Martin who explained he had left the premises at 6 p.m. the previous evening, just as people were arriving. "The police sergeant got most upset and kept asking about Frank. It was obvious he wanted to pin something on him, but what I don't know. He got most irate saying, 'There's a charge here!'"

After turning their attention to Keylock once again, the police sealed the house. Giving the keys to Mary, they informed her that no one was to enter the house or gounds unless accompanied by themselves. Then they left.

With the house quiet and locked tight, Michael Martin decided to go home. Clutching Brian's scorched Bible under his arm, he got into his van, took one last look at Cotchford and started the engine.

He checked his bank account the following week and realised he was no longer working for The Rolling Stones.

Mary had gone home that afternoon too. She had just settled in for the evening when the doorbell rang, setting her dogs off barking loudly in the hallway. She went out to the glass-panelled door where Frank Thorogood was standing, his finger resting firmly on the doorbell.

"He had come back to get his clothes out. I told him that I had police orders to keep the place all shut up and that I was told particularly to keep him shut out. He was very angry and called me a fair number of names."

Mary breathed a sigh of relief as Thorogood sloped off down her path muttering to himself and disappeared from her life to the sound of an unseen car revved to its limits. Two further strange incidents followed within days of Thorogood's return visit to Cotchford Lane.

In all her years working at Cotchford, Mary had never heard the burglar alarm sound at the farm, but she knew exactly what the ghostly wail was that froze her to the spot early the next day. The piercing shrill echoed up the line, like some unearthly banshee, as she fumbled for the phone. "Well, I was frightened out of my life. I said to Leslie, 'You go down to see if you can see what it is.' I had to stay where I was because the police would come straight to me in order to be let in." Les Hallett crept down to the sealed farmhouse and reached it just as the sound of distant police bells joined in with the resounding din. There he found, stuck between the outer and inner doors at the back of the house, Anna Wohlin curled up in a ball and crying hysterically. "She had crawled through the back door's catflap, she was so thin. The outer door wasn't alarmed, but the one inside was, so once inside she pushed the inner door and set the alarms off."

The police swung into Cotchford Lane and raced towards the farm, where by now, both Leslie and Mary were comforting the distraught girl. "Anna, like Frank, had wanted some of her clothes that had been locked in the house, but she had been warned by somebody never to go back to the house. It was silly really because if she had rung me, I would have let her in, but she was so frightened of being caught there by someone. I told the police to be kind to her because she was a nice girl and she didn't mean any harm, but they took her away and I never saw her again."

Mary didn't go to Cotchford for several weeks following Anna's visit. Neither did she hear a word from the Stones' office in London as to the property's future, apart from a "For Sale" sign which had grown mysteriously from the farm's hedgerow overnight.

There had been no other movement at the house until suddenly the alarm sounded again. The police arrived within minutes and searched the house and grounds but found no one. Confused and mystified the police got ready to leave when Mary noticed floating at the bottom of the pool something which looked like a large brown paper package tied with string.

The police, using a branch, managed to rake the bundle to one side and fish it out. They tore the soggy paper apart and found a collection of knitted baby clothes addressed to Brian.

10

Who Killed Christopher Robin?

Brian was an outsider right from childhood and remained one throughout his short and tragic life. He had an arrogant hedonistic attitude to life, something he fortunately passed on to The Stones, giving the group a lasting rebellious appeal and image that remains largely intact today. Keith and Mick were ordinary middle-class boys from the suburbs, and they had to work hard at their image; with Brian it was natural. Described as "a fashionable punk rocker" by Anita Pallenberg, he epitomised the 1960s rock star. Some say he wrote the definition, but added to this was a very troubled, dark side to his character. He was cruel and sadistic, particularly with his women, known at times to thrash some of them with a dog lead. He had many women in his life, and most of them suffered at his demented hands. Pat Andrews, his Cheltenham girlfriend, tried to analyze Brian's attitude to women. "He could never get close to any of them, he could never really give anything of himself. To him, making love to a woman meant something at the time because he was getting the love he needed, but it never went deep. He never had a lasting love for anyone and that is what turned him to drugs. He always felt that if he hadn't been Brian Jones of The Rolling Stones none of those girls would have looked at him, and that was really crushing to him. The only thing that meant more to him was his music." These sentiments have been echoed and matched by most women in his life, romantically involved or not.

Former Stones secretary, Shirley Arnold, who was never romantically involved with Brian, grew to know him very well.

She said, "Even with millions of girls clamouring to meet him, and ready to do anything for him, he was lonely. He just couldn't communicate with people. He was frightened of people, especially girls. I knew about his children, but they were the result of his early days when he thought he had to prove himself by being a tearaway. Brian was a womaniser, but girls meant nothing to him. He would use them when he was high, but he never loved them. Brian couldn't love anyone except himself or his music. That was his problem. He used to use drink and drugs to overcome a deep self-induced loneliness."

Despite his dismissive and abusive behaviour, all of his women clung firmly to futile hopes and dreams that theirs would be the relationship to succeed. Retrospectively, they were blind to all his faults, allowing their memories to paper over such flaws and cracks with a maternal-like wonder. Whether this was due to a cold and calculated pattern of behaviour cultivated on Brian's part or the desire of women to tame the untameable, can never be said for sure, but whatever the truth, it certainly worked. Linda Lawrence said, "I was always in love with Brian. Even when he went out with other girls I never gave up hope that one day he would eventually come back to me."

Even Pat Andrews, who had more reason than most to rebuff such a theory, doesn't. Abandoned with a child by Brian to the loneliness of a refuge centre for the homeless in late 1963, she maintains her loving bond with the dead rock star today. She said, "He was always very insecure and unsure of himself. He wanted terribly to be loved by everybody, but he had a knack of turning people against him. He was afraid of life. I'm sure that is why he took drugs – to give himself confidence. He could be very rough with me – he gave me quite a few black eyes but I was never jealous of any of the girls he had while he was with me or after. Because I knew he could never get close to any of them."

He was a heavy drinker from as early as 1964 when warning signs flashed to drummer Charlie Watts. He cared enough to try and help him stop drinking before abandoning the cause, resigned to the fact that Brian was aleady becoming an alcoholic, a fact verified by his autopsy in 1969. This lethal intake of drink, combined with his excessive drug use in the intervening years, undoubtedly proved to be the catalyst for his unacceptable, unpredictable and destructive behaviour, a type of behaviour he imposed on all and sundry. Anita Pallenberg said, "He was quite a bully, you know, like small guys are. Like when he got drunk, what he would do if he felt threatened, that's when I knew trouble was coming. He would break a bottle on the table edge and put the glass in his pocket. I think he got away with slashing someone's face in a New York club. He was quite vicious at the end."

At the time of his death Brian, along with the rest of The Stones and three-quarters of The Beatles, was managed by Alan Klein, the tough Jewish streetwise business accountant from New York. His infatuation with English bands and musicians was ignited by first hearing The Beatles in 1963 and this had brought about his transformation in business affairs to specialising in the field of music and entertainment management.

With the help of some well placed rumour-mongering and speculation, mostly of the Chicago/New York mob connection type, and combined with an overbearing personal presence, he was able to cross the Atlantic and bring about major changes in contracts and conditions for the English groups and acts in his charge. Klein's form of intimidating tactics were hitherto unheard of in England at the time and earned him the very English title of "The Robin Hood of Pop". Over the years, however, closer in-spection of Klein's Mafia and family connections suggest that these so-called mob connections were more likely the brainchild and furtive working of his press-manoeuvring and former partner Andrew Oldham.

Klein had a debonair attitude to his client's money, taking what he thought he was owed as opposed to whatever percentage he was legally entitled to. Klein, who began representing The Stones in 1965, had by late 1967 recognised that the true force behind the band was now Jagger and Richards and that Brian Jones had lost his way completely, both personally and professionally; he was simply a liability to The Stones. He had gone on to make almost no musical contribution to the band throughout 1968 and, as far as Klein was concerned, the sooner Jones was out of the band the better.

By 1969, facing a crippling tax demand and with a classic album *Beggars Banquet* under their belts and needing promoting, The Stones wanted and desperately needed to tour again. But Brian, even without his drug conviction fouling up the possibility of a visa, was not physically or mentally capable of sustaining a tour. It was obvious that there was never going to be a better or easier time to rid themselves of their one-time leader.

When Mick and Keith came up with the idea, inspired by both loyalty to Brian for his major contribution to the music of The Stones and for his actual formation of the band, of paying him a conscience-easing £100,000 as an initial settlement for leaving the group, plus £20,000 per year for as long as The Stones stayed together as a band, Klein became furious. "You must be crazy paying him all that money," he said to Mick and Keith. "There must be a better solution than that. Surely we can work something else out."

In 1968 Brian had sat in the Revolution Club in London pouring his heart out to John Lennon. Jones complained that he was being forced out of the band that he had started and that "they" were taking his band away from him and didn't want to play the blues any more. Interviews with Brian at this time curiously show his referring to the band as them, never we.

Lennon, who was having similar internal problems of his own with Paul McCartney, sympathised with Jones and told him, "Stop feeling sorry for youself. To the fans you are still the leader of The Stones – you are the one they want to see. Go ahead, start up your own bloody band! And I might even come with you." Whether this was a throwaway comment or not on Lennon's part, it was enough to plant the seed of an idea with Brian about forming a new group.

It was through Lennon's problems within The Beatles that Brian was able to draw favourable comparisons. Both were founder members of Britain's, if not the world's, two biggest bands. Both bands were managed by Alan Klein and at one time both were considered leaders. Jones was being forced out of The Stones and Lennon had, to all intents and purposes, left The Beatles (only the public announcement was needed to dot the "i"'s and cross the "t"'s).

After Mick, Keith and Charlie had broken the news to Brian that they were kicking him out of the band, and to all intents and purposes had already replaced him with ex-Mayall guitarist Mick Taylor, Brian's women, past and present once again came out in sympathy with him. Marianne Faithful said, "They have finished him off now. Poor, beautiful, bewildered Brian. Whatever is going to happen to him?" Keith protested, "For Christ's sake, the guy is getting a hundred grand for sitting on his bum. I don't know what everyone is moaning about."

Most people who saw or spoke to Brian following his departure from The Stones are quick to say that he seemed to be in the best state of mind he had been in for nearly a year. Encouraged and coached by Alexis Korner, who visited him every day except the day he died, they are convinced his plans to form a "a band bigger than anyone can imagine" would have reached some sort of fruition. Brian continued to let rumour fly that this band would in fact feature a collaboration with him and Lennon. What effect this would have had on the fortunes and future of The Rolling Stones if the most popular Stone fan-wise (Brian was receiving as many fanclub letters as Jagger in 1969) and one of The Beatles got together, needed careful consideration. By this time The Beatles were almost finished as a band.

All that was left to argue about, it seemed, was the dividing-up and control of Northern Songs, an argument that was to prove long and bitter and prompted Lennon's famous challenge to big business, "I'm not going to be fucked around by men in suits sitting on their fat arses." While The Rolling Stones were certainly alive and kicking, recording-wise, financially they were almost bankrupt. But unlike The Beatles, they still had long-term plans. None of them included Brian Jones.

When in 1969 after a visit to Cotchford Farm Tom Keylock reported to Alan Klein that Jones was in the process of forming his new group – and that Brian was repeatedly boasting that it might include John Lennon – it was finally taken as a serious thought that a Jones/Lennon partnership was a very real proposition, one that could really rock both the already shaky Stones and Beatles boats. Apart from finishing The Beatles for good, something Klein was desperately fighting to stop happening, it would also have taken a considerable edge off the new-look Stones.

"Will someone tell me," Klein screamed in angry frustration, "why we are paying that little shit all of that money – and he's still making trouble?"

For once, Klein's anger with Jones became apparent within the Stones' organisation. He was already perceived as a nuisance but now he was considered as a threat, and a serious one at that.

Brian's predictable but untimely death stopped any such super-group being formed but Klein could never have foreseen that eventuality.

His thoughts at the time, as those of Jagger and Richards, were that although Brian was no longer a Rolling Stone, his name would forever be synonymous with the band. Wary of Jones's bad and unpredictable behaviour, the Stones' organisation was very keen to keep a close eye on his activities, fully aware that any bad publicity that Jones could and did attract with an unbelievable ease would be tied and lead back to The Stones.

Back in 1966, it had been decided that The Stones would hire a full-time public-relations man, Les Perrin. It was Les Perrin's tireless publicity work for the band that proved invaluable in the 1960s, especially during their various drug raids and trials. It was his job to keep the band's bad press and publicity down to a minimum, using his well established and respected connections in Fleet Street. He was largely successful, particularly where Brian – who Perrin constantly referred to as a persistent headache – was concerned. Photographer Etan Russell, who had been appointed in 1968 to shoot pictures of The Stones in their individual surroundings by band secretary Jo Bergman, had pictures of Brian stopped on the orders of Perrin who, after seeing the results, told him, "We have enough trouble just getting that boy a visa."

1966 was also the year when it was considered that the band's popularity had risen to a point where it was deemed important enough to appoint individual chauffeurs and security people to each group member. Up until this point the group had been both driven and looked after en masse. Tom Keylock, driver, minder and self-proclaimed hardman, was appointed Jones's personal minder and chauffeur in 1966. Keylock's origins are traceable back to a car-hire firm in North London – used by the likes of Don Arden, Kit Lambert and John Gunnel, managers, promoters and businessmen – to which The Stones had first been exposed via their association with Arden, who had featured The Stones on his early 1963-64 package tours before going on to manage fellow Decca label-mates, The Small Faces. Keylock, described by Brian's friend Christopher Gibbs as, "a hairier Michael Caine", was brought into the Stones' organisation to act as driver for the band on their sixth major tour of Britain. He worked his way up through the Stones' camp to become their tour manager by 1969.

Keylock stayed and worked exclusively with Brian for one year (1966-67) and drove him on his first trip to Morocco, with Anita and Christopher Gibbs. Gibbs remembered, "I don't think Tom liked Brian very much. He didn't seem to like music very much. He was meant to be working for Brian but he was really there for his own good always. He wasn't interested in looking after Brian, just interested in what he could make out of the situation. He was the type that would sell stories to the newspapers."

In early 1967, Brian, Anita and Keith made that fateful trip back to Morocco, once again driven by Keylock, still working for Brian but by now astute enough to recognise the shifting balance of power within the band. Gibbs continued, "They had absolutely no respect for each other by then, but then Brian never had a great deal of respect for anybody. But somebody had to look after him, somebody had to get him up in the morning and literally dress him and make sure he had everything he needed. Keylock had to do that . . . obviously he's not going to have a great deal of respect for him, but no one else had the patience."

Keylock's patience was sorely tried and had run out completely on that trip. The love-hate triangle that was Brian, Keith and Anita was Keylock's perfect opportunity to switch allegiances.

Keylock had left Brian by his clever ploy of telling Brion Gysin, painter and resident of Tangier, the party's host, that a planeload of unwanted reporters had landed, and, in the light of recent developments amongst the Stones' camp, were intent on making life difficult for the band. He told Gysin to take Brian out of harm's way and keep him there, when in reality he was aiding the back-handed elopement of Keith and Anita, driving them at high speed back to London, leaving Brian alone and stranded.

It had been an important move for Keylock and one which gave the minder a much higher profile within the band's organisation. Keylock quickly advanced his way up the Stones' ladder, his influence on the hiring of chauffeurs and minders becoming highly pronounced.

He was now the one to find and recruit them and they, in turn, were answerable to him. He effectively built a close-knit network of people loyal to him within the Stones' structure. People like Alan Dunn, John Corey, Frank Thorogood and Brian Palasanga were all brought in by Tom Keylock, and hired exclusively to look after Brian. They all knew they would pay considerably if they crossed him, as Palasanga in particular found out when Keylock parted him from his teeth. Keylock, although ruthless, had a basic code of honour.

This inner organisation was made all the more possible when The Stones themselves are examined. They had long held and nurtured an image that flirted with the harsh and brutal side of life, shamelessly flaunted in songs like *Street Fighting Man*, *Sympathy for the Devil* and *Midnight Rambler*. They had a fascination and genuine admiration for the hardmen, thugs, tearaways and petty crooks that emanated from South London and the East End. These people, they felt, gave The Stones a 1960s version of street cool. This was, after all, an era when two vicious psychopathic twins from the East End, a team of train robbers and a family of scrapmetal-dealers from South London had become bona-fide English folk-heroes. The Stones did not go to the extremes of hiring the likes of the Krays or the Richardsons, but they certainly hired people who behaved like them. While Keith and Mick had few, if any, problems controlling these drivers and bodyguards, who became known unto themselves as the Stones' Mafia, Jones was never mentally strong enough to stand up to them. He was a middle-class boy from Cheltenham who was well used to dominating people of a similar ilk, but found himself entirely out of his depth with people who made up their own rules, having spurned society.

Alan Dunn, one of Brian's numerous aides, worked for him in early 1968, but he, like so many others, eventually abandoned him, preferring to work exclusively for Jagger. Dunn witnessed the helpless Stone's plight at the hands of these characters first-hand. "He was being taken for a ride by his roadies, drivers and employees. It was a crazy situation. Someone would work for Brian and all of a sudden you'd need somebody to work for that guy 'cause his ego had got so big. You'd ask Brian where his car was and he'd say someone else had it. So you'd find Brian's car outside the Speakeasy or some place and his roadie would be in there telling women that he was the band's manager or something." These employees were workers for The Rolling Stones, a company that had its own corporate structure as similar to and as basic as that of any large or small business. It had its own levels of executives, middle management and workers. The worker levels consisted of the drivers, minders, roadies and soundmen, plus office staff, accountants and secretaries – people like John Corey, Sam Cutler, Jo Bergman, Shirley Arnold and Fiona Fraser.

Middle management had its Les Perrins and Tom Keylocks while the executive level was split into four distinct departments: Alan Klein, Mick Jagger and Keith Richards, Brian Jones, Bill Wyman and Charlie Watts. Like most big companies, some departments were better to work for than others. There was the decidedly unglamorous department of Bill and Charlie, who Keith laughingly referred to as the real fun part of the band. The drummer and bassist were steadfast and predictable, preferring to look after themselves; not much room for a determined opportunist here and certainly not the place to start climbing the ladder to a better and more privileged position within the affluent Stones society. For this you had to work for someone closer to the top. Before 1967 the route to the top was accessible by working for one of the three main Stones, Mick, Keith or Brian. But by 1968 Brian was no longer seen as an equal part of that triangle since its balance had shifted sideways to allow Alan Klein to move in at his expense. Jones was now seen as no more than a stepping stone to pass over on the way up the structure. Keylock had perceived this shift when he handed over his role as Brian's consort to Brian Palasanga, in senior to apprentice like fashion, after advancing on to Keith and beyond. Palasanga in turn passed the position on to John Corey.

By now, Keylock was firmly established in the very strong position of tour manager. He had seen that the only route Brian was destined to take was the one that took him out of the band, and he knew that, as in most big companies, when the boss goes the employees go too. Keylock, although not a paying employer as such, was nonetheless still relied upon and responsible for recommending and supplying many of Brian's and the band's personal workforce, most noticeably his old and trusted schoolfriend Frank Thorogood. If he felt the writing was on the wall for Brian, then the least Keylock could do for Thorogood was to tip him off.

Thorogood was the last in a chain of people to look after Brian Jones and was heading his household entourage at the time of his death. He was originally brought into the organisation as a maintenance man and builder for the band, a role he combined with the tag of unofficial minder and driver when moving over to Brian. (He had moved into Cotchford a little over a week after

Brian and stayed in a small flat above the garage, which during the week he shared, without asking or getting permission from Brian, with a string of girlfriends, the latest apparently being a young nurse, Janet Lawson, a friend of Tom Keylock. Thorogood returned to his wife at the weekends.)

In turn, Thorogood brought in two other builders, Mo and Johnny, both from West Wittering, plus two labourers, Reg and David, recruited from the local village of Hartfield and used for specific tasks at different intervals. Keylock had first brought in Thorogood to work on Keith Richards' house Redlands a year before, but he was eventually suspected of thieving and in 1968 Keith, via Keylock, kindly passed him on to Brian at his newly acquired farmhouse, Cotchford. Christopher Gibbs, who was helping with the interior of the house during this extraordinary swop, said, "This wasn't a particular good pick-up. Brian was no kind of judge of people at all. If you've never employed anyone before and suddenly you've got loads of money and you are famous and have a gift whereby you are more interested in your music than anything else, there is no reason why you should be clever at finding the right sort of person to work for you or look after you. Especially if you don't, like he didn't, know how to tell them what to do.

"It was a very uneven relationship which stemmed from his time with Keylock. You see, up until Keylock, Brian had thought that a chauffeur's job was to simply sit about in a car and wait until he felt like going somewhere, even if it was at five in the morning. It could be anywhere, go out into the country, go to a nightclub, anywhere. It was a very difficult role to play the minder, driver, bodyguard. So if anybody is going to put up with it and stay and work with Brian, then they are going to stay and work with him for the wrong reasons, to rip him off, use him or whatever." Gered Mankowitz said it was a dodgy role for anyone to play. People like Keylock or Thorogood were expected to act as bodyguard and maitre d', a difficult role to play at the best of times, especially it if was for Brian.

The obvious differences between employee and employer are too numerous and complex to define. Needless to say, resentment, jealousy and hopeless ambition all combine in the age-old process of manager and worker strife, whether you work for ICI or The Rolling Stones.

In Brian's case there were two added antagonisms; one was his age, the other his class. There was a vast age difference between Brian and the people employed to look after him. People like Keylock were well into their late 30s, almost ten years his senior, whereas Thorogood was already in his 40s. Hardened working-class men, born prior to the War, who had suffered both the hardship and heartbreak of evacuation and the restrictions of rationing during their early and formative years, they were brought up in a time of strife that Brian had only heard about. "Nothing sticks in my mind at all about the War. All I know is what I read in magazines since," he once said.

Undoubtedly, things had improved for the likes of Keylock and Thorogood in the post-War period. Tory Prime Minister Harold Macmillan had been right when he proclaimed, "You've never had it so good," but that was nothing compared to what was to follow. The 1960s generation was the unmuzzled society whose emphasis was on youth and freedom. They had the look, the money and, most importantly, the time to enjoy it.

It was a time and era that happened as quickly as an explosion and literally passed the previous generation of Keylocks and Thorogoods by. People like Robert Fraser, Christopher Gibbs, Tara Brown, Talitha and Paul Getty Jnr, although born to be part of the Establishment, were turning society on its head and enhancing the popular thinking of the time that the 1960s had broken down the class barriers and offered the opportunity for everyone to make good. Working-class youngsters no longer had to rely on the examples of Henry Cooper and Jimmy Greaves and depend on boxing and football as the only means of escaping a life of dull, anonymous drudgery. Glamorous professions like photography and modelling were now accessible to all. Or were they?

True, the working class had their token representatives in David Bailey, George Best, Twiggy, Terrance Stamp and Michael Caine, but they were undoubtedly exceptions to the rule, few and very far between, offered up for public consumption in the hope that one underlying reality of the 1960s myth would go unnoticed – the fact that the opportunities to make good for the average working-class boy or girl had not and were not going to change at all. It was in the light of this that the glamorization of the likes of the Kray brothers, Ronnie Biggs and Charlie Richardson was able to make such an impact. This, along with an upgraded image of the no-nonsense, moralistic and strangely fair-playing cockney rogue that was greatly romanticiscd in the cinema with 1960s films like *The Italian Job* and *Alfie*, goes some way to explaining the exaltation of such characters to role-model status among the ordinary working classes. It was, in reality, left almost solely to the music business to cut across these class barriers and prejudices, the only really accessible industry that could offer anything like an alternative and exciting career for all. It brought about the chance of attaining a lifestyle that was previously unobtainable elsewhere and its many-faceted openings meant that anyone could find their niche, from heroes to villains.

The announcement that Brian Jones had left The Stones possibly to rejoin them at some later date was made in May 1969. Simultaneously it was annoucned that ex John Mayall's Blues Breakers guitarist, 21-year-old Mick Taylor would be joining.

Brian was quoted in the newspapers as saying, "I no longer see eye to eye with the others over the discs we are cutting. We no longer communicate musically. The Stones' music is not to my taste any more. The work of Mick and Keith has progressed at a tangent, at least to my way of thinking. I have a desire to play my own brand of music rather than that of others no matter how I appreciate their musical concepts. We had a friendly meeting and agreed that an amicable termination, temporary or permanent, was the only answer. The only solution was to go our separate ways but we shall still remain friends. I love those fellows."

Interestingly enough, although the press made a big deal out of it, mostly of the "Did he jump or was he pushed?" variety, the fans seemed to have met the news with a certain resignation.

The slow and deliberate watering-down of his profile within the band for months was typically defined in the group's promotion videos shot for the last few singles. Two versions of *Jumping Jack Flash* had been filmed at right-angles to the band's front line-up, excluding Brian from view with him only appearing in second-quick flashes. *Children of the Moon* had him off on his own peering from behind trees and bushes at the other four. Previous to these clips had come *2000 Light Years from Home* and *We Love You*, both of which awarded Brian the same treatment. This treatment continued throughout the entire filming of Jean-Luc Godard's intimate insight into the Stones' recording process, the film *One Plus One*.

By 1968 Brian's path from The Stones had led him to the door of author A.A. Milne's hideaway on the outskirts of the Ashdown Forest, Cotchford Farm in Sussex, the scene of Brian's final weeks alive. By 1969 he was no longer a Rolling Stone, he was out on his own. Following a typical helter-skelter affair with drink and drugs, he began to set about rebuilding his life and was, as many people said, full of hope for the future.

He appeared to have greatly recovered from his emotional watershed and his plans for a new group were coming to fruition. Brian had even visited the Stones at Olympic Studios in London, where he had enthused excitedly about their progression after spending the day with former Jeff Beck drummer, Mick Waller, and Alexis Korner.

This jubilation and optimism could not hide the issue that money had, by 1969, become a big problem for Brian, just as it had for all The Stones. Klein's tight rein on the band's resources and payment was now presenting the very real possibility of the band going broke. Bill Wyman had reported in February that he was almost £12,000 in debt and even Keith, normally a lot better off than Bill, Charlie and Brian, had telegrammed their New York office with the news that his bank account was £3,720 overdrawn and sent Tom Keylock over to New York to personally persuade Klein to hand over much-needed funds. Brian's account, however, did have a miraculously healthy balance of £4,000 in credit, but his first settlement from the band wasn't due for at least another eight months.

He had expressed his money fears to Tony Sanchez when referring to his household workforce and expenditure which, if counting Leslie Hallett as a helper in the gardens for Michael Martin, was now standing at seven full-time staff. "I'm really worried about how I'm going to pay for everything until I get that first £100,000."

Money worries aside, it was Brian's diagnosed paranoia which was causing him his greatest concern. It was inevitable, following the years of persistent and prolonged drink and drug abuse, highlighted by months of relentless police and press harassment, and a near jail sentence, that it would manifest itself as a very deep-rooted emotional problem.

Instances of his paranoiac outbursts were by now legendary. Mick Jagger was well known to mockingly call him paranoid given the slightest reason and even Bob Dylan, upon greeting Brian, was once heard to laughingly say, "Hey man, how's your paranoia?" By 1969 it was a joke that had worn thin and turned in on itself in the most classic of scenarios. Brian was convinced that if anything was seriously amiss now, he'd already become the boy that cried wolf. No one would come and help.

His frantic calls to the Stones' office in the past concerning minor crisis after crisis were, if not put on hold, dealt with by Jo Bergman. "He would often call me at three or four in the morning. He would sound high as a kite and he would say, 'Sorry to disturb you, what time is it?' and when I would tell him, he would say, 'Oh, it's not that late. Sorry but you must listen.' He needed constant attention."

When, in previous times, Brian had said that both the Stones' organisation and the police were out to get him, it was a convenient cop-out to simply accuse him of being paranoid rather than deal with the problem. Yet he had been thrown out of the band and had realised that someone in the Stones' organisation had continuously leaked information to the police about him. They had even planted the marijuana that led to his arrest on 21st May 1968, which subsequently prevented him from touring and led to his dismissal. This was confirmed by Trevor Kempson.

He started complaining that for weeks there were lights being shone into his house at night. He maintained that somebody had the house under constant surveillance, although this could have been accounted for by the likely actions of the local constabulary who were well known to keep a watchful eye on the comings and goings at Cotchford Farm. After all, Brian was a convicted drug-user and was suspected of still practising.

Also, he had become something of a nuisance in the area. Although some people thought his behaviour had modified recently, this view was certainly not shared by all. His previous drunken escapades in Cotchford Village were well remembered. Keith Altham said, "I think he was worse at the end. People who get into that condition by consuming what they are consuming, something takes them over and you lose that person. I don't think he was even Brian Jones at that time. I mean the Brian Jones that I knew initially was a much nicer person than the Brian Jones I knew at the end."

The dye was considered cast as far as people's attitudes were concerned, but was it all completely justifiable?

Both the Stones' accountant Fred Trowbridge and Les Perrin remained in close daily contact with Brian via their London office throughout those final days. Perrin has remarked on how lonely Brian appeared then and has told how shocked he had been to receive a 63-word telegram in which Brian poured out his heart about his feelings and the extent of his solitude, even stating categorically how he had serious fears for his life.

"Brian needed someone who really cared for him and would protect him and there wasn't anybody at the end prepared to undertake such a job. He had made things so difficult for himself, you'd have to be a saint. It was something that intensified once he was no longer in the band, but he had pushed himself to the very · fringe. It was obvious that it had been the band that kept him together."

Mary Hallett was also getting increasingly concerned about Brian's fits of depression, loneliness and paranoia. "He became like a little boy lost. That's why I think he turned to the Bible. He began talking about it quite a lot. It's funny, but when I spoke to Philip Norman, he wrote in his book that Brian had a big Bible down there but I never saw it. He must have had one though, because he knew it back to front, Old Testament and New. He told me he thought that the earth was hell and above was heaven. He said, 'I'm sure I'm living in hell,' and I said that if that was true then he was in for a better time presently. That didn't cheer him up. He was saying he must have been a terrible person in a previous life because his life was so bad now.

"It was as if he had lost part of himself somewhere. He told me the only girl he would have married wasn't having anything to do with him any more and that she was the only girl he had ever really loved and she was gone. He wanted to open his heart to me and I was ready to listen. He made me make a solemn promise never to repeat to anyone the girl's name, but it wasn't Anita or Linda. I never even told Leslie, I never repeated it. He would ring me, ever so woebegone, about the slightest silly thing and ask me to go down to him. He would be ever so appreciateive, he didn't seem to be able to do the smallest of things. He made everything harder work than it needed to be."

The first indication that Mary had that Brian's monetary affairs were in disarray was the arrival of Fred Trowbridge's memo to Cotchford concerning her overspending on the feeding of Brian's cats. "They tried to say that I was spending the money on myself." It was more likely Brian's insistence on covering Mary's phone-bills that proved to be a bigger bone of contention for the prudent bookkeeper. This particular period of petty-mindedness and penny-pinching only came to an end a couple of weeks prior to Brian's death.

Then Brian told Mary that confirmation of his settlement had come through from Klein's New York office. "He was so excited, he kept saying, 'At last we'll be alright. My money is coming.'" This put Brian's mind at rest as before he had made no secret of the fact that he had been very sceptical as to the validity of the Stones' generous offer ever since accepting it.

The news also signalled a renewed determination in Brian to regain control of his financial and household concerns and put a stop to what he referred to as the constant rip-off being orchestrated by his wayward gang of workmen. Brian had complained endlessly to old friends Peter Jones and Alexis Korner that he was being taken advantage of, but seemed to do little to stop it.

Michael Martin had found the workmen's treatment of his boss difficult to take and confirmed that, in addition to Brian feeling undermined on a daily basis, he was being physically intimidated as well. Martin, by no means a small man, had been threatened on more than one occasion for interfering on his behalf. "They had threatened to rearrange my face a couple of times for what they considered my sticking my nose in."

Brian, Martin felt, had done nothing to bring about a correct and proper running order at the farm. Up until then Brian had been dependent on the Stones' office to choose his staff and provide the money to pay the everyday expenditure. It was now clear that he had made up his mind that the whole entourage would have to go. Even, it appears, Anna Wohlin.

The day before his death he told Mary of this decision in no uncertain terms, but what remains unclear at this point is whether he, in turn, made these intentions known to everyone else. The only indication that others knew of his plans was a conversation Mary subsequently overheard between Anna and the builders. "They were discussing Brian and saying how he'd be so and so and how they'd do so and so and he'd be sorry. I was trying not to take any notice because it was really nothing to do with me, but I couldn't help hear something about what they would do to him.

It was just a thing I overheard without meaning to. It's a pity I didn't listen more closely. You see, they had always said they liked Brian but it never sounded like it to me. I wouldn't have said that it was a very friendly discussion, I would have said that they were up to something but what I don't know. Whether it was to do with money or what, I can't say, but they were definitely planning something; you could tell they were just up to something or other." This conversation in no way proves that Brian had actually carried out his plan to dismiss his Crotchford workforce as the fact remains that they were still very much in evidence and gainfully employed on the morning of his death and mixing freely with Brian's guests that evening.

What is easy to assume is the likelihood of their knowing that their time was up. Naturally, this would have caused feelings of resentment and anger, particularly in Thorogood, as he had grown accustomed to a lifestyle based around the high-flying Stones and there was no guarantee of a further position within that society. He had already well and truly queered his pitch while working for Keith at Redlands.

Cotchford had proved a lucrative time for all and Thorogood had even come to look upon it as home. It is easy to conclude therefore that feelings were running high and must surely have added to the generally unpleasant and tense atmosphere that surrounded the farm at the time, and probably aggravated Brian's asthmatic attacks, one of which he had on the morning of his death.

If, on the night of Brian's death, he had announced that he was dismissing the Cotchford staff in the midst of a full-blown party, something that would have befitted his theatrical manner, then an already bad situation would have been turned into a powerfully explosive one.

Gered Mankowitz agreed. "Yes, it's one of those things that happens to humans. If you see someone abuse their situation or if you touch the very fringes of extreme wealth and affluence only to have it taken away by someone who is seen to abuse it, you become pretty embittered. Why the fuck has he got all that and I've got nothing, he's a piece of shit, I'm a hard-working bloke, look at him, he's a pathetic shit, I've had to wipe his arse! It's going to lead to frustration and bitterness."

Brian had no one to protect him from it. "So what happened to

Brian was somehow written . . . there was nothing you could do about it." Brian had arranged a rehearsal with Steve Marriott and the fledgling Humble Pie on 3rd July and when he didn't show up, Marriott rang Cotchford and was told the news. "I couldn't believe it, we were just sitting around and waiting for him, didn't guess for a minute what had happened."

The tributes to Brian appeared on the front pages of all the daily news and weekly music papers with quotes from the likes of Pete Townsend of The Who and George Harrison.

Townsend said, "Oh, it's a normal day for Brian, like he died every day, you know?" He later wrote and recorded a song entitled *A normal day for Brian, a man who died every day.*

"The Stones," said Harrison, "have always been a group that I dug very much . . . dug all the dodgy aspects of them as well, and Brian Jones had always been what I've regarded as one of the dodgy aspects. The way he fitted in there and the way he didn't fit in, I always felt that when he stopped playing with them that dynamism was going to be missing, but somehow it's still there. I credited him with a lot. I think the thing is that The Stones have just managed by some miracle to kind of replace him. Not with Mick Taylor. I mean, he's like a musician but they've kind of filled the hole, either that or the fact that his death has made that dynamic. I don't know.

"He was a good fellow, you know. I got to know him very well and I felt close to him. You know how it is with some people, you feel for them, you feel near to them. He was born on 29 February 1943 and I was born on 25 February 1943 and he was with Mick and Keith and I was with John and Paul in the groups, so there was a sort of understanding between the two of us . . . I often seemed to meet him in his times of trouble. There was nothing the matter with him that a little extra love wouldn't have cured. I don't think he had enough love or understanding. He was a very nice and sincere and sensitive and we must remember that's what he was."

Pat Andrews heard about Brian's death at a bleak South London refuge where she was living with her and Brian's little son Mark. "They woke me up at half-past six in the morning and told me, 'We've just heard on the news, Brian is dead – now you'll be able to get some money.' It didn't sink in till about ten o'clock, when I heard myself. I just broke down and cried." Brian hadn't left a will and Mark's birth certificate showing no father's name meant that legally both Pat and her son were entitled to nothing.

Dick Hattrell was a hotel manager in Swansea when he got the news of Brian's death. "Brian's father sent me a telegram. I was so overcome with grief that I burnt every photograph and correspondence I ever had from him. I suppose it was a mark of respect to him, a respect to his music, a private funeral if you will."

Linda Lawrence, who was twenty-two and living with Brian's other son Julian, running a boutique in Hollywood, said, "I remember Brian as the kindest, most gentle person I have ever met."

Shirley Arnold, the Rolling Stones' secretary added a most poignant insight into Brian when she said, "The sadness of his dying is somehow not so bad as the sadness of seeing him try to live."

Shirley Arnold had just had her telephone connected. Only one person knew the number. Shirley had given it to Tom Keylock's wife Joan, because The Stones were recording at Olympic Studios in Barnes that night and might have needed it.

Shirley's phone rang at one o'clock in the morning; it could only have been Joan. It was the first phonecall she received on her newly installed telephone. She picked up the receiver. Joan Keylock said, "Are you awake?" Shirley replied, "Yeah, I'm downstairs, what's wrong?" Joan said, "I've got some bad news." Shirley said, "Brian," Joan said, "He's dead."

Shirley continued, "She was in a state, she'd only just heard, she heard before anyone else. Frank Thorogood, who was down there with Brian, was a very good friend of Tom's. As they pulled Brian from the pool, they realised he was dead. The first thing Frank did was to ring Joan and say, 'Brian's dead, someone get Tom down, because Tom was great at getting things sorted out. I was the first to be rung, even before the studio, to tell Stu and the boys. John said, 'Frank and Brian went for a swim and Brian didn't come out.' I then went upstairs and became hysterical."

Joan Keylock rang the studio after speaking to Shirley and said, "Is Tom there? Tom's got to go down to Cotchford." Stu snapped "Oh, what's the silly bugger done now?" Joan replied, "He's dead." Tom Keylock had not arrived at the studio.

The Stones had booked a recording session at Olympic Studios in Barnes for the evening of 3rd July. As normal, the actual session was not going to start until after midnight and earlier in the day Tom had gone to Redlands from Cotchford to pick up Keith. On arriving at Olympic, Keith had sent Keylock back to Redlands in order to pick up a guitar he needed for that night's recording.

Redlands, like Cotchford, is in Sussex. They are roughly 48 miles apart, but both a good two hours drive from the Olympic Studios in Barnes, London. Keylock knew that the session would not start until late, very late, and probably go on to the early hours of the morning. He had made the journey to Redlands to pick up the guitar in good time, giving himself plenty of time to return to London at a more leisurely pace, stopping for dinner at what he later described as 'some sort of country club'.

Nicholas Fitzgerald and his friend Richard Cadbury, two of Brian's rich associates, were also in Sussex and had been to Cotchford earlier that day. Fitzgerald claimed in his book *The Inside Story of the Original Rolling Stone* that they arrived there at much the same time as the first of Brian's evening guests. "It was always open house at Brian's." After staying a short time the pair went on to the nearby town of Haywards Heath to drink in the bar of the Hayworth Hotel which closed at 10.30 p.m.

They returned to Hartfield and reached Brian's by 11.15 p.m. Turning into the lane, they were stopped by a solitary car blocking the driveway. Leaving the car they continued on foot towards the house, which was now silent. Mary Hallett had already witnessed the mass car evacuation of the lane earlier. When they reached the ground's perimeter bushes, they were confronted by a man Fitzgerald described as burly and wearing glasses, who grabbed him and, shaking him violently by the collar, growled in a thick cockney accent, "Get out of here, Fitzgerald, or you'll be next." Releasing Fitzgerald, both he and Cadbury fled immediately. Fitzgerald said later that he had not seen the man before but he did see him again once more, days later at the Rolling Stones' Hyde Park concert in London.

Because of the witnesses' many conflicting recollections involving Brian's entering the water, it is unclear as to the exact time of his death. All that is certain is the time the police received the call from Cotchford at the police station in East Grinstead, six miles away, which was 12.10 a.m. If Fitzgerald had left the farm earlier at 11.15 p.m. that would leave almost 50 minutes unaccounted for.

Who Killed Christopher Robin?

Ian Stewart received a phonecall at Olympic Studios from Joan Keylock at 1.10 a.m. She asked for her husband who had still not returned, and broke the news of Brian's death to the band. Keylock arrived at the studio with Keith's guitar in time to meet the group (minus Bill Wyman who had left the studios just as Tom arrived, a little before 2.00) sitting together stunned and dazed. It was then that Jagger told Keylock, "We think Brian is dead." Les Perrin was notified and collected by Keylock in order to take charge of the ensuing press invasion. Both he and Keylock then left London. They drove to Hartfield in an hour and a half and arrived at Cotchford a little after 3.30 a.m. Brian's body had already been removed and the house was in the control of Detective Chief Inspector Ron Marshall, the head of East Grinstead's CID who told them the first officer to arrive on the scene had been PC Albert Evans of Hartfield, who, he said, was called to the farm at ten minutes past midnight. When he got to Cotchford he saw the body of Brian Jones lying next to the pool with his head slightly raised by a towel, indicating that there had been some attempts to revive him. The police then conducted a thorough inspection of the house and grounds and took possession of a number of empty and partially empty bottles of alcohol and pills.

Later, at first light, Keylock and Perrin inspected the grounds themselves and found a 'Riker Medihailer' which they gave to the police still at the house. Oddly enough the police hadn't found it during their previous search when it was Brian's habit to keep four such inhalers, one at each corner of the pool, while swimming. This prompted the terse police reply to Perrin, "Very clever, Mr Perrin, you're working like a good PR man, what did you do, drop it down your trouser leg?"

Before Keylock had gone to East Grinstead police station to pick up the now sober Frank Thorogood, who had been giving his statement as to the events of that night, he had held an unofficial press conference at the garden gate where he introduced himself to reporters and photographers as the Rolling Stones' road manager and told them that he had spoken to Brian the previous lunchtime and he had been in very good shape and in tip-top spirits. Speaking about Brian's country surroundings, he said, "He came here to rest and think and had put a lot of time into the renovations and landscape. He was enjoying every minute of his new outlook."

Frank's statement made absolutely no mention to the authorities that there had been several other people besides Brian, Anna, Janet and himself at the house that evening. Added to this was the even more dubious failure by the police to find any inhalers by the poolside. This could possibly have indicated that Brian had no intention of going swimming that night, or else they had been moved during the course of the night. Either way, it all adds up to a very sketchy picture.

Keith Richards observed, "I take all the story from that night with a pinch of salt. I've no doubt it's the same with anybody when those things happen. There's a crowd of people, then suddenly there's nobody there. Instead of trying to help the guy, they think of their own skins and run. I don't really know what happened on that night. I know that there was a lot of people there and suddenly there wasn't." Keith expressed further misgivings about the mysterious circumstances surrounding that night when he said, "We had these chauffeurs working for us and we tried to find out . . . some of them had a wierd hold over Brian. There were a lot of chicks there and there was a whole lot going on, they were having a party. I just don't know what happened to Brian that night. There was no one there that'd want to murder him. Someone didn't take care of him and they should have done because he had someone there who was supposed to take care of him. Everyone knew what Brian was like, expecially at a party. Maybe he did just go for a swim and have an asthma attack . . . We were completely shocked. I got straight into it and wanted to know who was there and couldn't find out. The only cat I could ask was the one I think got rid of everybody and did the whole disappearing trick so that when the cops arrived, it looked like it was just an accident.

"Maybe it was. Maybe the cat just wanted to get everyone out of the way so it wasn't all names involved, etc. Maybe he did the right thing, but I don't know. I don't even know who was there that night and finding out is impossible. It's the same feeling with who killed Kennedy. You can't get to the bottom of it."

The most unreliable witness that evening appears to be Anna Wohlin, who, following the inquest on 7th July, told Brian's father that Brian had used Janet Lawon as an excuse for wanting them to leave, saying that he wanted to avoid any unwanted trouble or gossip she would attract from the village. She went on to say that in fact Brian had gone to bed with a sleeping pill that night, but woke and then asked Frank to leave, but he wouldn't.

He then had a few drinks with them at what she termed a party and then decided to go for a swim with Frank. Both men, she said, appeared to be under the influence of drink.

Lewis Jones, Brian's father, later said, "I couldn't never understand that statement the papers supposedly got from Anna about a party. If one were planning a party, would he take sleeping pills first? I was horrified by the *People's* knowing that a doctor had prescribed the drugs Brian had taken and their saying nothing at all about it. Nobody asked any questions. I wrote the police a letter telling them the drugs were prescribed so they could investigate and have that cleared up, at any rate that the drugs were prescribed for Brian by a doctor. I sent the letter on a Friday and by Monday the doctor was out of the country. I have no idea what it means." This differs entirely to the account Anna supposedly gave her friend, Jim Caterfae, the manager of the London club The Speakeasy, who said some time later, "the night Brian died I got a call from Anna maybe about ten minutes after it happened. Somebody got the phone and put it down and she called me a bit later. She was very upset. She was moved out of the country so fast that it wasn't true, and told to say nothing. I don't know who made her do this. Anna told me she had never seen Brian so happy as he was the night he died, with the way things were going with the band. She had gone upstairs to sleep, then suddenly she came down. Frank and the nurse were standing by the pool, Brian was there and they were doing nothing at all. Anna dived in and tried to fish him out. Brian was floating under the water in the pool and they wouldn't help her at all. They were just standing by the pool watching and after that Anna said everything disappeared from the house."

Wohlin testified at the inquest, where she was asked by the coroner, Dr Angus Sommerville, if she had ever seen Brian have an asthma attack. She replied, no, but she had seen him use an inhaler, particularly when in the pool and he had difficulty breathing. He asked if she had ever seen him take a black pill called Duraphil, to which she said, yes, once on that night.

Following the inquest Anna went to stay with Bill Wyman and his girlfriend Astrid, a fellow Swede. Two days later she took a hired Chauffeur-driven car, charged to Brian's account, to the airport and flew back to Stockholm never to be seen again.

At this time Brian's parents drove to Cotchford. They wanted to see Mrs Hallett in order to collect Brian's personal belongings from the locked farmhouse, which they had rightly expected to find still lavishly furnished and kept, along with his many personal items, such as antiques and musical equipment. But on entering they were shocked to discover just how little their son owned. They left that day with scarcely a dozen items, including Brian's favourite black and white jumper and pink snakeskin boots which Mrs Jones gave to Helen Spittal as a lasting and touching reminder. Lewis and Louisa did keep in touch with Mary for several months. While the house was up for sale, they sent several parcels of baby clothes for Mary's recently born granddaughter, Tabitha, who they said reminded them of Brian. One day the correpsondence simply ceased.

Brian's chauffeur, Brian Palasanga, wasted no time and spared no one's feelings when on 6th July he sold the exlusive rights to his story of working for Brian to the *People* newspaper, respect-fully entitled, "The Shocking Life of Brian Jones, by the man who knew him intimately, his former chauffeur."

Meanwhile a self-confessed 25-year-old black witch, Lorraine Faithless, claimed in an Australian newpaper she was the mother of Brian's illegitimate son, Timmy.

Brian was buried on 10th July at the Priory Road Cemetery in Cheltenham, only yards from the church where he sang as a choirboy. Cannon Hopkins, who conducted the service, read aloud to the crowd Brian's own epitaph which ended, "Please don't judge me too harshly."

Pat Andrews' father died shortly after Brian, suffering with mental illness. "What finished him off was Brian's funeral," Pat stated. "He felt it was like winning the pools and not posting the coupon. He just couldn't cope with the thought or the feeling of 'Look what I've done to Pat and Mark, if only I had Brian's name registered as the father they wouldn't be in this mess'."

The death of Brian that night remains shrouded in mystery. What is clear is that his death was more than a mere case of mis-adventure. The many strange and conflicting accounts of that night, coupled with the bizarre and menacing behind-the-scenes activities involving his position in and out of the band, do point to something a lot more complex and sinister. Several obvious con-clusions can be drawn as to that night's true events, but in the absence of police willingness to investigate fully, these will never be proven.

On 7th August, 1969, Detective Chief Inspector Lawrence Finley of Chichester CID said that the police had no further interest in the death of Brian Jones and the case was officially closed. He added that "his (Brian's) name had come up several times since during their enquiries into a serious case; this being one of attempted murder."

Mr Finley said his name was included in reports to the Director of Public Prosecutions "but we know he had little significance in the matter and we certainly have no interest in his death." Finley explained that they had made enquiries into rumours surounding Jones's death, but found them "without foundation."

A spokesman for the Director of Public Prosecutions added that they could not discuss the matter further.

So the mystery deepens and continues up until this day, despite new evidence and revelations presenting themselves, frequently in bizarre fashion, and from the most unexpected sources. An article that appeared in the August issue of the American magazine *Circus* in 1974 read, "In a world where artists play musical chairs more often than old gummers play checkers, it seems that the swap of the century was cancelled due to circumstances beyond the player's control.

"Lifting the cloak of secrecy which has shrouded Brian Jones's last days on earth, recent revelations suggest the blond Welshman was to join The Beatles after leaving The Stones."

Brian did make recordings with The Beatles (*You Know My Name, Look Up My Number*) which featured the multi-talented Mr Jones on sax while The Stones helped out The Beatles in this same period, providing harmonies on *Dandelion*. The story concerning Brian's death has some interesting twists as well. Somebody tried to charge photographers £200 for pictures of Brian's body. For this Mick and Keith had the entrepreneur chased out of Europe. This gent is supposedly still on the run. Half truths, high suspicion or innuendos? Keith Altham thinks a bit of all three. "Yeah, Brian was going to join The Beatles and perhaps it would have been a good thing if he had. He and Lennon might still be alive today if he had."

A much more recent and relevant interview conducted by *Q Magazine* and Keith Richards in 1988 gives an altogether more even and level-headed insight into Brian's death when he said, "I don't think you would find anyone who liked Brian. Brian was not a likeable guy. He had so many hang-ups, he was unreliable, he wanted to be a star. I admired his grit and determination . . . Listen, I'm being honest, right, I could say, oh yeah, Brian, lovely guy, but I'm being honest and he had so many hang-ups, he didn't know where to hang himself so he drowned himself. I wasn't surprised when he died, not at all. There were extra hassles between Brian and me because I took his old lady. You know he enjoyed beating chicks up, not a likeable guy. At the same time he had a likeable charm and we all tried to get on with him but then he'd shit on you. It sounds like I'm just putting him down but you ask anyone in The Stones and if they are honest they'll say the same thing. So no, I wasn't surprised about Brian. I didn't wish him dead and there were a few guys who did, but in all honesty it was no surprise, he was out there and I really don't think he expected to live."

So the veil of secrecy still persists, perpetuated by the very people who could and should throw light on to the matter but for one reason or another remain silent, even to this day. In the words of Michael Martin, "some evil men got hold of him and they just wouldn't let go. Poor Brian just didn't have a chance but it is all in the past and if the police didn't get anywhere, how is anyone else going to."

In January 1969 Brian Jones was one of the highest-paid musicians and performers in the pop-music world, but at the time of his death on 3rd August 1969 the ex-Rolling Stone was broke. His promised pay-off settlement from the band of £100,000 had never materialised, neither had any of his retainer totalling £20,000 per annum.

Brian had many personal expenses and accounts for travelling, publicity and entertaining. He assumed that most of these bills would be met by deductions at source from his earnings and dealt with by the Stones' accountants at their London office. This however, was not the case. By as early as 1968 Brian's affairs were wildly out of hand and he was deeply in debt. The true extent of these debts were disclosed at a creditors' meeting, held in London on 13th May 1970. Brian left liabilities exceeding £157,920. His gross estate amounted to £33,787 with further liabilities totalling £191,707. His assets consisted chiefly of his country house, cars and a small cash resource of an undisclosed amount. A close friend, speaking on behalf of Brian after the hearing said, "Brian was no spendthrift, he had his Rolls Royce and his clothes but he didn't waste money. He was milked dry by a few monsters although he was a very intelligent individual. You have got to remember that Brian was not the richest member of The Stones. Mick Jagger and Keith Richards received the lion's share of the royalties as they were the band's songwriters."

On 23rd July that same year the Stones filed a 29 million dollar lawsuit against Alan Klein and ABKCO Industires Inc. claiming mishandling of Rolling Stones funds saying, "Klein persuaded the band to sign over all the North American rights to their songs to a company called 'Nanker Phelge Music Inc.'." The Stones claimed they were led to believe they ran the company themselves when in truth it was controlled solely by Klein. The suit was signed by the four remainging original band-members and Lewis Jones, Brian's father. This was followed in August by another High Court writ against ex -managers Andrew Oldham and Eric Eason, charging that they had made a secret deal with Decca Records in 1963 which deprived the group of record royalties. The suit alleged that Oldham persuaded Brian Jones to accept a 6 per cent share of wholesale record prices for The Stones, while Decca was paying Oldham and Easton 14 per cent. At the same time Oldham had a 25 per cent management contract with The Stones themselves. Once again Lews Jones sued on Brian's behalf. Both cases were settled out of court in favour of The Stones.

It is somewhat macabre and ironic that Brian's desperate search for love and understanding and his determined visionary quest for musical fulfilment should now benefit parents who had so vehemently discouraged both.

The 4th of July 1991 marked the 22nd anniversary of Brian's death. A requiem service that was held at St Philip's and St James' church in Hatherley Road, Cheltenham, united Brian's two sons, Mark and Julian, for the first time and it is here that Pat Andrews' vows brought Brian Jones's chaotic story to a typically unfulfilling update. Lewis, Louisa and Barbara Jones, still resident in Cheltenham, did not attend the service.

"I hope that the people gave him a better deal in death than they did in life." said Alexis Korner, July 1969

11

Jigsaw Puzzle

On Sunday 7th November 1993, Tom Keylock went to the North Middlesex Hospital to visit his old friend Frank Thorogood. Thorogood had been in and out of hospital over the preceding four years with various health problems relating to his heart, kidneys and lungs. On this particular occasion, Thorogood was in bad shape. His health had deteriorated so badly that he had specifically asked his worried daughter Jan to ring Uncle Tom Keylock (Jan had always called him Uncle Tom since her childhood) the night before and ask him to visit him. This Jan did and Tom duly arrived at the hospital at eleven o'clock the next morning. On his way to the hospital, Keylock had sensed by Jan's shaky message that Frank's time was approaching, an impression that Thorogood's gaunt appearance did nothing to dispel.

"When I saw Frank I feared the worst," Keylock says. "He looked really rough. We started talking and he told me that he wanted to put his house in order. I thought he was talking about a will and in that sense he had made some provisions regarding his possessions. I knew that he wanted to leave everything, including his jewellery and his money, to Jan. I told him that he was a fighter, that he shouldn't give up the struggle but Frank told me he was too weak. It was too late for him."

The pair spoke together for almost an hour, before Frank suddenly changed the tone of his conversation.

"Frank said to me," Keylock recalls, "'There's something I have to tell you. It will probably shock you but we've been friends for so many years that I feel I can tell you.' I didn't know what he

The Stones at the filming of *One Plus One*, 1968 (Tony Gale)

The Stones at the filming of *One Plus One*, 1968 (Tony Gale)

Brian takes time out with Jean Luc Godard (Tony Gale)

Brian joins Ringo Starr and the other Beatles at a launch party for Apple's new signing The Grapefruit. January 1968. (Hulton Deutsch)

otchford's ancient history meant little Brian. What thrilled him was to live in he House At Pooh Corner. He is ctured here with the life size statue of hristopher Robin. (Brian Jones Fanclub)

July 3rd 1969. Tom Keylock meets the press outside Cotchford the morning after Brian's death. (Hulton Deutsch)

Press shot of Tom Keylock the day after the death. Brian's clothes lie in a pile on the ground. Keylock was soon to burn them along with Brian's other possessions. (Popperfoto)

Anna Vohlin. She gave Brian the kiss of life but it was too late. Like others present that night she was told never to return to Cotchford. (Popperfoto)

Brian's son Julian with Linda Lawrence

Pat Andrews and Brian's son Mark. 1979

Tom Keylock and Frank Thorogood return to Cotchford in June 1993 to reconstruct the events of twenty-four years ago. (Excel Productions)

rank Thorogood (right) explains the ɔgistics of Cotchford to Terry Rawlings, ɪne 1993 (Excel)

Tom Keylock relives the impromptu press call at the gate of the house. (Excel Productions)

Frank Thorogood, Cotchford, June 1993. (Excel Productions)

Pat Andrews and Tom Keylock at Brian's grave, July 1993 (Excel Productions)

was talking about and then he said, 'But you must promise me one thing, that you do not say a word to Jan or anybody about what I'm about to tell you while I'm still alive.' Naturally, I promised him that."

It was then that Frank confessed to Tom the awful truth, "It was me that did Brian." Keylock reeled back in surprise. This was what Frank meant by putting his house in order. He was getting everything off his chest. Tom had known Frank practically all his life and considered him a close friend. For Thorogood to have withheld this information for so long and not share it with him initially annoyed and disappointed Keylock.

"I was gutted and surprised but looking back on it I understood it," Keylock says. "After all, he coudn't say anything to anybody, not even me. How could he? When he told me about Brian, I replied, 'You must be joking.' Even though in the past, I, like a lot of people, had had my suspicions. I was genuinely shocked when Frank told me about Brian. I really thought he was winding me up but he was adamant, he wanted it out in the open, he had lived with it right to the end. At that stage, a nurse came in and gave him his daily tablets. After she left, I said to him, 'How did you do it?' He said, 'Well, I just finally snapped, it just happened. That's all there is to it.' Obviously I wanted to ask him a lot more but Frank refused to say anything other than 'It just happened. It just happened'.

"He was getting very emotional. He was really rough and I didn't feel that I could press him further about it. He was dozing off by now so I got ready to leave. I promised to see him on the Tuesday and left. I thought that then I could ask him more about what had gone on. But the next night his daughter Jan called me to say that Frank had died in his sleep."

Jan told Tom later that her father had seemed relieved by his visit and afterwards had appeared very calm.

Three months later I interviewed Tom Keylock to clear up details about the Moroccan trip that he had accompanied Keith, Anita, Mick, Brian and Marianne on. From the start of the interview it was quite obvious that Tom, who is normally a very self-assured character, was quite uptight and a little nervous. Halfway through our conversation, Keylock said to me, "People have been trying for twenty-five years to get me to talk about The Stones and I have never said a word, I have never been interested in any of those books, they are all a lot of crap. I still feel very responsible for them and I will never stitch them up, but there is something you should know and I'm only telling you now because all those stories and rumours are going to carry on unless someone finally puts it right. It's time to let both Brian and Frank rest in peace once and for all."

It was then that Keylock told me about Frank Thorogood's bedside confession. After he had finished, I immediately thought of the day we had spent during the summer filming a documentary at Cotchford Farm to accompany this book.

On the day of that shoot, we had arranged to interview both Tom Keylock and Frank Thorogood down at Cotchford Farm. Tom was driven down to Cotchford in his car by his driver and friend, Dean Halkins. Thorogood was picked up from his North London home by a friend of mine called Tony Perfect.

We spent the day interviewing both men in the house and around the pool that Brian died in. Halfway through filming Tony took me aside, and said to me, "Frank was very jittery and nervous on the way down here. He kept wanting constant reassuring that Tom would be at Cotchford when he arrived. It was like he felt he was being set up. He kept asking questions about you and going through the events of that night parrot fashion. I don't really know or understand the story of Brian Jones or what he was getting at, but something's really dodgy about what you're trying to do here."

That day Frank spoke to me for several hours and we were able for the first time to put together the most concise and complete picture of the events leading up to that night in 1969.

After filming what turned out to be Frank Thorogood's last-ever interview, we all retired to a hotel in East Grinstead to spend the night. The next day Tony again told me of his suspicions about Thorogood which, I have to confess, I did not pay much attention to. For my part, I believed that we would never uncover the real truth about Brian Jones's untimely demise. Since starting this project I have been convinced that there had been more people at Cotchford that night than had been previously reported and it was this factor that would yield new evidence.

This was the angle I was working to establish. So when Tony told me about Frank, I didn't really take much notice. Before I could question Frank again, he fell ill and had to be taken home.

Jigsaw Puzzle

Going on Frank's confession, we are now able to paint a truthful and complete picture of what exactly occurred that fateful night at Cotchford and finally extinguish the suspicions, rumours and innuendos that have dogged Brian's death for 25 years.

At 12 noon on 2nd July 1969, after spending the night at the farm, Tom Keylock left Cotchford and drove over to Redlands in West Wittering, to join up with Keith Richards. Keylock spent the rest of the day with Richards, and at about 8.30 p.m. drove the hour and 45-minute journey to Olympic Studios. It was on arriving that Keith asked Tom to return to Redlands in order to pick up a certain guitar that he required for the recording session that night. Tom was none too pleased at the thought of the return journey, but agreed to go and left immediately.

Brian woke that day just in time to see Keylock off at lunchtime. Turning on a reel to reel tape-player, he turned the volume up full tilt before talking briefly to Mrs Hallett. Both Hallett and Keylock remarked later that Brian had been in high spirits although he did have a touch of asthma, but this was dispelled with the use of his inhaler. Brian did not know it at the time, but the day would bring several major arguments. The first would be with his old girlfriend, Suki Potier. She had arranged to return to Cotchford to pick up the rest of her belongings. She had arrived alone, but was joined later by three of her girlfriends. It transpires that she harboured the idea that maybe she could persuade Brian to continue their relationship. For despite all his misdemeanours, Suki truly loved Brian.

Earlier that morning, Frank Thorogood had caught the train form East Grinstead to Victoria station where he was picked up by Jackie, the minicab-driver. She drove him to David Bailey's house in Regents Park where he had been commissioned by the famous photographer to carry out renovations.

After his meeting was over, Frank and Jackie drove over to see Fred Trowbridge at his Maddox Street office to pick up wages for himself and the workmen at Cotchford. In the 1960s, and throughout the major part of the 1970s, everyone in the building trade was paid on a Thursday. This practice was eventually stopped when it was noted that a significant amount of people would not show up for work on a Friday.

Trowbridge had some bad news for Thorogood. Brian had requested all payments to Frank and his team of builders to cease immediately. In true Brian fashion, Thorogood had not been told directly by his employer. Once again, Brian was relying on other people to carry out his awkward orders.

Thorogood was both shocked and enraged by Brian's cowardly actions and it was in that mood that he and Jackie drove back to Cotchford. On their arrival, Brian was in the middle of a heated argument with Suki. Her friends awkwardly busied themselves by wandering around the grounds while she tried to cajole Brian into restarting the doomed relationship. They were joined by Gary Leeds, the Walker Brothers drummer who had come down to Cotchford earlier in the hope of rehearsing with Brian.

After the spat was finished, it was obvious that their relationship was finally over. Matters were made worse for Suki by the presence of Anna Wholin who was present throughout the couple's altercations. Suki who had stood by Brian diligently for the duration of their long-suffering relationship, realised she had been coldly and cruelly dispensed with in favour of a girl he hardly knew. She was especially hurt by Brian's obvious enjoyment of her embarrassing predicament. Frustrated, she channelled her anger towards Anna and an explosive row erupted between the two girls, delighting Brian all the more. The distraught Suki was eventually prised out of the house by her friends who loaded her belongings into their cars and together screeched out of the lane. Anxious to avoid witnessing any other confrontations, Gary Leeds hastily made his excuses and also left. It was these cars Mary Hallett overheard leaving.

It was now Frank's turn to confront Brian, who, finally faced with his secretive actions, had no alternative other than to make good his plans to sack the builders. Brian told Frank that he and his girlfriend Janet Lawson were to move out and all work was to cease.

Frank contested he was owed a considerable amount of money by Jones, almost £8000, and wouldn't be leaving until he was paid.

Between November 1968 and July 1969, Brian had paid out the sum of £18,000 on building work and the upkeep of Cotchford. This translates to the incredible equivalent of £180,000 in today's money. Brian reasoned that it was impossible for him to still owe an extra £8000 when the house was no nearer completion and was still in such a state of disarray. The drainage system was still to be installed and the drive continued to look like a building site.

For Frank to be owed such a considerable sum meant the builder was drawing approximately £250 a week at a time when the average working wage was between £15 and £20 a week.

A stalemate was reached and the volatile situation was temporarily resolved. Brian had stuck to his guns and used the money owed as leverage by negotiating a deal that would see both Frank and his builders paid in full on the condition of their leaving.

It has to be understood that to Frank and the builders, Brian was a rich, spoiled brat. To them, he dressed as a dandy, he was rarely sober and lived in a style that they both envied and considered he was undeserving of. Now, behind their backs, he had unceremoniously dumped them, just as he had dumped so many others throughout his life. Thorogood was accountable for his builders' wages and his allegiance was to these men. Brian had placed Frank in a very unenviable position. Add this to the fact that the builder's obvious high times of living the life of luxury were now over, and Frank had every reason in mind to be greatly upset.

Even so, it is more than probable that it was agreed between Jones and Thorogood that his departure should take place the following day. Frank's next action was to accompany Jackie to the local pub and buy various bottles of alcohol. The pair then returned to Cotchford where Frank, together with Jackie, Mo, Dave and Johnny, huddled around the bench at the end of the pool to talk over this latest development. The builders and Jackie stayed until about eight and then left, leaving Brian alone in the house with Frank, Anna and Janet.

Frank and Janet retired to the guest flat above the garage to start packing up their belongings, while Brian went to one of the upstairs bedrooms in the main house and flopped down in front of the TV, while Anna readied herself for bed (Brian did not use one particular bedroom as his own, preferring to alternate between the three main bedrooms). After dozing for a few minutes, Brian suddenly woke with a renewed energy, and at about 10.00 p.m., crossed over to the flat to see Frank. Brian wanted to show there were no hard feelings between them and explain that necessity, as much as anything else, had guided his actions. He invited the pair to join him and Anna for another drink back at the house. Janet and Frank's statement testify that Brian was quite drunk as he led them unsteadily by torchlight.

Sitting around the farmhouse table, all four of them continued drinking and it was now that Frank resumed the argument. Brian, in another attempt to pacify the builder, suggested a swim to cool things down. He and Frank went upstairs to search for some swimwear while Janet and Anna went out to the pool with a tray of drinks and one of Brian's inhalers. They set the tray down by the bench which was already surrounded by an impressive array of bottles – brandy, whisky and vodka left over from earlier in the day.

Anna stripped down to her knickers and slipped into the water and began swimming as Brian and Frank reached the pool. Janet meanwhile had walked a little way back towards the house where she sat out of sight on another bench that was positioned adjacent to the dining-room doors. It was from here that she watched Brian being helped up on to the diving board by Frank who himself retired to the shallow end of the pool as Brian swam at the opposite end. At this point, Janet retired to the house to answer the phone. It was for Anna. She called to Anna, who joined her in the house, leaving the two men alone in the pool.

Based on Thorogood's confession, we now know that the argument flared up again for the third and final time. He knew Brian well and was unconvinced by his promise of payment upon leaving. Frank, now quite drunk himself, flew into a complete rage. He began plunging Brian repeatedly under the water. Consumed with rage he held Brian firmly beneath the surface until his body went limp.

Brian's lungs filled with water and he sank silently to the bottom of the pool, coming to rest in the right-hand corner of the deep end.

The two girls were unaware of what had happened. They were still inside. Still dripping wet, Thorogood then appeared in the house, ostensibly to find a towel. He nervously lit a cigarette as Janet Lawson asked where Brian was. Frank told her he was still in the pool. Janet went outside to check on him. Which is when the body was discovered.

On seeing his body, Janet Lawson went screaming back into the house, yelling for help. Anna Wohlin was the first person to respond. Both women rushed out to the pool and jumped in. They desperately began to try and drag Jones's body out of the pool. Significantly, Thorogood hesitated so much that both girls

190

had to scream at him for help. Eventually, the reluctant Thorogood helped to drag the body out whilst Janet ran into the house to phone for help.

As Anna had been on the phone at the time of Janet's cries for help, the phone was still off the hook on one of the bedroom's extensions. Janet then went back to the pool and asked Thorogood to get the phone working. This he finally did but not before ringing up Tom Keylock's wife in the hope of locating the minder who was known as Mr Get It Together Man. He was never more needed than right now.

Keylock himself was driving back to Olympic Studios with Keith's guitar. When he arrived at the studios in Barnes he was told that his wife had called the studio at midnight and informed the band of the tragedy. The shocked Stones, minus Bill Wyman who had already gone for the night, ordered Keylock once again to drive down to Cotchford. He arrived at 3.30 a.m. (the ambulance had taken away the lifeless body of Brian Jones at 1.30 a.m.) and started to secure the house. The police had tried to seal off the grounds but the farm's sprawling gardens made this an impossible task so Keylock, being familiar with Cotchford's lay-out, began making his own checks. He patrolled the length of the lane and spotted two men hiding amongst the hedgerows. He made a grab for the nearest and forcibly shoved him back out into the lane and watched while the other scampered away.

The police had taken everyone down to the station and, after questioning Anna and Janet, they released the two women. The police's initial suspicions led them to believe that Frank Thorogood was the man responsible for Brian's death. They told him that they would be pressing charges against him accordingly. The police kept Thorogood all night and repeatedly quizzed him about the night's events. Thorogood kept to his story which was fast turning into a perfect alibi. This story was the one that Frank would stick to word for word for the next 25 years. Brian had been swimming happily in the pool when he left him in search of a cigarette, and, as there were no witnesses to say otherwise, the police reluctantly let him go. Mrs Hallett highlighted this reluctance of the police, when she told me, "The police sergeant that was in charge said he intended to make an arrest."

In a separate version of that night's events Nicholas Fitzgerald claimed in his book *Brian Jones: The Inside Story of The Original Stone* that he had called Brian from a hotel at Haywards Heath at about 8.20 p.m., and a girl had picked up the phone and then left it off the hook as she apparently went to look for Brian. Fitzgerald said that he was surprised to hear shouting and music as if a party was in progress. He said he had seen Brian earlier that day and he had made no mention of throwing a party. As he listened in, someone then replaced the receiver, cutting him off.

Fitzgerald and his companion, Richard Cadbury, had one final drink before driving over to Cotchford. The journey took them half an hour. As they approached the house, Fitzgerald claimed that he and Cadbury hid behind some bushes and watched three men repeatedly dunk Brian Jones in the pool.

It was then that, in Fitzgerald's words, "a burly minder with glasses and a cockney accent" suddenly appeared out of nowhere and told them to clear off in no uncertain terms. Fitzgerald said that he did not know the identity of the man, but he saw him three days later at the Stones' free concert in Hyde Park, which was held in Brian's honour. By his description of that man in Hyde Park, Fitzgerald was placing Tom Keylock at the scene of the crime.

However, Fitzgerald and Cadbury's failure to intervene and help out their friend, who was obviously in great distress, coupled with Fitzgerald's constant refusal to sign a police state-ment to this fact, leaves his version of events highly questionable. Keylock, for his part, does confirm that he threw two men off the property and that his language had been far more colourful than Fitzgerald had previously reported.

I viewed Fitzgerald's written police statement at the coroner's office at Bex Hill, in Sussex.

Set out in the form of a questionnaire there is no mention of Fitzgerald being at the scene, nor does he state any times relating to the night's events. He was given three separate chances to con-firm that he indeed witnessed what in his mind amounted to a criminal act. Fitzgerald passed on all three.

The day following Brian's death reporters laid seige to Cotch-ford Farm. Keylock, in the absence of the Stones' publicist, fended off all their enquiries. He had already been instructed by Brian's father to remove as many of his son's personal posses-sions as possible and burn the remains.

Keylock full-heartedly instructed Thorogood's aggrieved

builders to act as removal men. It was to prove a costly mistake as the workmen, feeling rightly entitled to some sort of severance pay, liberally helped themselves to the pick of Brian's belongings, before delivering the remnants to Cheltenham.

On Thorogood's instructions the builders also loaded the now redundant supply of building materials, including the farm's ornate front gate and railings, on to a low-sided lorry. They then left Cotchford for the last time.

Keylock told me of his dismay at carrying out the bizarre orders given by Brian's father and was at a loss to explain them. "The only reason I could possibly imagine old man Jones wanting Brian's clothes burned was to stop people getting them and keeping them as some sort of morbid trophy or for some equally sordid reason, but not all of them went back to Cheltenham. A big trunk of gear went back to the office and I don't know what happened to that. Brian's father was one of the strangest blokes I've ever met, which is saying something. Brian never got on with him, but everyone knows that. He had disowned them. I remember once when The Stones played in Cheltenham, his parents came backstage and Brian turned to me and said, 'Don't let them in, I don't want to see them'. I asked him why and he said, 'I'll fucking freak out if you let them in,' so I had to stand on the dressing-room door and wait for them. I barred everyone that night so it wouldn't look like it was only directed at them."

The bizarre relationship between Brian and his father went as far as the grave with Brian, where once again Keylock found himself in the role of intermediary. "I had ordered a coffin from the States after talking to the funeral parlour. The undertaker had an eye to sending Brian off in a certain fashion, because he was a star, so he showed me pictures of all these coffins and I spotted this bronze one which was beautiful, but we couldn't get one in England so we had to have it flown over from the US. It cost a lot more money than normal, but the funeral parlour were getting right into it. It was the biggest funeral they had ever performed and their attitude was, Brian wasn't gonna spend any more of his money and he should have the best send-off. But Brian's father was totally put out by it, which amazed me. He even asked me if I couldn't have found a cheaper coffin. I never spoke to him from that day onwards, not even at the funeral. Mistakes were made and things could have been handled better but that was the final insult."

Who Killed Christopher Robin?

A few days after Brian's death on 7th July the coroner recorded a verdict of death by misadventure.

Appendix

I, Thomas Richard Keylock, of 29 Brandon Road, Booker, High Wycombe, Bucks HP12 4PG MAKE OATH and say as follows:

"On the Saturday evening of 6th November 1993, at the request of Frank Thorogood, as relayed by his family, I visited him at the North Middlesex Hospital in Silver Street, Edmonton, North London on Sunday 7th November 1993. Mr Thorogood was terminally ill and close to death.

I spent many hours with him and during our conversation, Mr Thorogood stated that he would finally like to set the record straight in relation to the death of Brian Jones, a former member of The Rolling Stones pop group.

Mr Thorogood confirmed that, on the evening of 2nd July 1969, he was swimming with Brian Jones in the private pool at Cotchford Farm. He stated that he physically held Brian Jones under the water and that this resulted in the death of Brian Jones. Following this incident, Mr Thorogood stated he left the pool in order to get a cigarette and that the events which followed are as detailed in the various witnesses statements of the time.

Mr Thorogood also stated that many more people were at Cotchford Farm on 2nd July 1969 than admitted to. These people included his employed builders.

A few hours following my meeting with Mr Thorogood, he died."

SWORN at 20 Balcombe Street
Dorset Square, London NW1 6NB
this 16th day of ~~February~~ March 1994

Before me

H.S. KINGS

Beckman & Beckman
20 Balcombe Street
Dorset Square
London NW1 6NB

A Solicitor/~~Commissioner of Oaths~~

D. Cert.
SR.

CAUTION - It is an offence to falsify a certificate or to make or knowingly use a false certificate or a copy of a false certificate intending it to be accepted as genuine to the prejudice of any person, or to possess a certificate knowing it to be false without lawful authority.

CERTIFIED COPY
Pursuant to the Births and

OF AN ENTRY
Deaths Registration Act 1953

DEATH	Entry Number	108

| Registration District | Uckfield |
| Sub-district | East Grinstead |

Administrative area
County of East Sussex

1. Date and place of death
Second July 1969
Cotchford Farm, Hartfield

2. Name and surname
Lewis Brian JONES

3. Sex **Male**

4. Maiden surname of woman who has married —

5. Date and place of birth
28th February 1942
Cheltenham Glos.

6. Occupation and usual address
Entertainer
Cotchford Farm Hartfield

7. (a) Name and surname of informant
Certificate received from A.C. Sommerville. Coroner for East Sussex. Inquest held 7th July 1969

(b) Qualification

(c) Usual address —

8. Cause of death
1a Drowning
b Immersion in Fresh Water

11 Severe liver dysfunction due to fatty degeneration and the ingestion of alcohol and drugs. Swimming whilst under the influence of alcohol and drugs.
MISADVENTURE

9. I certify that the particulars given by me above are true to the best of my knowledge and belief. —
Signature of informant

10. Date of registration
Ninth July 1969

11. Signature of registrar
M. P. Lacey Registrar

Certified to be a true copy of an entry in a register in my custody.
J Purcell Deputy Superintendent Registrar 10th July 1992 Date

GA 53561

CERTIFIED COPY OF AN ENTRY OF BIRTH

BIRTH in the Sub-district of _Cheltenham_ in the _County of Gloucester_

REGISTRATION DISTRICT _Cheltenham_

Columns:—

1	2	3	4	5	6	7	8	9	10*
When and where born	Name, if any	Sex	Name and surname of father	Name, surname and maiden surname of mother	Occupation of father	Signature, description and residence of informant	When registered	Signature of registrar	Name entered after registration
1942 Twenty fourth October 1942 189 The Park Tunning Hospital Cheltenham u.d.	Lewis Brian Roy Jones	Boy	Lewis Blount Jones	Louisa Beatrice Jones formerly Hammond Eldorado Road Cheltenham u.d.	aircraft Daughtsman 33 Jones father Eldorado Road Cheltenham u.d.	Beatrice Jones mother	Second March 1943	Second March J. Snell Registrar	

CERTIFIED to be a true copy of an entry in the certified copy of a Register of Births in the District above mentioned.
Given at the GENERAL REGISTER OFFICE, LONDON, under the Seal of the said Office, the 25th day of November 1983

BXA 897775

*See note overleaf

Form A502M Dd 8364376 100M 6/83 Mcr (301297)

The University of Sheffield

Department of Forensic Pathology

Professor M A Green
Dr J C Clark
Dr C M Milroy

The Medico-Legal Centre
Watery Street
Sheffield S3 7ES
Tel: (0742) 738721
Fax No. (0742) 726247

Our ref: CMM/JR

17 March 1994

Mr R Santilli
Managing Director
The Merlin Group
40 Balcombe Street
LONDON
NW1 6ND

Dear Mr Santilli

RE: BRIAN JONES

I have examined the inquest records and post mortem examination report of Dr Sachs. I cannot exclude the possibility that Jones was held under water. The absence of injury on the body does not exclude this. If pressure was applied to the head or shoulders, bruising would not be expected and if held under water then drowning could follow. Holding someone under water would be easier when the victim was under the influence of alcohol and other drugs. If someone was taken by surprise in being pushed under water, inhalation of water could take place quickly and death from drowning would follow soon after.

Yours sincerely

DR C M MILROY
MB ChB MRCPath DMJ
Senior Lecturer in Forensic Pathology
Consultant Pathologist to the Home Office

200

DEPARTMENT OF FORENSIC PATHOLOGY
UNIVERSITY OF SHEFFIELD

Report on the death of Brian Jones

NAME: Lewis Brian JONES (Deceased)   **AGE:** 27 years

The post mortem examination of Lewis Brian JONES, formerly of Cotchford Farm, Hartfield, Sussex, was conducted by Dr Albert Sachs who was a Consultant Pathologist at Queen Victoria Hospital, East Grinstead, Sussex.

Lewis Brian Jones was involved in drowning incident between 2330 hrs and 2359 hrs on 2nd July 1969. A post mortem examination was conducted on 3rd July 1969. The post mortem examination showed changes seen in drowning. The lungs were heavy weighing 632g and 643g. Frothy fluid exuded from the surface of the lungs. Microscopic examination of the lungs was also in keeping with drowning. There was some frothy fluid around the nostrils which is also seen in drowning.

The post mortem examination also showed that there was organ damage as a result of alcohol and drug abuse. The liver was fatty and grossly enlarged weighing 3000g which is twice the normal size.

The heart also showed evidence of damage, being enlarged and weighing 411g; the normal maximum being 380g. The chambers of the heart were dilated and the heart muscle was described as fatty and flabby. The damage to the heart was probably caused by alcohol which can have a direct toxic effect on the heart producing alcoholic cardiomyopathy.

Jones was described as being 5'11" tall of powerful build with a tendency to obesity. Under the section 'injuries', Dr Sachs records 'nil'. Examination of blood and urine revealed the blood alcohol of 140mg/100ml and 1720μg/100ml of a basic amphetamine-like substance in the urine.

Report on the death of Brian Jones

The first question to arise from the post mortem examination is how Jones died. It is my opinion there is clear evidence that Jones drowned. In view of the fact that drowning was the cause of death, the question arises as to why Jones drowned when he was said to be a competent swimmer. The question was raised as to whether Jones had suffered an asthma attack. It was pointed out by Dr Sachs at the inquest that in asthma, the lungs are light and bulky, indented by the ribs with thick mucus in the airways. These features were not present in this case and therefore there is no evidence of Jones suffering an asthma attack and drowning as a consequence.

The verdict at the inquest was that death was as the result of misadventure. Jones drowning whilst under the influence of alcohol and drugs.

The circulating blood alcohol level is equivalent to a consumption of around 4-5 pints of beer. However, this is difficult to be accurate about, in view of the fact that Jones was a regular and heavy drinker, the circulating levels may have been produced by a higher consumption.

Deaths from amphetamine abuse are rare. High levels can be tolerated in habituated abusers.

Dr C M MILROY
MB ChB MRCPath DMJ
Senior Lecturer in Forensic Pathology
Consultant Pathologist to the Home Office

Form

SUSSEX CONSTABULARY

REPORT TO THE CORONER CONCERNING A DEATH

Sudden Death * / Accident * / Suspected Suicide * /

Name, age, occupation and address ....Lewis Brian JONES. 26 years. Born 28.2.42. Chlllnh- 27
of deceased. If married woman, ...Cotchford Farm, Hartfield, Sussex.
widow, divorced, or child (under
16), state husband's or father's ....Entertainer.
name, occupation and address.

Next of Kin (relationship) ....Father.

Time and date when :-
    (a) last seen alive ....11.30 p.m. approx. 2/7/69.
    and by whom ....Mr. Frank David THOROUGHGOOD.

    (b) died/found dead ....
    where ....Swimming pool at above address.
    found by ....Miss Janette Ann LAWSON.

Conditions under which body found

(a) Road * / Grass * / Under cover out Doors * / Water * / Vehicle * / ....

(b) Fully clothed * / Partly clothed * / Pyjamas * / Naked * / ....

(c) Face upwards * / Face down * / Sitting * / ....

(d) Time and nature of last meal ....

Additional information required for accident and suspected suicides

(a) Road Accidents. Deceased was driver * / front * or rear * seat passenger / cyclist * /
    pedestrian * / ....

(b) Note of any drugs etc. found at scene ....Box of various drugs, herewith sent.
    ....Capsules found at deceased's home identified as DUROPHET (retained by Police).

If under care of a Doctor

Name, address and telephone number of Doctor attending deceased ....

Nature of illness or complaint ....

Treatment given and drugs prescribed ....

Date when last seen by Doctor ....
Doctor confirming death ....Dr. R. R. EVANS, 'Snowdenham' Hartfield.

Name and address of Undertaker or other ....Queen Victoria Hospital mortuary by
person moving body to Mortuary (State ....ambulance.
where body now lying)

Name, address and telephone number of ....
Undertaker attending to funeral

Cremation * / Burial *

*To be completed in triplicate. Original and second copy (together with statements) to the
Coroner's Officer, first copy to be left at Mortuary with body.   * Delete as necessary.*   10/67

Brief circumstances of death ...At about 00.10, as a result of a call received of a s...,ected drowning I went to Cotchford Farm Hartfield and there saw the body of a man I know as Brian JONES laying beside the swimming pool. East Grinstead Ambulance was already at the scene and artificial resusitation was being carried out. It would appear that the deceased, a chronic asthmatic had also been drinking, and had decided to go for a swim with friends. After about a half an hour the friends left the pool and went indoors leaving JONES swimming on his own. Soon afterwards another guest went to the pool and saw JONES lying face down in the bottom of the pool. Dr. Evans of Hartfield was called, and pronounced life extinct. Drugs, samples of which are herewith sent, were found in the house, as deceased is supposed to have taken some before swimming.

Report submitted by ...A.V.Evans. ... P.C. AE.887

Division ...'F'... Station ...East Grinstead... Telephone number ...21155.

Section below to be completed by Coroner's Officer

Death reported to Coroner (name and district) on and by whom. — Dr. A. C. SOMERVILLE at 9.30 a.m. by Det. C/Insp. MARSHALL.

Name of Pathologist who carried out post mortem examination, giving place and date —

Cause of death

1(a) ....

1(b) ....

1(c) ....

2 ....

Registrar' District —

Witnesses/relatives names, addresses and telephone numbers.

Frank David THOROUGHGOOD. 7, Albert Close, Wood Green.N.22.

Janette Ann LAWSON. 20, Netherton Road, Gosport, Hants.

Anna WOHLIN (Swedish) c/o Cotchford Farm, Hartfield.

Inquest held with/without Jury, place and time —

Verdict —

Remarks —

Signature of Coroner's Officer .... Date ....

Division .... Station ....

Sudden Death - Brian JONES

The Deceased was under the care of Dr. A.L. GREENBURGH of
73 Eaton Place, Belgravia, W.1., telephone Belgravia 3232.

Dr. GREENBURGH is away in Majorca until late evening of
Sunday, 6th July. Will be contacted at his surgery at 9.15 a.m.
on Monday, 7th July.

The Doctor's secretary confirmed that the Deceased was regularly
prescribed:

MANDREX - as sleeping tablets.

VALIUM (believed 10 mg) - as tranquillizers, which 'he needed
all of the time'.

MEDIHALER - regular prescriptions

DUROPHET - ("black bombers")

It is known to the secretary that about ten days ago, the
Deceased made an urgent telephone call to Dr. GREENBURGH,
requesting Durophet and a prescription for ten or so was given.

Above information passed by me to Dr. SACHS at 2.30 p.m. 4.7.69.

Sudden Death - Brian JONES

The Deceased was under the care of Dr. A.L. GREENBURGH of 73 Eaton Place, Belgravia, W.1., telephone Belgravia 3232.

Dr. GREENBURGH was away in Majorca until the late evening of Sunday, 6th July. Was contacted at his surgery at 9.15 a.m. on Monday, 7th July.

The Doctor confirmed that the Deceased was regularly prescribed:

MANDREX - as sleeping tablets, 2 to 3 per day.

VALIUM - (10 mg) - as tranquillizers, 3 per day, which, 'he needed all of the time'.

MEDIHALER - regular prescriptions - Doctor has never been consulted by the Deceased for asthma.

DUROPHET - ("black bombers") infrequently.

PIRITON - 4 mg., was prescribed day before death as a result of a telephone call from Deceased, complaining of hay-fever.

About ten days ago, the Deceased made an urgent telephone call to Dr. GREENBURGH, requesting Durophet and a prescription for ten or so was given.

Dr. GREENBURGH stated that the Deceased's drug requirements were becoming less and he had shown considerable improvement of late. Prescriptions were made in small quantities at frequent intervals rather than large prescriptions, which, experience had shown, resulted in the Deceased taking larger doses.

Kinnanhan
D.C.1.
7/7/69

206

TUNBRIDGE WELLS GROUP HOSPITAL MANAGEMENT COMMITTEE

THE QUEEN VICTORIA HOSPITAL
EAST GRINSTEAD, SUSSEX

PATRON
H.M. QUEEN ELIZABETH, THE QUEEN MOTHER

HONORARY PRESIDENT
GLADYS, LADY KINDERSLEY

PHONE: EAST GRINSTEAD 24111
TELEGRAMS: QUVICHOS, EAST GRINSTEAD

PATHOLOGIST:
A. SACHS, C.B., C.B.E.,
M.Sc., M.D.,

PATHOLOGICAL LABORATORY
F.R.C.P. F.C. Path.

5th July, 1969.

Dr. C. Sommerville,
H.M. Coroner,
Beckford,
Lewes Road,
E. Grinstead.

Dear Dr. Sommerville,

Comments on the case of the:-

Late Lewis Brian Jones.

(1)   In an asthmatic attack the bronchi are in
spasm. This would tend to seal the lining
tissue and prevent the entry of a gas while
the spasm lasted. The viscid adherent mucus in
the bronchi which is present in an asthmatic
attack was not found.   As the interval
between his last being seen alive and found
in the bottom of the pool face downwards was
only five minutes, I feel it unlikely that he
had had an attack of asthma at the time of
death.

(2)   It is well documented that individuals with
liver dysfunction due to fatty degeneration
can die suddenly without any other cause
being found. Fatty degeneration of the
liver is produced by chronic alcoholism.
Drugs may also have an influence.

/livers.

----

(3)   In addition to their legitimate use to
relieve broncho-spasm, Medihalers have
been abused to 'produce a kick'. Deaths
have been recorded following excessive use,
and the danger is clearly marked on the
inhaler.

Yours sincerely,

A. Sachs

Consultant Pathologist.

207

UNBRIDGE WELLS GROUP HOSPITAL MANAGEMENT COMMITTEE

THE QUEEN VICTORIA HOSPITAL
EAST GRINSTEAD, SUSSEX

PATRON
H.M. QUEEN ELIZABETH, THE QUEEN MOTHER

HONORARY PRESIDENT
GLADYS, LADY KINDERSLEY

PHONE: EAST GRINSTEAD 24111
TELEGRAMS: QUVICHOS, EAST GRINSTEAD

PATHOLOGIST:
A. SACHS, C.B., C.B.E.,
M.Sc., M.D., FRCP. F.C. Path.

PATHOLOGICAL LABORATORY   7th July, 1969.

Telephone report from Mr. Cook, Biochemist, Royal Sussex
Hospital, Brighton.

1. **Blood barbiturate.**   Nil.

2. **Blood alcohol.**   140mgs% (Approx 7 whiskeys, or
                                   3½ pints of beer)

3. **Urine.**   Amphetamine like substance
                                   1720 micro-gms% (in normal
                                   urine this never exceeds
                                   200 micro gms%) These figure
                                   suggest ingestion of a fairly
                                   large quanity of a drug

4. **Thin layer chromatography.** Failed to reveal the presence
                                   of the following in an
                                   unchanged state.

                                   (a) Amphetamine.
                                   (b) Methedrine.
                                   (c) Morphine.
                                   (d) Methadrone.
                                   (e) Isoprenaline.

But did show the presence of 2 dense spots, one yellow
orange which has not been identified and the other a
purple spot. This could be due to diphenhydramine, which
is present together with methaqualone in mandrax, which
the deceased is known to have taken.

Form 832EG

HISTOLOGY

Pathological Report No. 669 Date received: 3.7.65 PM.

T QUEEN VICTORIA HOSPITAL,   Ward: Specimen:Liver-frozen.

EAST GRINSTEAD.   Site: Lungs x 2.

Name: Brian Jones.   Age:26   Surgeon or Physician: Dr. Sommerville.

Lungs. The alveolar spaces are dilated and show bullous areas due to breakdown of the alveolar septa. Albuminoid material is present in the alveolar spaces. Subpleural haemorrhage is present. This is the histology found in drowning.

Date: Signed: Pathologist.

209

Doctor A.SACHS, Consultant Pathologist,
Queen Victoria Hospital, East Grinstead, Sussex.

continued.........

H.H.CORONER:

"What are the Post-Mortem signs of an attack of Asthma"?

Doctor SACHS.

"Haemorrhages into the lungs. Lungs bulky, light, and
voluminous. Lung collapses when incised. Rib Markings.
No evidence of water in lung tissue. Bronchial bile - casts
of viscid mucus present."

"In this case, the lungs were heavy and exuding water.
Left side of heart- Haemolisis

"The liver showed gross fatty degeneration".

H.M.CORONER:

Have you any comment on the drugs referred to in the
previous evidence?".

Dr.SACHS:

"Mandrax should not be taken when gross liver disease is present.
It's effect is exaggerated by C2 H5 011".

"The action of Vallium is also intensified by C2 H5 011".

H.M.CORONER:

"Can gross liver damage be diagnosed clinically"?

Dr.SACHS:

"Not without liver function tests".

INQUISITION

123

An inquisition taken for our Sovereign Lady the Queen

At **THE MAGISTRATES COURT** in the **PARISH** of **EAST GRINSTEAD SUSSEX.**

On the **SEVENTH** day of **JULY,** , 19 69

[And by ~~adjournment on the~~] ~~day of~~ 19]

[Before and by] (1) me Angus Christopher SOMMERVILLE.

one of her Majesty's coroners for the said **County of Sussex.**

~~[and the undermentioned jurors]~~ touching the death of (2) Lewis Brian JONES.

whose body has been viewed by me (3)

~~[concerning a stillbirth]~~

1. Name of deceased: Lewis Brian JONES.

2. Injury or disease causing death: (4)
   1 (a) Drowning
   (b) Immersion in Fresh Water.
   II. Severe liver dysfunction due to fatty degeneration and the ingestion of alcohol and drugs.

3. Time, place and circumstances at or in which injury was sustained: (5) Approximately 11.30 p.m., on the 2nd July, 1969, at Cotchford Farm, Hartfield, Sussex. Deceased had been drinking earlier in the evening, and was seen to be obviously under the influence of Alcohol and apparently Drugs. Insisted on going for a bathe. Seen to stagger on the Diving Board before jumping off into Swimming Pool, but managed to swim with other companion in Pool. Latter left to get Towel, returned to find deceased at bottom of Pool.

4. Conclusion of the jury/coroner as to the death:
Drowning whilst/under the influence of Alcohol and Drugs.
                        Swimming
MISADVENTURE.

5. Particulars for the time being required by the Registration Acts to be registered concerning the death :

(1) When and where died	(2) Name and surname of deceased	(3) Sex	(4) Age or probable age	(5) Occupation and address
11.30 p.m. 2nd July, 1969. Cotchford Farm, Hartfield, Sussex.	Lewis Brian JONES.	M	27	Entertainer. of Cotchford Farm, Hartfield, Sussex.

Signature of jurors:

Signature of coroner:

P.T.O.

Notes of the Post-Mortem Examination of

Name of deceased ___ Lewis Brian Jones.   Age ___ 26   Sex ___ Male

Address of deceased ___ Cotchford Farm, Hartfield, Sussex.

Name of G.P. ___

Observers present at examination ___ C. L. D.

Date and time of examination ___ Mortuary, Queen Victoria Hospital,
Place where examination performed ___ E. Grinstead, 3rd July, 1969.

Estimated time of death ___ 11.30 - midnight 2nd July, 1969.

Chief points in the history of the case.	Deceased apparently went for a swim in a pool at his home with friends. Friends left the pool and the deceased decided to stay in the water. Last seen alive 11.30 p.m, 2nd July, 1969. Found dead shortly afterwards.

EXTERNAL EXAMINATION

Height(length). Weight	5' 9".
Apparent age	26 years of age.
Nourishment	Powerfully built, with a tendency to obesity.
Temperature at rectum	Not taken.
Rigor mortis, hypostasis, decomposition	Rigor mortis present. Hypostasis present.
Evidence of violence, burns	Nil.
Identification (tattoo marks, old scars, special deformities	Nil seen.
Body surface - Pallor, abnormal coloration	Pallor of face. Frothy fluid round nostrils.
Orifices of body, hair, teeth	Own teeth.

INTERNAL EXAMINATION

Cranial Cavity Skull, scalp and face	N.A.D.
Brain - weight, etc.	Wt. 1553gms. Congested and oedematous. Punctate haemorrhages in white matter.
Meninges and blood vessels	Congested.
Spinal column, cord and meninges	N.A.D.
Thoracic Cavity Mouth, tongue, tonsils, oesophagus	Little blood stained fluid in mouth. Could be due to artificial respiration.
Larynx, trachea, bronchi, thyroid and thymus glands	Respiratory tract. Mucosa congested. Bronchi contains a few flakes of glairy mucus, but this is not the viscid adherent mucus associated with death due to an asthmatic attack.
Lungs, pleurae, diaphragm	Wt. L 632gms, R 643gms. Adhesions left base to chest wall. No free fluid to pleural cavities. Both lungs voluminous. Some areas of collapse. Lungs pit on pressure. Frothy blood stained fluid exudes from lungs on section. Few subpleural petechial haemorrhages.
Pericardium	
Heart (size, weight, cavities and contents (valve orifices and valves), heart muscle and coronary arteries	Heart Wt. 411gms. General hypertrophy. Both sides dilated. Myocardium fatty and flabby. No evidence of vascular or valvular disease.

Aorta, pulmonary and other blood vessels	Blood from left side of heart showed 29% Hb plasma due to haemolysis. Aorta. Narrow but no Blood alcohol 140 mgs %
Internal injuries (thoracic)	Nil
Abdominal cavity Stomach and contents	About 1oz. of undigested food in fluid. Mucosa congested.
Peritoneum, intestines and contents, appendix, mesenteric glands, etc.	N.A.D.
Liver and gall bladder	Wt. 3000gms. Congested. Architecture lost. Sections show liver dysfunction due to extensive
Spleen	fatty degeneration. Gall bladder. Empty. Spleen Wt. 247gms. Congested.
Kidneys and ureters	Wt. L 190gms R 181gms. Congested.
Bladder and urine	Little urine present. Analysis showed 1720 micro-
Suprarenals, pancreas	gms. % of a basic amphetamine-like substance. Apparently normal.
Generative organs, breasts, prostate, etc.	Normal for age.
Internal injuries (abdominal)	Nil.
Are all other organs healthy?	Apparently.
Cause of death as shown by the examination :	In my opinion the cause of death was :-

I

Disease or condition directly leading to death * ... ... Antecedent causes ... ... Morbid conditions, if any, giving rise to the above cause stating the under-lying condition last ...	(a) Drowning. due to (or as a consequence of) (b) Immersion in fresh water. due to (or as a consequence of) (c)

II

Other significant conditions, contributing to the death, but not related to the disease or condition causing it ∮

II

Severe liver dysfunction due to fatty degeneration and the ingestion of alcohol and drugs.

* This does not mean the mode of dying, such as, e.g. heart failure, asphyxia, asthenia, etc., it means the disease, injury or complication which caused death.

∮ Conditions which do not in the pathologist's opinion contribute materially to the death should not be included under this heading

These notes should be short and concise records of the facts observed; if opinions are expressed the grounds upon which they are based should also be stated. Scientific terms should be avoided when possible.

Any further remarks . In death from an asthmatic attack lungs are light and bulky.

Signature and qualifications Albert Sachs, CB. CBE. MD. MSc. FRCP. F. C .Path

Address Queen Victoria Hospital. E. Grinstead. Sussex.

Date 5th July, 1969

11/67

CLE/394/3650/250

NAME :   Francis David THOROGOOD

OCCUPATION : Builder

ADDRESS :   7 Albert Close, Wood Green, N.22

TEL :   888 6712

I am a builder and for about three years I have been engaged by members of the Rolling Stones Group to carry out repairs and alterations to properties owned by them. At present I am carrying out such work at Cotchford Farm for Brian JONES since November, 1968.

I have been living at the flat over the garage to the farm.

I have known Brian JONES for about 18 months and have been on fairly close terms with him since working at his home.

Since February, 1969, he has spent his time at the farm and from my knowledge, he has always been a fairly heavy drinker but cannot be described as an alcoholic.

During Wednesday, 2nd July, 1969, I went to London during the day and came back to Hartfield between 6p.m. and 6.30p.m. I saw Brian on my return and he was his usual self, watching television. We talked for a while and he asked that I go to the public house to get some drink. I went in a taxi to the Dorset Arms, Hartfield, and bought a bottle of Vodka, bottle of Wine, Blue Nun, half bottle of brandy and half bottle of whiskey.

I left the bottles with Brian after having a drink with him. I had vodka, he brandy. His girlfriend Anna was there. I think she had wine.

I left them and went to my flat which is close by.

I stayed in my flat talking to Janet who was staying at the farm for a few days.

About 9.30p.m. Brian came to the flat and asked that we join him for a drink. I think it was nearer 10p.m. because it was dark and Brian had a torch. Janet and I went with Brian to the farmhouse where Brian and I had more to drink. I had vodka and he was drinking brandy.

We watched Rowan & Martins T.V. programme and when it finished at 9.50p.m., Brian suggested a swim in the pool. By this time we had had quite enough to drink. We got our costumes which were in the farmhouse and went to the pool.

Brian was staggering but I was not too concerned because I had seen him in a worse condition and he was able to swim safely. He was a good swimmer but he was an asthmatic and used an inhaler. He had some difficulty in balancing on the divingboard and I helped to steady him but this was not unusual for him. He went in off the board and I went in the shallow end. He was swimming quite normally. Anna was in the pool with us for some of the time, then she went indoors leaving us in the pool. Janet also went indoors.

After we had been in the pool for about twenty minutes or so, I got out and went to the house for a cigarette leaving Brian in the pool.

I honestly don't remember asking Janet for a towel but if she said I did, then I accept it. I know I got a cigarette and lit it and when I went back to the pool, Anna appeared from the house about the same time. She said to me "He is laying on the bottom" or something like that. I saw Brian face down in the deep end on the bottom of the pool. Anna and I got in the water and after a struggle, got him out. His body was limp and as we got him to the side, Janet joined us and helped get him out.

Janet said that she had had difficulty with the 'phone and I went to the house and dialled '999'.

I returned to the pool and the girls were trying to revive him. When the ambulance men came they took over. The doctor came and said he was dead.

On Tuesday night, 1st July, 1969, Brian spent sometime in the pool and Janet, Anna and myself watched. At one time, Brian came to the side and I could see he had an asthma attack. He asked us to pass his inhaler, which he used and went on swimming. I have noticed during the past couple of days that his asthma has been bad and he has suffered from hay fever.

I did not think of this when I went into the pool with him on the night of his death. If I had of thought he was in any danger, I would not have left him on his own.

This statement, consisting of 4 pages each signed by me, is true to the best of my knowledge and belief and I make it knowing that, if it is tendered in evidence, I shall be liable to prosecution if I have wilfully stated in it anything which I know to be false or do not believe to be true.

F.D.THOROGOOD

Dated this 3rd day of July, 1969.

The above statement was taken by me in the presence of Detective Chief Inspector MARSHALL, and signed by the maker after I had read it over to him and he had been invited to make any addition or alteration thereto.

Peter HUNTER, D.S.

<u>STATEMENT OF WITNESS</u>

NAME: Thomas Richard KEYLOCK

OCCUPATION: Tour Manager

ADDRESS: 15 Outram Road, Alexandra Park, London, N.22

TELEPHONE NO: 888 - 3436

I am the Tour Manager for the Rolling Stones and until four weeks ago Brian JONES was a member of that group, but, I continued to look after his interests under the order of Rolling Stones Ltd. He was making tentative arrangements to form a new group.

I have known Brian for four and a half years. He has always been of a restless and nervous disposition. I have been in frequent contact with him up to the time of his death and last spoke to him by telephone at midday on Wednesday 2nd July, 1969 when he was his normal self and discussed with me his plans for a holiday and the formation of his new group.

For some time Brian has been under treatment from Dr. GREENBOROUGH of 73 Eaton Place, Belgravia, who to my knowledge regularly prescribed tranquillizers and sleeping pills. He also had a supply of 'black bombers' but these were restricted on Doctor's orders. He always described his sleeping tablets as 'sleepers'.

Brian was a good drinker and enjoyed beer as well as spirits such as vodka and brandy. There were occasions when he became under the influence but I have seen him really drunk yet able to swim proficiently.

Brian was subject to asthma attacks and was issued with an inhaler.

This statement, consisting of 2 pages each signed by me, is true to the best of my knowledge and belief and I make it knowing that, if it is tendered in evidence, I shall be liable to prosecution if I have wilfully stated in it anything which I know to be false or do not believe to be true.   (signed) T.R. KEYLOCK.

Dated this 3rd day of July, 1969

The above statement was taken by me at 4 p.m. 3rd July, 1969 in the presence of Detective Chief Inspector MARSHALL at Cotchford Farm and signed by the maker after he had read it over and he had been invited to make any addition or alteration thereto.

(signed) Peter HUNTER, D.S.

NAME: Albert EVANS

OCCUPATION: Police Officer

ADDRESS: County Police Station, Hartfield, Sussex

TELEPHONE NO: Hartfield 206

AGE: Over 21.

At 12.10 a.m. on Thursday, 3rd July, as a result of information received, I went to Cotchford Mill Farm, Hartfield.

I was shown to a garden swimming pool about 35 yards to the rear of the farmhouse. On the pool edge I saw the body of a man on its back with the head slightly raised by a towel. The body was clothed in swimming trunks.

At the side of the pool I saw a RIKER 'Medihaler'.

Ambulance attendants were applying resuscitation.

I went to the house and took possession of half a bottle of brandy, 4/5ths consumed; a bottle of vodka, ⅔rds consumed, and half a bottle of whisky, half consumed.

I also took possession of a number of bottles which contained or had contained various types of pills.

Dr. EVANS of Hartfield pronounced life extinct in my presence and I accompanied the deceased to the Queen Victoria Hospital, East Grinstead, where I formally identified the body to Dr. SACHS, Pathologist, who conducted a post-mortem in my presence.

This statement is true to the best of my knowledge and belief and I make it knowing that, if it is tendered in evidence, I shall be liable to prosecution if I have wilfully stated in it anything which I know to be false or do not believe to be true.

(signed) A. EVANS, Police Constable AE.887

Dated this 3rd day of July, 1969.

About 12 Medihalers about the house. — most empty

The Pills (bottled) — 2 × Valium Tab
1 × Cohis Menthan
1 × Pimla-Tab.

There were also many empty bottles about

D' Dais (Lld)

What in the f.n. signs shall in an attack you hoone?. —

    Hq. in the camp
    h emp. Enethy. light's volum inan
      h my collapses when uncirea
    R. b. rulings
    no evidence of unilicin em, time
    Bronches like — carli j viscid mucus hosend.

   I n the res tie Lungs was h eamged according make
   hl. sichs death . hassudpu

The Lures showed gross felly degenenhen

Any comment in the dougs referred to in the freman evides'

    ~~Andreas~~
    M anduas should not by taken when gross huis Disease is hosend.
      It's effect is exaggelid by tells ou
    Valuum's action also intensified by la Uf ou

Con gpon livin damage be chied genered clinically ?
   nel. all al. levis func hintets

NAME: Janet Ann LAWSON

OCCUPATION: State Registered Nurse

ADDRESS: 20 Netherton Road, Gosport, Hants

TELEPHONE NO: Gosport 80919

AGE: Over 21.

I am a State Registered Nurse employed by an Agency.

I first met Brian JONES about 12 months ago in Chichester.

I next saw him on Tuesday, 1st July, 1969, when I decided to
spend a few days in the country. A friend, Frank THOROUGOOD was
engaged as a builder at Brian JONES' home at Cotchford Farm, Hartfield.
I rang Frank at the farm on Monday 30th June during the early evening
and it was agreed that I should take the train from London to East
Grinstead and Frank met me at the Railway Station.

I spent that evening in the garage flat.

I saw Brian that Tuesday evening when I dined with him and friends
at the farm.

We had wine with the meal and Brian attempted to persuade us to
use the outdoor pool. We all declined but he swam and we took drinks
out to the side of the pool. It was about 9 p.m. and the floodlighting
was on.

He was a good swimmer and was acrobatic in the water.

I think we watched him for about two hours and then I left to
return to the flat.

I stayed in the flat throughout the day and had no contact with
Brian JONES during the day.

I would like it to be made clear that I barely knew Brian JONES
and there is nothing significant in the fact that we did not meet
during the day.

Brian JONES visited the flat about 10.30 p.m. on Wednesday evening
and invited my friend and I to join him at the house. We did so and

-1-

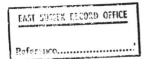

Brian guided us back to the house with a hand torch. It was clear that he was unsteady on his feet as the light was unreliable. He seemed to be talking quite sensibly, I believe about the drainage scheme. Nevertheless, it was obvious that he had been drinking.

My friend and I sat at the dining room table and drinks were there but I did not take it. Brian and my friend were drinking spirits.

Brian attempted conversation but it was a little garbled and he excused it by saying, "I've had my sleepers" or some such phrase. From this I gathered he had taken sleeping tablets.

He seemed anxious to be occupied and invited us to swim.

At about this point in time, Anna, Brian's friend, joined us and she, Frank and Brian decided to swim. I declined because I considered that Frank and Brian were in no fit condition to swim. I felt sufficiently strongly about this that I mentioned it to both the men. They disregarded my warning and it was obvious that they were drunk.

The men went upstairs to search for costumes and Anna took the dogs to the side of the pool. I followed her and watched her go into the water. She had been drinking but appeared capable to care for herself.

A few minutes later the men joined her in the water. I wanted to disassociate myself with the escapade and in order to keep an eye on the trio I partly hid myself in an effort to avoid their requests to join them.

I saw that Brian had great difficulty in holding his balance on the spring board. Frank was doing his best to assist him but not very successfully.

Eventually Brian flopped into the water and yet despite his condition seemed to be able to cope and made his strokes in the deep end. His movements wer e sluggish but I felt reasonably assured that they all were able to look after each other.

I returned to the music room in the house and played a guitar.

I heard Anna return to the house and talk to the dogs as she went upstairs.

I went to the garden and saw that the two men were still in the pool. I returned to the house.

About ten minutes later Frank returned to the house and asked for a towel. I went out to the pool and on the bottom I saw Brian. He was face down in the deep end. He was motionless and I sensed the worst straight away.

I shouted under the open window of the bedroom to Anna who was speaking on the telephone. I ran into the house and shouted to Frank. Both joined me - I was by then in the water but realized I couldn't manage him alone and I shouted to Frank to get into the pool to get Brian out.

I returned to the house to use the 'phone but I had difficulty as the line was engaged and there were several telephones in the house but I was not sure of the location of them all.

I returned to the pool to get Frank to use the 'phone and he and Anna were struggling to get Brian out of the water. I helped and we eventually got him out. He lay on his back and as Frank went to the house to 'phone I turned the body over and attempted to pump the water out of him. It was obvious to me he was dead but I turned the body back and I told Anna how to apply mouth to mouth resuscitation as I applied external cardiac massage.

I carried on for at least fifteen minutes but there was no pulse.

The three swimmers were in such a condition that I was tempted to return to the flat but I had a moral obligation to keep an eye on them because I sensed that they were all being very stupid - I suppose as a nurse I felt responsible.

I estimate that Brian and Frank were in the pool together for about half an hour before Frank joined me in the house to get a towel.

I met Frank in April 1968 and met him occasionally when he was a friend of a girl friend of mine. I knew Frank was working at Brian's home and I felt reasonably sure that Frank would give me house room for

-3-

a few days on request.

This statement, consisting of 5 pages each signed by me, is true to the best of my knowledge and belief and I make it knowing that, if it is tendered in evidence, I shall be liable to prosecution if I have wilfully stated in it anything which I know to be false or do not believe to be true.

(signed) J.A. LAWSON.

Dated this 3rd day of July, 1969.

The above statement was taken at East Grinstead Police Station and signed by the maker after she had read it over and she had been invited to make any addition or alteration thereto.

(signed) Peter HUNTER, Detective Sergeant.

NAME: Anna Ann Katherine WOHLIN

OCCUPATION: Student

ADDRESS: c/o Cotchford Farm, Hartfield, Sussex

TELEPHONE NO: Hartfield 536

AGE: Over 21

I am a Swedish National in the United Kingdom as a student. I first met Brian JONES about two or three months ago. I had two or three casual meetings with him and then six weeks ago he asked me to come and stay with him at Cotchford Farm, Hartfield. I agreed and once I moved there he didn't want me to leave and so I stayed with him. During those six weeks we were together nearly every minute of the day.

Frank THOROGOOD was living in the flat over the garage at Cotchford Farm and most week-days he was about there. At week-ends he went to London and also every Wednesday. Every evening when he was there Frank had dinner with Brian and myself at the farm. We used to always have wine with our dinner and sometimes a drink afterwards. Brian always drank brandy, Frank vodka and I usually drank wine.

On Tuesday evening the 1st July, 1969, Janet (LAWSON) came to stay for a couple of days. On that evening we all had dinner together and then had some drinks. After that Brian had a swim in the pool for a couple of hours. Frank, Janet and myself did not go in the pool that evening we sat with our drinks and watched Brian. While he was in the pool Brian came to the edge and asked me for his squirter which he used as a name for his inhaler. He often used it and I didn't think anything about it. He used the inhaler and then went on swimming. He suffered from asthma. On Tuesday night I told Brian I wouldn't go in the pool because I was too cold. I think that the temperature of the water that night was about 80°. The next day, Wednesday, the 2nd July, Brian had the temperature set up to 90°.

During Wednesday, 2nd July, Brian and I got up at about 11 a.m.

-1-

and watched the tennis on television for most of the day. We had a salad
for lunch and another snack later. During the evening of that day Brian
and I were watching television. At about 10.15 p.m. we were going to bed
and then Brian said that he wanted to go for a swim. I wasn't very keen
and he went over to Frank's flat and came back with Frank and Janet. I
came downstairs and they were sitting at the dining table with drinks.
Brian put the garden floodlights on and put the drinks on a tray to
take out. Then he and Frank changed into swimming trunks. They were
laughing about with each other. I went into the pool before they came
out and stayed there a while after they were both in there. They were
both a bit drunk. Janet didn't go in the water. After a while I went
up to my room to get dressed leaving the two men in the water and Janet
at the side. While I was in the house the 'phone rang, I answered it.
It was for me. I heard Frank come in then and he picked up the 'phone
in the kitchen. I told him the call was for me and he put the 'phone
down. Then I heard Janet shout, "Something has happened to Brian."
I rushed out about the same time as Frank. Janet was there and I saw
Brian lying on the bottom of the pool. I dived in and got him off the
bottom and Frank came in and helped me to pull him out. Janet went to
'phone for help. Then she came back and said she couldn't get through.
I think I must have left the phone off the hook. Then Frank went to
'phone and Janet and I applied artificial respiration. While we were
doing this I felt Brian's hand grip mine. We were still trying when the
ambulance men came. Then they took over. Then the doctor came and said
Brian was dead. When Brian was trying to slim he sometimes took a black
capsule, but only to try and slim, he didn't like taking them, he was
afraid of drugs. The black pills were called 'durophet'. As far as I
knew he got them on prescription. On Wednesday evening when I went into
the pool the water was too hot to cool us. I remember that before I
went upstairs to dress Brian came to the side of the pool and asked
me for his inhaler. I gave it to him and after using it he carried on

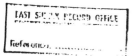

-2-

I have never seen him in an attack of asthma — but I have seen him
use his medihaler frequently

225

swimming.

    This statement, consisting of four pages each signed by me, is true to the best of my knowledge and belief and I make it knowing that, if it is tendered in evidence, I shall be liable to prosecution if I have wilfully stated in it anything which I know to be false or do not believe to be true.

(signed) Anna WOHLIN.

Dated this 3rd day of July, 1969

    The above statement was taken by me at 12.15 p.m. on 3rd July, 1969 in the presence of Detective Chief Inspector Marshall at East Grinstead Police Station and signed by the maker after I had read it over to her and she had been invited to make any addition or alteration thereto.

(signed) B. CARROLL, T/W.D.C. BC.40.

Name: LEWIS BLOUNT JONES.
Occupation of Witness: PROFESSIONAL ENGINEER.
Address: 335, Hatherley Road, CHELTENHAM.

Lewis Brian JONES was my son he was 27 years of age, born 28.2.42.
He lived alone at Cotchford Farm, Hartfield, Sussex, but usually had
friends staying at his home.   I last saw him on the 18th May, 1969
when my wife and I stayed the weekend at his home.   At that time he
seemed very fit and well.   He has suffered from Asthma since early
childhood, but he has gradually improved as he got older. I know he
used an inhaler at times to help.   He has always been a very keen
swimmer.   I spoke to him on the telephone about three weeks ago, and
at that time he was full of beans.

At 5 p.m. on Thursday 3rd July, 1969, I went to the Queen Victoria
Hospital, East Grinstead, where I identified the body of my son Lewis
BRIAN JONES to P. C. Duffett.

                                        Sgd. Lewis B. Jones.

The above statement was taken by me at 4.30 p.m. 3rd July, 1969.

                                    Sgd. C. Duffett. P.C.AD.755.

227